Gainsharing and Power

Denis Collins

Gainsharing and Power

LESSONS FROM

SIX SCANLON PLANS

ILR Press AN IMPRINT OF

Cornell University Press

ITHACA AND LONDON

First published 1998 by Cornell University Press.

Library of Congress Cataloging-in-Publication Data

Collins, Denis, b. 1956
    Gainsharing and power : lessons from six Scanlon plans / Denis
  Collins.
       p.   cm.
    Includes bibliographical references and index.
    ISBN 0-8014-3490-4 (cloth : alk. paper)
    1. Profit-sharing—United States—Case studies. 2. Management—
  Employee participation—United States—Case studies. 3. Bonus
  system—United States—Case studies. I. Title.
  HD2984.C65   1998   97-39573
  658.3'225—dc21

Cloth printing   10 9 8 7 6 5 4 3 2 1

CONTENTS

TABLES AND FIGURES

Tables

Figures

PREFACE

This book is dedicated to Timothy L. Ross, Larry Hatcher, and all management and nonmanagement employees who are sincerely involved in democratizing their organizations.

When I was obtaining my master's in philosophy at Bowling Green State University back in 1987, I knew that I wanted to document events that occurred at organizations actively engaged in ethical innovations. I went to the library and thumbed through hundreds of pages of names of consultants doing all sorts of consulting. As will be obvious from the final chapter of this book, I consider gainsharing to be an ethical innovation. To my pleasant surprise, there was a management consultant by the name of Timothy L. Ross located on campus in the business school who implemented gainsharing plans. Tim lives and breathes gainsharing, and it was extremely refreshing to locate an ethical idealist in an accounting department. From interviews with several employees at a gainsharing company, it was obvious that Tim had a profound impact on their everyday work lives. I am indebted to Tim for his insights and for opening the door to many gainsharing companies.

Conducting research for Tim led to a meeting with Larry Hatcher. Larry had obtained his Ph.D. in psychology from Bowling Green State University and was teaching at Winthrop College, South Carolina. During his so-called summer vacation, Larry was driving around the Midwest conducting research for Tim. We had the pleasure of sharing hotel rooms and thoughts of freeing all the chickens cooped up along the interstate highway while surveying and interviewing management and nonmanagement employees about their gainsharing experiences. I am indebted to Larry for his infinite amount of energy and for setting the highest standard for research excellence.

I am also indebted to William C. Frederick of the University of Pittsburgh, who chaired my dissertation committee in 1990. Bill provided me with the academic freedom to pursue my thoughts and intuitions about the ethical dimension of participatory management. These thoughts were sharpened by the other members of my dissertation committee—Gary Florkowski, Carrie Leana, Dick Moreland, and Donna Wood. I am also indebted to the School of Business at the University of Wisconsin–Madison for providing me with an unimaginable amount of professional autonomy and support to continue this line of research.

The field studies were made possible with the aid of several financial grants. I am grateful to the National Science Foundation Program for Decision, Risk, and Management Science, the Graduate School at the University of Wisconsin-Madison, and the Association for Quality and Participation for providing the necessary funding.

I also thank all the academic journal editors and anonymous reviewers who commented on the evolution of my theory, research methods, and interpretation of findings. Portions of this book have appeared in several articles published in academic journals: "Self-Interests and Group-Interests in Employee Involvement Programs: A Case Study," *Journal of Labor Research* 16, no. 1 (1995): 57–79; reprinted by permission. "A Socio-Political Theory of Workplace Democracy: Class Conflict, Constituent Reactions, and Organizational Outcomes at a Gainsharing Facility," *Organization Science* 6, no. 6 (June 1996): 628–644, copyright © 1996, and "The Ethical Superiority and Inevitability of Participatory Management as an Organizational System," *Organization Science* copyright © 1997, The Institute for Operations Research and the Management Sciences (INFORMS), 2 Charles Street, Suite 300, Providence, R.I. 02904. "The Death of a Gainsharing Plan: Power Politics and Participatory Management," in *Organizational Dynamics* 24, no. 1 (Summer 1995): 23–38, reprinted by permission of the publisher, © 1995, American Management Association, New York, New York, all rights reserved. "How and Why Participatory Management Improves a Company's Social Performance: Four Gainsharing Case Studies," *Business and Society* 35, no. 2 (1996): 176–210, copyright © 1996, reprinted by permission of Sage Publications.

You would not be reading the words of this book without the kind assistance of those associated with Cornell University Press. In particular, I wish to thank Robert Stern of Cornell University and Steven Markham of Virginia Polytechnic Institute for their very constructive comments on an earlier draft of this book, and Fran Benson for her editorial guidance.

If it were not for the wonderful doctors and staff of Meriter Hospital's Oncology Department, particularly Dr. Thomas McFarland, you also would not be reading this book. Tom had the unpleasant task of informing me that I had an advanced stage of Hodgkins' Disease shortly after I finished the first draft. Under his expert guidance, and with eight months of chemotherapy spread over ten months, the cancer entered remission and I began rewriting the final manuscript.

Last, this book is possible only because of the willingness of the management and nonmanagement employees at Cylinder Lifts, Foam Seats, Timberland, Innovations, Innovations-Brotherhood, and Packaging International to tell their stories. I am indebted to them for their insights, openness, and ability to survive in a very difficult work environment. It seems like yesterday that a welder responded to my question about whether work was now more enjoyable because of gainsharing with this statement: "You're _____ me! You want to know if I'm happier working sixty-hour weeks in one-hundred degree temperatures fixing little broken pieces because I hand in suggestions, evaluate them, and get a little extra money for it? Don't play games with me!" May they and their families all experience enriching, meaningful, and economically rewarding lives.

DENIS COLLINS

Madison, Wisconsin

Gainsharing and Power

Introduction

This book tells the heroic stories of management and nonmanagement employees at six facilities that implemented Scanlon-type gainsharing plans, a form of participatory management that includes a suggestion system, teams, and group-based bonuses. Like the leading characters in most good novels, some of these heroes have scars. Nonetheless, all six facilities realized significant benefits despite the many power games that were played out between and among management and nonmanagement employees.

Involving employees in decisions that directly affect them has been praised in the management literature for over a century. Most of the classic organization scholars—Argyris, Bennis, Drucker, Herzberg, Katz and Kahn, Lawrence and Lorsch, Lewin, Likert, March and Simon, Maslow, McClelland, McGregor—mention the benefits of participatory management. High praise for participatory management has dominated many best-selling management books published in the 1970s, 1980s, and 1990s. Management magazines are filled with brief, enthusiastic essays aimed at encouraging managers to get on the gainsharing bandwagon and improve facility performance.

Much scholarly research on gainsharing and participatory management suggests, however, that most efforts experience modest success. Some facilities have had tremendous success with Scanlon-type plans, even under very difficult economic conditions. Other facilities have failed miserably. If managed appropriately, the plans can work. But why are some plans managed effectively and not others? Given that so much has been written about how to do it right, why don't managers just design the plans right, implement them properly, and provide support so that the plans will succeed?

An essential factor underlying the research and commentaries on Scanlon-type gainsharing plan successes and failures is the role of power games. All attempts to decentralize organizations entail changes in power relationships. Implementing gainsharing is a threat to management power (and union power, if a union is present in the facility) and to traditional relationships between management and workers because each group's interests are being redefined. These fascinating issues are addressed in this book based on six field studies.

Chapter 1 places Scanlon-type gainsharing plans in a historical context. It reviews the most recent research on gainsharing plans and concludes with a call to consider comparative gainsharing case studies from a political science perspective, rather than human relations or human resource management perspectives.

Chapter 2 defends the need for a new theory of gainsharing based on conflicts of interest between management and nonmanagement employees. From political science research on changing from authoritarian rule to democracy, a conflict of interest theory of what happens when facilities implement Scanlon-type gainsharing plans is developed.

Chapter 3 describes how six facilities with Scanlon-type gainsharing plans were chosen for this study and the data collection methods used. These particular facilities were chosen because they differed according to union status, size of gainsharing bonuses, and type of ownership. Each facility was given a fictitious name to preserve anonymity.

Four of the facilities—Cylinder Lifts (Chapter 4), Foam Seats (Chapter 5), Forestland (Chapter 6), and Innovations (Chapter 7)—were non-union, and two—Innovations-Brotherhood (Chapter 8) and Packaging International (Chapter 9)—were union. Each of the nonunion facilities was chosen because of variances in gainsharing bonus payouts. Examining facilities with different gainsharing bonus payouts provided insight into how employee participation in decision making or the size of the financial bonus affects an organization. Cylinder Lifts (1.2 percent/$18) had a very small average monthly bonus payout; Foam Seats (5.2 percent/$63) and Forestland (6.8 percent/$85) had relatively modest monthly bonus payouts; and Innovations (19.3 percent/$370) had a large average monthly bonus payout. In addition, Cylinder Lifts was privately owned, whereas Foam Seats, Forestland, and Innovations were publicly owned.

The two union facilities were chosen after the four nonunion field studies had been conducted on the basis of how they could further an understanding of the gainsharing phenomenon. Innovations-Brother-hood, although part of the same publicly owned corporation as Innova-tions, had a very small average monthly gainsharing bonus (0.4 per-cent/$12). Packaging International, which also had a small average monthly gainsharing bonus payout (1.2 percent/$25), was employee-owned and abandoned gainsharing after six years.

Seventy-four semistructured interviews with key informants served as the primary source of data collection for each field study. Ten to four-teen semistructured interviews were conducted at each facility. Each in-terview lasted thirty to forty-five minutes, on facility time, and each in-terviewee was guaranteed anonymity. The seventy-four interviewees consisted of thirty-nine managers (six per facility), eighteen nonmanage-ment gainsharing team representatives (two to four per facility), and seventeen other nonmanagement production employees (two to four per facility). Managers were chosen based on their key positions at different levels of the facility's hierarchy (typically the president, facility manager, controller, engineering manager, supervisors, and so on). Nonmanage-ment employees were chosen based on whether they were supportive of gainsharing by submitting many suggestions and being elected team representatives (*go-getters*), unresponsive by submitting only one or two gainsharing suggestions every year (*fence-sitters*), or adversarial by hav-ing seldom or never submitted a suggestion and speaking strongly against gainsharing (*opponents*). This interview procedure allowed for cross-verification by those who represented a different role in the facility (i.e., stories told by managers were verified by a nonmanagement em-ployee) and the gainsharing coordinator. Gainsharing coordinators were interviewed first—at the end of each day, and just prior to departure.

Additional information about each facility was gathered from the gainsharing suggestion logs, minutes of gainsharing meetings, facility newsletters, and other relevant facility documents. I attended review board meetings at the five facilities that still had gainsharing plans, as well as employee meetings, gainsharing team meetings, and work cell meetings whenever possible.

Chapter 10 summarizes the six Scanlon-type gainsharing case studies in terms of trends related to power games and outcomes. In addition, the four nonunion facilities are compared based on the gainsharing evalua-tion and attitude surveys conducted at the time of the field study. Strate-gies for restricting and enhancing employee involvement and gainshar-ing bonus payouts are summarized. Each interest group is analyzed in terms of their reactions to the suggestion process, gainsharing teams and the group-based financial bonus. Gainsharing outcomes are summarized based on direct and indirect benefits to management and nonmanagement employees. Practical advice is provided on how to manage the power games that occurred at the six facilities.

Last, Chapter 11 defends the position that participatory management represents a form of workplace governance that is ethically superior to alternative forms of workplace governance. It investigates the social-philosophical assumptions that underlie prominent political and economic theories and applies them to workplace relationships. Debates in political and economic theory are framed in terms of the tension that exists within communitarian social philosophies and between communitarian and libertarian social philosophies, suggesting that communitarian social philosophy, as exemplified by democracy and the mixed economy, is ethically superior to the alternatives.

For similar reasons, participatory management is held to be an ethically superior way to manage workplace relationships. Unfortunately, many organizations, and much of the research in organization theory, assume an authoritarian model. Thus, those who experience significant benefits as a result of the central position of "liberty" in the social-philosophical assumptions of democracy and capitalism design authoritarian organizations that significantly restrict the liberty of their employees. Workplace practices, as exemplified by the participatory management movement, are very slowly evolving from an authoritarian to communitarian social philosophy. Societal problems may be reduced when business organizations adopt forms of workplace governance based on communitarian principles.

PART I

Employee Involvement

1 Participatory Management and Scanlon-Type Gainsharing Plans

Involving employees in decisions that directly affect them has been praised in the management literature for more than a century. Even a management consultant with such a brutish reputation as Frederick Winslow Taylor, who used a stopwatch to determine each worker's maximum output capacity, recommended that workers be encouraged to make job task suggestions and "if it proves to be better [based on scientific investigation], what I advocate every time is, not only that the new method shall be adopted, but that the man who made the suggestion be paid a big price for having improved on the old standard" (Taylor [1912] 1947: 199–200). In the 1920s, Elton Mayo declared that the failure to create collaborative mechanisms at the workplace was "the great stupidity of our time" (Mayo 1925: 231). Most of the classic organization scholars—Argyris, Bennis, Drucker, Herzberg, Katz and Kahn, Lawrence and Lorsch, Lewin, March and Simon, Maslow, McClelland—mention the benefits of participatory management.

During the 1960s, Douglas McGregor (1960) and Rensis Likert (1967) advocated that participatory management was the one best way, not just one of many ways, to manage people in any organization. Importantly, these passionate works on participatory management were a reaction to the prevalence of theoretical assumptions (Theory X) and patterns of management (System I) that greatly discouraged employee involvement in most companies. For instance, McGregor claimed that despite the obvious benefits documented in several case studies, participatory management had achieved very limited progress in organizations because

managers had failed to change their basic assumptions about employees. Many managers still believed that (1) "the average human being has
an inherent dislike of work and will avoid it if he can"; (2) "most people
must be coerced, controlled, directed, threatened with punishment to get
them to put forth an adequate effort toward the achievement of organizational objectives"; and (3) "the average human being prefers to be
directed, wishes to avoid responsibility, has relatively little ambition,
wants security above all" (McGregor 1960: 33–34). McGregor maintained
that little change would occur in organizations unless these beliefs were
replaced by assumptions, which he called Theory Y, that recognized the
possibility of human growth and development. According to McGregor,
"The assumptions of Theory Y point up to the fact that the limits on human collaboration in the organizational setting are not limits of human
nature but of management's ingenuity in discovering how to realize the
potential represented by its human resources" (48).

Dachler and Wilpert (1978) added significantly to participatory management by distinguishing four defining dimensions of participatory social arrangements. Their conceptual framework included (1) contextual
boundaries, such as the characteristics of a particular society; (2) the values, assumptions and goals of implementers; (3) properties of participation, such as formal-informal, direct-indirect; and (4) individual, group,
organizational, and societal outcomes. McGregor's emphasis on human
growth and development as an underlying value has been superseded
by an emphasis on the impact of participation on productivity and efficiency. During the 1980s, participatory management mechanisms became an often stated solution to America's low rate of productivity
growth.

High praise for participatory management has dominated many best-
selling management books of the 1970s and 1980s. One example is the
1982 best-seller *In Search of Excellence*, by Tom Peters and Robert Waterman. Truisms abound in this book, for example:

> Treat people as adults. Treat them as partners; treat them with dignity;
> treat them with respect. Treat *them*—not capital spending and automa-
> tion—as the primary source of productivity gain. These are fundamental
> lessons from the excellent companies' research. . . .
> Let us make clear one final prefatory point. We are not talking about
> mollycoddling. We are talking about tough-minded respect for the indi-
> vidual and the willingness to train him, to set reasonable and clear ex-
> pectations for him, and to grant him practical autonomy to step up and
> contribute directly to his job. (Peters and Waterman 1982: 238, 239)

In his later best-seller, *Thriving on Chaos* (1988), Peters maintained that total responsiveness to customers and fast-paced innovation require "empowered" employees. What does Peters mean by the "empowerment"? "Involve all personnel at all levels in all functions in virtually everything: for example, quality improvement programs and 100 percent self-inspection; productivity improvement programs; measuring and monitoring results; budget development, monitoring, and adjustment; layout of work areas; assessment of new technology; recruiting and hiring; making customer calls and participating in customer visit programs" (284). And how is this to be accomplished? "Organize as much as possible around teams, to achieve enhanced focus, task orientation, innovativeness, and individual commitment. . . . Regardless of whether or not the fit is perfect, organize *every function* into ten- to thirty-person, largely self-managing teams" (296).

The number of management experts who advocate flat, participatory forms of organization has increased dramatically. For instance, employee involvement in decisions that affect them plays a central role in the popularization of the writings of W. Edwards Deming (Walton 1991). Ed Lawler (1992) argues that participatory management represents the ultimate competitive advantage. For Peter Senge (1990), a "learning organization" emphasizes local autonomy, letting those closest to the problem solve it. Paradoxically, this approach fosters greater—not less—control by central authorities, a lesson learned in democratic societies. Ackoff (1994) embraces this concept in his description of a circular organization. He asserts that a democratic hierarchy has three essential characteristics: "(1) the absence of an ultimate authority, the circularity of power; (2) the ability of each member to participate directly or through representation in all decisions that affect him or her directly; and (3) the ability of members, individually or collectively, to make and implement decisions that affect no one other than the decision-maker or decision-makers" (117).

Scanlon-Type Gainsharing Plans

The Scanlon plan is one example of the participatory management ingenuity that McGregor (1960) advocated. During the Great Depression, Joe Scanlon, a cost accountant and local union official of the United Steelworkers, developed a cooperative solution between union members and managers of the Empire Steel and Tin Plate Company of Cleveland on how to link increases in employee wages to productivity improvements. One union production committee suggestion—purchase a new machine—saved the firm $150,000 in one year (Davenport 1958). Scanlon implemented similar cooperative labor-management mechanisms at other companies through his union connections and the management connections he had made as an instructor at Massachusetts Institute of Technology. He also drew on Scanlon plan case studies of the Adamson Company and the Lapointe Machine Tool Company, which had been published in the popular press to reach more companies (Lesieur 1958).

Scanlon plans are now more commonly referred to as "gainsharing," although not all management systems known as gainsharing are Scanlon plans (Miller and Schuster 1987). For instance, profit sharing, Employee Stock Option Plans (ESOPs), and Improshare are often referred to as gainsharing plans, but they do not necessarily entail employee involvement in decision making. Some gainsharing plans limit financial rewards to particular teams rather than all company employees, and others limit the type of financial rewards to the accumulation of points that can be exchanged for merchandise (Doherty, Nord, and McAdams 1989). The term *gain sharing* can be traced to an 1889 article by Henry R. Towne that describes how he documented a work unit's costs and productivity, and shared future gains in these areas with the work unit (Towne 1889). Thus, throughout this book the term *Scanlon-type gainsharing plans* (or Scanlon-type plans) will be used. These plans constitute just one of many ways managers can involve nonmanagement employees in decisions that affect them (Lawler 1986).

Scanlon-type gainsharing plans have four unique features: a suggestion system, department teams, a review board, and a group-based bonus. First, Scanlon-type gainsharing plans consist of a highly structured suggestion system whereby nonmanagement employees submit suggestions for inproving production which are analyzed by department teams. The suggestions typically pertain to process concerns, such as redesigning jobs and reorganizing an area's work flow.

Second, department teams, which have substantial decision-making powers, usually consist of the department supervisor and three to seven nonmanagement employees who are elected by their peers. The team usually meets monthly but, in some companies, weekly. Team members solicit and evaluate the suggestions from nonmanagement employees in their work area. The team is empowered to implement any production-related suggestion that meets three criteria: there is a favorable consensus for it; the implementation cost falls within the team's monthly budget of approximately $400; and the suggestion does not directly affect the functioning of other departments. Suggestions that do not receive a favorable consensus are often rejected or revised, although the suggestion-giver may appeal the department team's unfavorable evaluation at a review board meeting. Any suggestion that receives a favorable consensus but exceeds the team's monthly budget authority or affects the functioning of other departments is immediately forwarded to the review board.

Third, the review board typically consists of one elected department representative from each team and an equal number of high-ranking managers chosen by management. The review board members discuss and evaluate all the suggestions that have been forwarded to it by the department teams. Any suggestion that receives a favorable consensus at the review board meeting is implemented.

Fourth, a group-based financial bonus calculation is devised that compares expected costs and actual costs for a given period of time, usually monthly. The expected costs are determined from the facility's historical performance, usually an average of the previous three to five years. Other factors may serve as the basis of the calculation, such as profit improvements or expected versus actual time required for production output. Assuming a monthly cost-based calculation, when the actual costs are lower than the expected costs, the financial difference is shared equally between the facility and its employees. Half of the employees' share is distributed to the employees as a percentage of each person's wage rate. The other half of the employees' share is set aside in a year-end reserve pool that accounts for months where actual costs exceed expected costs. Any amount left over in the reserve pool is then distributed at the end of the year.

Many Scanlon-type gainsharing plans are customized by the company (Graham-Moore and Ross 1990; Masternak 1991/92). For instance, some companies have three people on department teams, whereas others have all department employees on a team. Some companies have monthly department meetings; others have weekly meetings. Some companies have very broad bonus calculations that include many factors, and some have very narrow bonus calculations that include only a few factors. Most companies also hold monthly meetings where upper-level managers discuss the bonus results, company operations, and economic conditions with nonmanagement employees.

The particulars of a Scanlon-type plan are typically approved by a screening committee consisting of both management and nonmanagement employees, sometimes voted on by nonmanagement employees, and distributed as a document to all employees. The gainsharing plan statement often includes information on company history, company mission, purpose of gainsharing (e.g., total customer satisfaction, improve competitive position through cost reductions, increased employee satis-faction), gainsharing goals (high quality, greater employee involvement, productivity improvements, eliminate waste), employee responsibilities (cooperation, problem solving), management responsibilities (establish business plan, assist employees, cooperation), involvement structure (gainsharing coordinator, steering committee, gainsharing teams, and review board), group-based financial bonus calculation, and decisions not affected by the gainsharing plan (such as pay, promotion, and pric-ing).

Scanlon-type gainsharing plans are often presented as an ideal form of gainsharing. For example, Markham, Scott, and Little (1992) note that "Scanlon Plans are usually considered a high-end form of gainsharing because they incorporate a large amount of employee involvement in the design and administration of the plan" (34). Scanlon-type plans inte-grate employee involvement with group-based financial bonuses be-cause both financial and participation motives are considered essential (Graham-Moore and Ross 1990). Some companies have added Scanlon-type plans to quality circles, total quality management, and self-directed work teams because of the financial bonus incentive (Ross 1994). Simi-larly, the plans have been implemented in companies with ESOPs and profit-•haring because of the employee involvement incentive (Freund and Epstein 1984).

Gainsharing Implementation Rates

Unfortunately, one can only estimate the number of companies with Scanlon-type plans because of two major problems with interpreting the research. First, as noted earlier, researchers usually group a plethora of programs under the gainsharing heading and do not always distinguish Scanlon-type plans from other forms of gainsharing. Second, researchers who do distinguish among the different plans often provide a custom-designed option that may incorporate Scanlon-type gainsharing ele-ments. For instance, Masternak (1991/92) discussed two custom gain-sharing plans that may have been Scanlon-type. Similarly, I have interviewed human resource professionals who called their Scanlon-type plans a custom plan because they were unaware of the Scanlon con-nection.

Another problem with interpreting gainsharing implementation rate research pertains to the unit of analysis—the company. Although many research articles report the implementation of gainsharing on the company level of analysis, some companies have many facilities. For instance, BF Goodrich has several manufacturing plants in the United States. A few of these plants may have gainsharing plans, but many may not. Some very large companies who respond positively to survey questions on gainsharing may have gainsharing at only one of their many locations. Therefore, it is more meaningful to know the number of facilities rather than companies in the United States that have gainsharing.

From published survey data, a historical trend since the early 1980s can be developed. In 1982, the New York Stock Exchange surveyed the human resource management practices of a representative sample of U.S. companies with one hundred or more employees (Freund and Epstein 1984). Of the 1,158 respondents, only 14 percent had any formal human resource programs to improve productivity. Scanlon-type plans were not on the list of human resource activities surveyed. But two key ingredients of these plans were on the list: suggestion systems and group productivity financial incentives. Only 13 percent of the companies had the former, and only 2 percent had the latter. According to Dulworth and Usilaner (1987), an earlier report of these findings issued by the NYSE stated that 15 percent of companies with five hundred or more employees had some type of gainsharing plan, and at least 63 percent of these companies reported that employees participated in decision making, thus suggesting that as many as 9 percent of companies with more than five hundred employees may have had a Scanlon-type plan.

O'Dell and McAdams (1987) surveyed members of the American Productivity Center, the American Compensation Association, and other companies using gainsharing plans. Of the 1,598 respondents from different organizations or operating units, 223 (14 percent) responded to the section of the survey on gainsharing plans (defined as Scanlon plans, Improshare, profit sharing, and customized). Thirty-four companies had Scanlon plans, and ninety-five had custom plans. The latter were described as company-designed plans whereby "they can tailor the formula and supporting human resource practices to fit their objectives" (O'Dell and McAdams 1987: 35). Approximately 25 percent of the custom gainsharing plan companies also had problem-solving teams and department committees, so at most, twenty-four custom plans could have been Scanlon-type plans. By combining the Scanlon plans and the custom Scanlon-type plans, approximately fifty-eight companies (4 percent) had the latter plans. This may overestimate the general population of companies, however, since some companies were added to the sample specifically because they had gainsharing plans.

In 1990, Lawler, Mohrman, and Ledford (1992) surveyed Fortune 1000 companies and categorized them according to the percentage of employ-ees covered by participatory management practices. The gainsharing category included Scanlon plans, Improshare, the Rucker plan, and cus-tom-designed plans; it excluded ESOPs and profit sharing. Of the 313 re-spondents, 39 percent had gainsharing plans, an increase from the 26 percent who responded to a similar survey by the authors in 1987. If we compare their findings with those of Freund and Epstein (1984) and O'Dell and McAdams (1987), it becomes clear that gainsharing plans are more widely used by larger companies. Another important factor associ-ated with the larger companies surveyed by Lawler, Mohrman, and Led-ford (1992) is that most of the gainsharing plans covered less than 20 per-cent of a company's employees. Only 3 percent of the companies had gainsharing plans that covered more than 40 percent of employees. Gainsharing plans were, therefore, being applied in particular organiza-tional units but not company-wide.

In 1991, Markham, Scott, and Little (1992) surveyed 10,000 of the more than 40,000 members of the Society for Human Resource Management with job titles of plant-level human resource professional or higher. Of the 1,639 respondents, 219 (13 percent) had active gainsharing plans at their companies. Twenty-one companies had Scanlon plans and ninety-six had custom plans. In a personal communication, Steven Markham, the lead author, estimated that about half the customized plans were ac-tually modified Scanlon-type plans. Thus, of the 1,629 respondents, ap-proximately 4 percent had Scanlon-type gainsharing plans.

How widespread, then, are such plans? Using high-end estimates, the plans may be found in 26 percent of the Fortune 1000 companies (Lawler, Mohrman, and Ledford 1992), 9 percent of companies with more than five hundred employees (Dulworth and Usilaner 1987; Freund and Epstein 1984), 4 percent of the companies belonging to the American Productivity Center (O'Dell and McAdams 1987), and 4 per-cent of the companies that employ human resource professionals (Markham, Scott, and Little 1992).

The success stories of larger companies appear to encourage other companies to experiment with gainsharing plans. When 143 attendees of a Society for Human Resource Management conference were asked to identify the five most critical human resource issues their organizations would face in the 1990s, the second most critical set of issues, after health care, were gainsharing, productivity, and skill-based rewards issues ("Health Care Costs," 1992). Nonetheless, proclamations by some acade-mics that workplace democracy has arrived because "the pyramid-shaped organization chart has gone the way of the Edsel" (Slater and

Bennis 1990: 174) or that the participatory management "revolution itself is clearly underway" (Preston and Post 1974: 484) are still premature.

More important than the exact number of companies with Scanlon-type plans are the experiences these companies have had. What are the outcomes of the plans? When answering this question, it is helpful to divide the research on Scanlon-type plans into three categories: descriptive case studies; multiple company studies and literature reviews; and studies primarily examining factors leading to success. Excellent reviews of the Scanlon-type gainsharing plan literature include Frost, Wakely, and Ruh (1974); White (1979); Schuster (1983b); Lawler (1988); Gowen (1990); and Graham-Moore (1990a).

Descriptive Case Studies

Management research abounds with descriptive case studies of companies with Scanlon-type gainsharing plans. The company most often mentioned is Herman Miller, which has been operating under a Scanlon plan since 1950 (Azzarello 1992/93; Geber 1987; Olsen 1979; Ramquist 1982). Table 1-1 summarizes the findings of twenty-one articles published since 1979 that included information about organizational outcomes. The year 1979 was used as a cutoff date because White (1979) provides an excellent review of the most thorough Scanlon-type plan case studies prior to that year. There are many other gainsharing case studies, but most of them are about companies with an Improshare-type plan that does not include employee involvement. As noted earlier, most articles on gainsharing are brief essays encouraging companies to try gainsharing. The published case studies listed in Table 1-1 typically document the tremendous success companies have had with Scanlon-type plans, even under very difficult economic conditions. These improvements include increased productivity, product quality improvements, and reductions in turnover, scrap, and labor costs.

Multiple Company Studies and Literature Reviews

A second set of research studies examines whether Scanlon-type gainsharing plans have increased company performance across several companies. In one of the first multiple company studies, Puckett (1958) examined ten applications of the Scanlon plan, of which nine were implemented in unionized companies. After dismissing various factors

Table 1–1. Gainsharing case studies published since 1979

Authors	Company; Study Findings
Azzarello (1992/93)	Herman Miller; significant reductions in environmental costs (e.g., scrap, wastes).
Foxenberger (1994)	Men's tailored slacks facility; productivity increased by 10–11%; costs increased only by 1%.
Graham-Moore (1990b)	DeSoto facility, 17 years; continual increase in output per work-hour, suggestions per employee ranged from 0.6 to 1.6 every year, with the highest rate being achieved the 17th year, and the highest percentage of suggestions related to how the quantity of production could be increased.
Green and Berry (1985)	Motorola facility, 15 years; 50% reduction of work-in-progress inventory and 50% reduction in turnover.
Hanlon, Meyer and Taylor (1994)	One company; higher levels of moral commitment, prosocial behavior, and less intention to leave were observed in the experimental group than in the control group.
Hatcher and Ross (1985)	Duncan facility, 18 months; 49% reduction in scrap costs, 17.3% increase in direct-labor efficiency, 14.5% reduction in warranty costs, 6.6% reduction in indirect-labor costs, and a decline in grievances from 120 to 10.
Markham, Little, Scott, and Berman (1992)	Catherine McAuley Health Center laboratory department, 2 years; significant savings in wastage and rework resulted in an average employee bonus of $2,000.
Markham, Scott, and Cox (1992)	Xaloy facility, 6 years; substantial productivity increases and $2,100 average savings per suggestion during the most recent year.
Masternak (1991/92)	Two facilities owned by the same Fortune 500 company, first year; first facility—product quality rose 69% over target and costs were 96% of budget; second facility—productivity increased by 5% and significant safety improvements were achieved, but costs were 2% over target.
Masternak (1993)	BFGoodrich facility (Calif.), 2 years; first year—50% improvement in product quality, significant reduction in returned goods, costs 3% below budget, productivity increase of 4.5%, and improvement from 96% to 98% in on-time shipments; second year—18.5% quality improvement and 2% reduction in costs.
Masternak and Ross (1992)	BFGoodrich facility (Ind.), 1 year; quality improved 28%, productivity increased 6%, costs decreased 11%, and customer complaints declined 79%.
Moskal (1994)	General Tire facility, 9 years; 11,000 suggestions, $30 million in cost savings, and creation of 1,000 new jobs.

Table 1–1. (*Continued*)

Authors	Company; Study Findings
Olsen (1979)	Herman Miller; summary includes longitudinal data on number of suggestions and absenteeism.
Ramquist (1982)	Herman Miller; summary of the evolution of its Scanlon Plan over forty years, particularly major changes in 1978.
Ross and Collins (1987)	Tech Form Industries facility, 1 year; improved product quality, $750,000 in savings, decrease in direct labor for repair, decrease in absenteeism, decrease in employee grievances, and decrease in scrap.
Ross and Hatcher (1992)	Evart Products Co. facility, 4 years; defect rate decreased from 437 to 2 parts per 10,000, and more than 3,500 employee suggestions were implemented.
Ross, Hatcher and Ross (1989)	Tech Form Industries facility, 4 years; 83% decrease in defective product returns, 50% decrease in direct labor hours for repairs, and 41% decrease in grievances.
Ross, Ross, and Hatcher (1986)	Peabody Barnes facility, 2 years; 24% improvement in direct-labor efficiency, 58% decrease in scrap costs, and 58% decrease in warranty costs.
Schulhof (1979)	Rocky Mountain Data Systems facility, 5 years; eliminated employees peaking out in a pay category and middle-management empire building, 70% decline in turnover, and greater communication, cooperation, and integration.
Schuster (1983a)	Four companies; three companies implementing the plan increased productivity (one by nearly 40%), but the fourth company that was renewing it did not.
Schuster (1984)	A unionized manufacturing facility, 5 years; an abrupt positive change in productivity followed by positive trends for two product lines, and employment and turnover remained stable in contrast to wider shifts for the industry.

as the primary cause for productivity improvements, Puckett concluded that "the most significant conclusion to be drawn from the study is not that productivity achievements have been substantial, although this too is important. The most significant conclusion suggested in these data is that our human resources contain a potential that is apparently not fully utilized in even relatively efficient and profitable manufacturing companies. To tap this reservoir of human potential is the great challenge facing labor-management relations today" (116–17).

As more research was conducted, some of the clear findings became ambiguous. Frost, Wakely, and Ruh (1974) concluded that "few unambiguous conclusions concerning the effects of the Scanlon Plan can be drawn from the research conducted to date" (150). A decade later, Schuster (1983b) hesitantly concluded that empirical research suggests that Scanlon-type plans can increase organizational effectiveness, increase productivity, and stabilize employment. Schuster's comprehensive conclusion is worth citing in detail:

> Because so few empirical studies have been conducted, the evidence which does exist must be treated solely as preliminary, and by some authors' own acknowledgments often tentative due to design and statistical limitations. Based upon existing empirical evidence, albeit limited, there is basis to suggest that Scanlon Plans can be instrumental in mobilizing an entire workforce's efforts and talents to increase organizational effectiveness. Moreover, productivity may increase and employment can be stabilized. There is some evidence to suggest that the plan encourages people to work harder and leads to a series of positive work outcomes. It is also clear that the plan works better in some companies than in others and that the degree of employee participation varies significantly across organizations. One factor which may explain this result is the strength of management attitudes and commitment to employee participation through Scanlon. Additional research is needed to give greater support and credibility to existing findings (69).

Bullock and Lawler (1984) summarized the findings of thirty-three gainsharing case studies in reference to organizational outcomes. They found that improvements related to gainsharing pertained to organizational effectiveness (73 percent of the plans), quality of work life (64 percent), innovation (76 percent), labor-management cooperation (55 percent), pay (91 percent), and program success (67 percent). A U.S. Government Accounting Office (1981) report on thirty-eight companies with some form of gainsharing found that there was, on average, a 17 percent savings in workforce costs, improved labor-management relations (81 percent of the plans), fewer grievances (47 percent), less absenteeism (36 percent), and reduced turnover (36 percent).

Mitchell, Lewin, and Lawler (1990) list the following outcomes from research studies on gainsharing: coordination, teamwork, and sharing of knowledge are enhanced at lower levels; social needs are recognized through employee participation and mutually reinforcing group behavior; attention is focused on cost savings, not just quantity of production; acceptance of change due to technology, market demands, and new methods is greater because higher efficiency leads to bonuses; workers attitudes change, and they demand more efficient management and better planning; employees try to reduce overtime; employees produce ideas as well as effort; when unions are present, union-management relations or more flexible; and unorganized locations tend to remain nonunion.

An interesting debate has evolved as to the degree of certainty that empirical findings support the implementation of participatory management mechanisms. The most recent flare-up began with the work of Cotton et al. (1988), who categorized participatory management research studies according to several important distinguishing features. Scanlon plans were categorized as representative of a "consultative participation" form of management. The researchers noted that four out of five review articles found a positive relationship between consultative participation plans and performance factors, and three out of four review articles found a positive relationship between consultative participation plans and employee satisfaction factors. Unfortunately, quality circles were also categorized as a consultative participation form of management. It is a theoretical mistake to group Scanlon plans and quality circles under the same heading because the former have a group-based monetary incentive, and the latter do not. The authors also made several other mistakes in categorization, selection of studies, and interpretation of research results (Leana, Locke, and Schweiger 1990).

Therefore, Wagner (1994) collected the studies cited by Cotton et al. (1988) and performed a meta-analytic replication to test the statistical validity of Cotton's general claims. Wagner found no statistically significant support for concluding that consultative participation forms of management had a positive relationship with either performance or satisfaction outcomes. After performing a meta-analysis on ten other review articles, Wagner found "inconclusive" evidence regarding the impact of consultative participation on both performance and satisfaction. Wagner's summary of his meta-analysis results for all types of employee participation indicates how managers probably think about employee involvement:

Instead, support is provided for the conclusion that research has produced evidence of statistically significant but small relationships between participation and performance or satisfaction and that it has failed to verify the presence of strong, large relationships. Evidence from the findings of 10 other reviews of participation research upholds the same conclusion. Together, the conclusions of this article give cause to question the practical significance of participation as a means of influencing performance or satisfaction at work. (327)

This type of empirical analysis of research studies is misdirected be- cause it collapses successful and unsuccessful applications of Scanlon- type plans into the same database, thus generating neutral results when all the studies are aggregated. As is demonstrated by the many individ- ual case studies, the plans can greatly improve company operations. Some companies are not successful, however. Timothy L. Ross (1990), a Scanlon-type gainsharing consultant, notes that "most experts in the field of gainsharing would probably say that the success rate is not over 65 percent. (This percentage does not include firms with marginal plans, which is a common practice.) No one really knows the failure rate, since most of the plans have been installed by consultants who are frequently unwilling to share their client's experience with others" (100).

A much more productive and meaningful understanding of the Scan- lon-type gainsharing literature is gained by examining studies that at- tempt to determine the factors that distinguish between the successful and unsuccessful applications. If managed appropriately, Scanlon-type gainsharing plans can work. But why are some managed appropriately and others not?

Successful versus Unsuccessful Applications

What factors influence the success of Scanlon-type gainsharing plans? A very long list has been proposed by organization theorists involved in the implementation of these plans (Graham-Moore and Ross 1990; Lawler 1981; O'Dell and McAdams 1987; Schuster 1987) or who have conducted research on factors that may predict success (Bullock and Lawler 1984; Hatcher, Ross, and Collins 1989; Ruh, Wallace, and Frost 1973; Welbourne and Gomez-Mejia 1988; White 1979; White and Ruh 1973). For instance, Lawler (1981) and Schuster (1987) note that gain- sharing is most feasible in facilities that have less than five hundred em- ployees, single product lines, workforce interdependence, and underuti- lized employees, among many other factors. Lawler (1988) argues that gainsharing is most successful when there is a congruent fit among the group-based financial reward, participatory structures, and manage- ment philosophy. Similarly, Masternak (1991/92), in comparing two case studies, one much more successful than the other, attributed Scanlon plan success to five factors: employees rating bonus expectations low, rather than high, on a list of gainsharing goals; employees' perceived fairness of the bonus calculation; job stability of the gainsharing coordinator; better attitudes about employee participation prior to gainsharing implementation; and communication and teamwork training sessions.

The first thorough statistical analysis of factors that might predict the success of Scanlon-type plans was conducted by White (1979). He identified three groups of variables that previous research suggested were related to success: situational factors, personnel characteristics, and process variables. Based on employee survey results from twenty-two facilities, White found that Scanlon plan success was related to the average level of participation in decision making reported by employees, the number of years a company had a Scanlon plan, managerial attitudes, the chief executive officer's attitudes, and the expected level of success for the plan. Lawler's suggestion that success is related to company size was not supported by White's data.

Bullock and Tubbs (1990) performed a meta-analysis of thirty-three case studies in the gainsharing literature to determine whether particular structural features, implementation factors, or situational conditions predicted gainsharing success. They found that overall gainsharing intervention success (an aggregate of five success measures) was related to structural factors (in particular, formal employee involvement and monthly payout periods) and implementation factors (in particular, employee involvement in design and favorable employee attitudes toward implementation) but not to situational conditions. No relationship was found between overall intervention success and payout percentage, management style, company size, union status, type of technology, and external market or product environment. When success was measured in terms of plan retention, the statistically significant factors were monthly payout periods, favorable employee attitudes toward implementation, and participative management style.

In a survey of eighty-three companies with some form of gainsharing, Imberman (1992) found that about two-thirds of the gainsharing plans did not meet expectations due to lack of top management support, inadequate middle management involvement, lack of training for first-level supervisors, inadequate assessment of suggestions, and failure to use some expert guidance. Similarly, Kim (1994a) surveyed managers from 622 facilities with gainsharing plans (some of which lacked employee involvement) in terms of five factors: design factors (what was done), implementation factors (how it was done), situation factors (when and where was it done), labor relations factors (who did it and to whom was it applied), and gainsharing results. Of the 269 respondents, 63 percent reported that their gainsharing plans were successful. Kim found that the degree of gainsharing success was related to the first four factors. Gainsharing success was not related to the employees' percentage of the bonus, the type of bonus plan, the average educational level of employees, or the number of years of the program was in operation.

What conclusion should be drawn from these studies? With the exception of Kim (1994a), the research studies discount the importance of situation. In some circumstances, certain situational variables may be daunting. But in other circumstances, they can be overcome. For instance, some consultants have expressed exasperation at establishing Scanlon plans in unionized facilities (Ross, Hatcher, and Adams 1985). However, union companies were the first to implement Scanlon plans. Both Joe Scanlon and Frederick Lesieur, an early and influential advocate of Scanlon plans, were former union officials who refused to work with companies that they suspected were trying to decertify a union (Driscoll 1979). Scanlon-type gainsharing plans are certainly easier to implement when everyone in the company is an avid supporter, but this is rarely the case for any organizational change, particularly change that is likely to affect an organization's structure, processes, and reward system. Nonetheless, some companies implemented Scanlon-type plans successfully because labor relations were so terrible that either management or the union was desperate to try anything. According to Ewing (1989), "Even when not all conditions are favorable, gainsharing can still work and work well. An organization must be willing to put forth the effort needed to identify and offset any unfavorable factors. More often than not, the payoff is substantial enough to be well worth the effort" (52–53).

The variables that appear to best predict success have more to do with the design of the employee involvement mechanisms, how the plan was implemented, and employee attitudes—particularly those of management—toward implementing and supporting the Scanlon plan. This leads to a very interesting question: Given that so much has been written about how to do the plans right, why don't more companies implement them appropriately and give them the support they need to succeed?

2 Conflicts of Interest: At Work and in Political Systems

As we have seen, some facilities have successful Scanlon-type gain-sharing plans and others fail in the attempt. Why the mixed results? One's answer to the question is guided by one's theory of workplace relationships. When a problem is explored, theory usually guides the investigation. Theories are often but not necessarily fully grounded in either personal experience or what one learns about the subject.

Sometimes people misunderstand the nature of problems and solutions because they apply incorrect or insufficient theoretical assumptions. Thomas Kuhn (1970) has pointed this out in relation to scientific discoveries. When exploring celestial matters, most astronomers prior to the 1500s assumed that all planets revolved around the earth. They wanted the facts of the case to fit their theory, and when the facts didn't, they questioned the nature of the facts rather than the nature of the theory. It took Copernicus to point out that a different theory, based on different assumptions, was needed. Similarly, business people design organizations and incentive systems based on the theoretical assumptions they make about human nature. As noted earlier, McGregor (1960) advocated participatory management as a superior system because its Theory Y assumptions about workers were closer to the truth.

Thus, in exploring a problem such as why the aggregate results of Scanlon-type plans have been disappointing, the analysis is based on theoretical assumptions about workplace relations. For instance, much research on participatory management is grounded in either human relations or human resource management theory. Many researchers seek theoretical explanations about participatory management based on these theories (Hammer, 1988; Leana and Florkowski, 1992), which assume that workers' behavior is driven by a desire for personal fulfillment and harmonious work relations (human relations theory) or personal satisfaction (human resource management theory).

Nonetheless, my experience in conducting interviews with employees at Scanlon-type gainsharing facilities has led me to discount the explanatory power of both theories. This is best exemplified by an interview I conducted with a welder who was actively involved with gainsharing teams and extremely pleased with the facility's experience. With sweat pouring from his face and hands in the air-conditioned meeting room, I asked if he felt greater satisfaction in his work or personal development and fulfillment as a result of gainsharing. His response: "You're !@#$%& me. You want to know if I'm happier working sixty-hour weeks in one hundred-degree temperatures fixing little broken pieces because I hand in suggestions, evaluate them, and get a little extra money for it? Don't play games with me!" Similar sentiments have been expressed by workers performing a variety of job tasks. They hoped gainsharing would last forever, but their sentiments were not linked to feelings of personal satisfaction or fulfillment. For these employees, work was still tedious and frustrating despite gainsharing. A different sort of theoretical lens is needed to understand what happens at facilities that implement Scanlon-type gainsharing plans.

Interest Groups and Power Differentials

One may begin reconstructing a theory of workplace relationships associated with Scanlon-type plans by exploring the original intentions of Joe Scanlon. What did Scanlon expect when facilities adopted the plans? As discussed earlier, Joe Scanlon was a steelworkers' union official at a time when the United States was suffering through an economic depression. Strikes were often the only recourse nonmanagement employees had to increase wages. He believed that unions had to go beyond collective bargaining and seek alternative, cooperative solutions for reconciling the sometimes competing interests of management and nonmanagement employees.

Unfortunately, Joe Scanlon did not write much, not even about Scanlon plans. But he did write an article on profit-sharing case studies that was published in *Industrial Relations Review* in October 1948 and reprinted in Frederick Lesieur's *The Scanlon Plan* (1958). His theory of workplace relationships can be found in his response to profit-sharing skeptics:

> In any event, success [of union-management cooperation plans] can be achieved only if the employees, through their union, are taken into management's confidence. This is admittedly a broad statement; but let us consider its ramifications.What are the problems affecting the industry, the company, or the plan? The worker would like to know about them. He is anxious to contribute his know-how and intelligence in helping solve these problems. He is not, as a rule, the unthinking, selfish person many people would have us believe. He needs an outline and a proper sense of direction. Granted that a normal evolutionary development has taken him from the area of strife and suspicion, fighting for the very existence of his union, into the area of complete acceptance, a new and different set of constructive activities and responsibilities must replace those he has discarded.
>
> If management expects to gain anything beneficial from these new relationships, it must now devote just as much time and effort in building with the union a complete sense of participation as it has probably spent in the past in fighting the union. As the industrial psychologist might put it, the egoistic needs of the group must be satisfied. Participation and partnership on a democratic basis will furnish these satisfactions. (148–49)

This passage shows that Joe Scanlon did rely on such ideas as workplace harmony and worker satisfaction. More important, though, is his underlying assumption that workplace relations should be defined as a conflict of interest between management and nonmanagement employees, with the union representing the latter's interests. He believed that these conflicts of interests could be dealt with more reasonably by developing workplace structures and rewards that encouraged nonmanagement employees to participate in decisions that could make the facility a better competitor which, in turn, meant better job security and wages for nonmanagement employees. Thus, Scanlon assumed that workplace relations are best understood in terms of interest group behavior.

An essential factor in the research and commentaries on Scanlon-type gainsharing plan successes and failures is the role of organizational politics. Gainsharing threatens management power (and union power, if the facility has one) and traditional relationships between management and

nonmanagement employees, because each group's interests are being redefined. For instance, when facilities implement a Scanlon plan it is in
the interests of both groups to meet and discuss production problems.
Management's fears about changes in the power dynamics is revealed in
the following exchange between John F. Donnelly, president of Donnelly
Mirrors, which has had a Scanlon plan since the 1950s, and *Harvard Business Review* ("Participative Management," 1977):

> HBR: People often like the sound of industrial democracy, and yet it
> hasn't taken hold very fast in the United States. Why do you think peo-
> ple are skeptical about approaches like Donnelly's?
>
> Mr. Donnelly: They're afraid of losing authority.
>
> HBR: Why do you think they believe authority works better?
>
> Mr. Donnelly: Because that's the way it's been done, and that's the
> way organizations are structured. They're most modeled after the
> military, and it's difficult for people to conceive of any other system
> working. I would be the last one to say that we don't use authority
> in this company. We do. But, to the extent that you have to rely on
> the authority of your position, you're a questionable manager. If
> you are in the position to get people to accept ideas because they're
> sound and if you are not willing to accept an idea because it's
> sound, then you're really not a good manager. (117)

Similar sentiments appear in the early scholarly articles on Scanlon
plans. Regarding the bonus calculation, Lesieur (1958) warns managers
that "it is most important, whatever measurement is used, to put all of
the cards on the table and hide nothing" (43). Regarding employee participation in decisions, Schultz (1958) warns managers that "success
from participation stems from hard work and from willingness at all levels of the management organization to face criticism" (51–52). Shultz
(1958) further asserted that the major obstacle with Scanlon plan implementation is not the typical management concern about getting previously adversarial workers to cooperate; rather, it rests with "the initial
loss of prestige and consequent opposition of middle and lower management people" (61). Getting supervisors to redefine their interests and
buy into gainsharing mechanisms remains a prominent issue in the literature (Hatcher, Ross, and Collins 1992).

What sort of interest group behaviors are managers likely to exhibit?
Schulhof (1979), president of a company that implemented a Scanlon

plan, notes that managers are tempted to take the extra efforts generated by nonmanagement employees for granted and thus eliminate the financial bonus in the hope of getting the same effort without the expense:

> It [a Scanlon Plan] costs a lot. When you begin productivity sharing, you are paying a bonus that doesn't cost you anything until performance is improved. However, after several years when you look and see that bonus payments are equal to profits and you could have twice as much profit if you cancelled the bonus payments, management begins to question the program. The fact is, we do find ourselves at times paying more than what the same person might be making in a different company. It is therefore necessary to always remember that, although you are paying more, by definition you are getting more, because the employees are more productive. We are still paying less per unit than formerly. (62)

Nonmanagement employees also face threats to the interests they had prior to gainsharing implementation. According to Schulhof (1979: 58), when his company implemented a Scanlon plan, "the marginal workers who were previously 'ripping off the company' were now 'ripping off the workers.'" He also found that "the real performers, who had been holding back, became more highly motivated than ever!" (59). At Xaloy, many of the first-year suggestions "were offered either to test management's sincerity, or to take care of some aggravation on the plant floor" (Markham, Scott, and Cox 1992). All of these interest-group activities suggest very prominent political behaviors.

Political behaviors continue after gainsharing is implemented. Because Scanlon-type plans must evolve constantly, a static plan will become a failed plan (Graham-Moore and Ross, 1990; Markham Scott, and Cox 1992). Scanlon plans at Donnelly Mirrors ("Participative Management," 1977) and Herman Miller (Ramquist 1982), which have been in operation since the 1950s, are continually changing. For instance, the bonus calculation needs to be constantly revised to meet changes in a facility's business environment. At every step of the evolutionary process, a new political situation arises.

Organization theorists are recognizing that conceptualizing organizations as political systems, wherein relationships between management and nonmanagement employees are interpreted in terms of conflicts of interest and power differences, enhances our understanding of why individuals and institutions fail to achieve their goals (Aktouf 1992; Astley and Zajac 1991; Braverman 1974; Clegg 1979, 1990; March 1962; Morgan 1986; Pfeffer 1981, 1992). The next step is to place Scanlon-type plans within the historical context of workplace conflicts of interest.

Workplace Conflicts of Interest

Organizational relationships between management and nonmanagement employees have always been marked by conflicts of interest. Adam Smith ([1776] 1976), in his economic treatise *Wealth of Nations*, predicted two socially undesirable outcomes for nonmanagement employees under a market economy—low wages and worker alienation—that he unsuccessfully attempted to solve by appealing to the moral sentiments of owners (Collins 1988). Smith forecasts that by pursuing their economic interests, owners would (1) successfully drive wages below the level of worker subsistence because owners had an unfair bargaining position (Smith [1776] 1976, i: 74) and (2) apply the division of labor in such excess that it would make employees as "stupid and ignorant as it is possible for a human creature to become" (Smith [1776] 1976, ii: 302–03). In both circumstances, Smith appealed to the moral sentiments of owners to restrain these selfish temptations.

The failure of owners and managers to heed Smith's moral appeals has fueled writings on capitalism and organization theory ranging from Karl Marx (abandon capitalism) to Taylor (tinker with incentive systems). Taylor's ideas are examined closely here because it was Taylorism that both Joe Scanlon and Douglas McGregor were combating. Like Adam Smith, Taylor was concerned with the relationship among the division of labor, production output, and employee wages. At the time of the American Industrial Revolution, there was a need to organize a large number of workers to perform a large variety of unfamiliar tasks. There was no common body of managerial knowledge, no common code of management behavior, a shortage of skilled labor, a lack of professionals to train the work force, and a managerial problem of disciplining and motivating formerly self-employed agrarian workers or craftsmen. Foremen possessed the authority to hire and fire workers, yet they lacked control over worker behavior in terms of overall production performance (Braverman 1974; Farnham 1921; Wren 1979). Production standards were dominated by "rule-of-thumb" calculations. According to Taylor ([1903] 1947), the managerial system of nineteenth-century America operated under the notion of "ignorance and deceit" (45). Workers deceived their employer about production output capacity, and the employer deceived workers about the wage value of their output. Both interest groups were ignorant of each other's knowledge.

Because of these deceptive practices, Taylor argued, industrial organizations were unable to produce efficiently. Production efficiency was the function of workers adopting the best methodology for performing particular work tasks in exchange for higher wages. Further investigation into the production efficiency led Taylor to highlight what he perceived to be a set of primary conflicts of interest between managers and workers over output and wages. First, managers want high production output, whereas workers want to restrict their output. Second, workers want high wage payments, whereas managers want to hold down wages. For the most part, managers control the wage factor, and workers control the production output factor. This primary conflict of interest is diagrammed in Figure 2-1.

How and why did workers restrict output? According to Taylor, workers restricted output by "soldiering," which was the purposeful slowdown by workers in performing their tasks. Taylor ([1903] 1947) differentiated between natural soldiering and systematic soldiering. Natural soldiering, which Taylor believed to be a universal principle, is the natural tendency of people not to exert themselves unnecessarily. Taylor pointed out that managers could appeal to workers' conscience to perform their duties more efficiently; he noted, however, that a threat from management would achieve the desired result much quicker.

Taylor was more concerned with systematic soldiering, a collaboration among workers to restrict output "done by the men with the deliberate object of keeping their employers ignorant of how fast work can be done" (Taylor [1911] 1947: 21). Taylor provided two reasons why workers adopted this practice. First, workers believed they were securing their own jobs by restricting output; if each worker increased output by 10 percent, workers feared that management would no longer need the

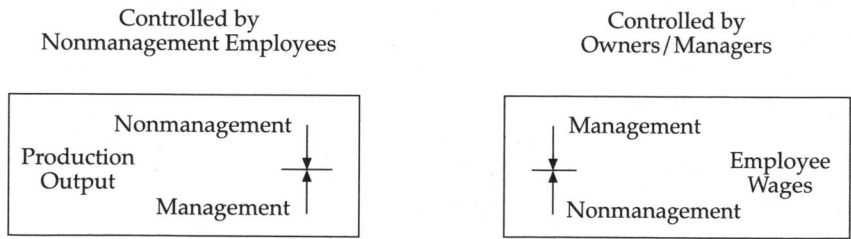

Figure 2-1.   Conflict of interest between management and nonmanagement employees

services of 10 percent of the workforce. Unrestricted output, therefore, meant unemployment for some workers. Although this may be true in the short term, Taylor maintained that capitalist theory showed that increased production efficiency led to more sales and, thus, more jobs. Second, workers restricted their output because of management's misuse of the piece-rate system. Taylor argued that management's penchant for setting piece rates created an unhealthy tension between the two interest groups. Workers became skeptical of future attempts by management to increase their productivity after management reduced their piece-rate incentive. According to Taylor ([1912] 1947), after a worker's piece rate has been cut once, "it would take an exceedingly broadminded man to do anything else than adopt soldiering as his permanent policy" (24).

Unlike Smith, Taylor did not appeal to the moral sentiments of either managers or workers to resolve this conflict of interest. Instead, he sought to devise an organizational mechanism for exchanges between the two disputing interest groups—improved production output in exchange for higher wages—designed and enforced by a technological engineer, such as himself. Instead of letting each worker determine for himself how a job task should be performed or depending on rule-of-thumb estimation by management, a technocrat would determine the best method of production. Taylor then took Adam Smith's concept of division of labor and did what Smith feared most by applying it to an extreme: he performed time and motion studies for each step of the production process.

Taylor argued that employers should not expect workers to simply adopt the best work methods. Workers would want something in return for changing their behavior, and what they wanted most were higher wages. The wage rate system Taylor proposed was differential; outstanding work would be rewarded, financially and inadequate work would be punished financially. He believed that such a system was democratic, for workers would receive financial compensation based on individual merit. The technocrat's determination of wage differentials was to be scientifically derived. Workers would receive their regular wages based on labor market rates plus a premium for performing according to the technocrat's production standards.

Taylor maintained that both disputing interest groups would benefit from this exchange. The workers were being asked to sacrifice productivity restrictions in exchange for higher wages, whereas the employer would sacrifice minimal wages in exchange for improved production performance. Both the employer and the workers had to temper one interest in order to achieve another.

Taylor often referred to scientific management as a "mental revolution." Workers were to change their attitudes toward production performance, and the employer was to change his attitude toward wages. Taylor ([1912] 1947) testified before the U.S. Congress on this issue:

> Now, in its essence, scientific management involves a complete mental revolution on the part of the *workingman* engaged in any particular establishment or industry—a complete mental revolution on the part of these men as their duties toward their work, toward their fellow men, and toward their employers. And it involves the equally complete mental revolution on the part of those on the *management's side*—the foreman, the superintendent, the owner of the business, the board of directors— a complete mental revolution on their part as to their duties toward their fellow workers in management, toward their workmen, and toward all their daily problems. And without this complete mental revolution on *both* sides scientific management does not exist. (26–27) [emphasis mine]

A distinction must be made between the theory and practice of scientific management. Taylor entered facilities promising that scientific management would increase efficiency and soothe the adversarial nature of relationships between management and nonmanagement employees. In many instances, scientific management led to more efficient use of material and human resources, but management and nonmanagement employee relations worsened. Taylor was not well liked by either workers or management. Taylor's own managerial track record was not entirely successful: he would be hired, promise better labor relations, arrogantly declare his system of management better than any other, restructure and redefine the manager's realm of responsibility, overrule objections from other managers, cause trouble with the workers, and then resign or get fired (Copley 1923; Kakar 1970; Nelson 1980).

Managers and workers were particularly sensitive to the redefinition of their job responsibilities. Under scientific management, managers were assigned four duties: scientifically determine the best work method, scientifically select and train workers, supervise workers closely, and organize all work activity (Taylor [1911] 1947: 36). Whereas managers were assigned additional responsibilities, workers were assigned fewer responsibilities. They were no longer involved in planning decisions. Instead, they were limited to adopting the best work method as prescribed by technocrats.

Taylor ([1912] 1947) told Congress that his greatest difficulty was "almost entirely with the management" (153). Taking these problems into consideration, Taylor skewed the implementation of scientific management to offset managerial objections. In a pragmatic gesture, Taylor recognized that the technocrat must be invited the workplace by the employer. Thereafter, Taylor perceived his chore as threefold: first, convince the employer to hire him; second, convince the employer to offer higher wages to workers; third, convince workers to increase production output. The major stumbling block for Taylor was obtaining an invitation from employers to restructure a facility. As a result, Taylor took shortcuts in order to minimize implementation costs and never implemented scientific management as he had theoretically explained it (Nelson 1980; Wrege and Peroni 1974). When asked by Congress how many companies had fully implemented scientific management, Taylor responded, "in its entirety—none; not one" ([1912] 1947: 280).

Taylor's alternative approach favored employers, not workers. In many instances the implementation of scientific management meant average pay for extraordinary work. Production quotas were sometimes scientifically derived and sometimes haphazardly derived. Regardless of methodology, production quotas tended to be high. Taylor admitted that it was not beyond managerial trickery to use scientific management "as a club to drive the workmen into doing a larger day's work for approximately the same pay that they had received in the past" ([1911] 1947: 134). As a result, the technocrat became an advocate of employers' interests—higher production output and minimum worker wages—and an adversary of workers' interests—higher wages and restricted output.

Taylor proposed that scientific management would result in harmony between managers and workers. He sought "the elimination of almost all causes for dispute and disagreement" between management and workers (Taylor [1911] 1947: 142). Facilities that adopted scientific management would be free of unnecessary quarrels and bickering. With each disputing interest group offering what the opposing interest group desired—higher wages for workers and higher output for owners—the end result would be "friendly cooperation" at the workplace. Following the withering away of adversarial relations between management and nonmanagement employees, Taylor foresaw the withering away of trade unions. Workers, content with the higher wages achieved without overexertion, would reject all overtures to unionize (Taylor [1903] 1947: 195). Such was his utopian vision. The result, however, was increased resentment by both interest groups toward each other.

Scanlon-Type Gainsharing Plan Solution

Scanlon-type plans highlight a secondary set of conflicts of interest between management and nonmanagement employees and link them to the primary wage-output conflict of interest highlighted by Taylor. First, some managers want information about the production process, whereas some workers want to withhold this information. Second, some workers want to be involved in decision making, whereas some managers want to restrict employee access to facility decisions. For the most part, managers control the level of employee involvement in facility decisions, and workers control the amount of information they share with managers about the production process (Graham-Moore and Ross 1990).

Scientific management, though it improved production efficiency, was unable to resolve all production process problems. Taylor foresaw this weakness in his theory; because the workplace environment was changing rapidly, he expected problems to arise that technocrats could not predict with any certainty. Technocrats could theoretically determine the best production methods but in practice needed feedback from workers (Taylor [1912] 1947). Taylor incorrectly assumed that workers would inform management about production problems because workers' pay was dependent on their production output. Workers know what is wrong with the production process, but they are unwilling to inform management for a variety of reasons: some may believe it is management's job, not their job, to determine process errors; some may hold a grudge with management and refuse to cooperate; and still others may use production process failures as a means of restricting their output. Similarly, some managers may believe that it is their job, not the job of workers, to determine process errors.

Though workers may be unwilling to offer production process suggestions to managers, and managers may be reticent to ask for them, workers may still want to be involved in production-related decisions. Hugo Munsterberg (1913) spearheaded industrial psychology by arguing that an efficient worker was a well-adjusted person who needed challenges beyond monotonous and boring work assignments. Elton Mayo (1933) spearheaded the human relations school of management by documenting the importance of fulfilling an employee's social needs at the workplace.

Importantly, this is not to say that all workers want to participate or that all workers will perform well under a participatory management system. For instance, Brownell (1981) has shown through laboratory and field studies that participation has a positive effect on a particular personality type, namely, those workers who tend to believe that they control their destiny. Nonetheless, when participatory plans are implemented, there is seldom a lack of willing volunteers. Lawler (1986) reports that when quality circles are introduced in a facility, up to 80 percent of its employees volunteer to participate. Similarly, Tannenbaum (1986) has provided extensive empirical research to support the view that if the proper organizational reward mechanisms are in place, workers will perform well in a participatory setting.

Whereas workers are reluctant to offer suggestions under traditional systems of management, managers are quite reluctant to allow nonmanagement employees to participate in facility decisions. As discussed in Chapter 1, managers are very slowly jumping on the participatory management bandwagon. The major objection of facility executives is that workers' involvement in decisions will lead to less, not greater, efficiency. For instance, when the West German government passed the 1976 co-determination law giving workers broader representation in the decision-making process of large corporations, managerial personnel objected on the grounds that such representation would politicize technical questions, increase bureaucratization, hamper entrepreneurial drive, dilute responsibilities, delay decisions, and endanger the unity and flexibility of management (Bergmann 1975). Commenting on the American experience with participatory management, Halal and Brown (1981) list its weaknesses as (1) creating unrealistic expectations and promises, (2) being time-consuming, (3) generating mediocre decisions, (4) confusing accountability, and (5) instigating disruptive conflicts.

The primary and secondary conflicts of interests between management and nonmanagement employees are interrelated. Managers, for the most part, control nonmanagement employee access to wages and the decision-making process. Nonmanagement employees, for the most part, control management access to their production output and information about the efficiency and effectiveness of the production process. Managers, believing it is in their interest, restrain employee wages and employee involvement in the decision-making process. Similarly, nonmanagement employees, believing it is in their interests, restrain production output and essential information about what is wrong with the production process. Both interest groups want what the other interest group is restraining.

These behaviors are reinforced on a daily basis through standard workplace operating policies and procedures and are further exacerbated by the authoritarian tendencies of top management. Whether referred to as a "bureaucratic culture" (Kilmann 1984), "control paradigm"

(Lawler 1986), "traditional paradigm" (Veltrop and Harrington 1988), a "rational model" (Peters and Waterman 1982) or the "Old Guard" (O'Toole 1985), this is the type of culture that organizational development consultants commonly find in modern organizations.

Scanlon-type gainsharing plans establish interest-group exchanges that link the strengths and weaknesses of both management and nonmanagement control factors. In this sense, management unfreezes the quasi-stationary equilibrium levels, shifts them to a more socially desirable level (greater employee participation, information sharing, output, and wages), and refreezes them (Lewin 1947). As shown in Figure 2-2, by implementing a Scanlon-type plan, managers allow nonmanagement employees greater access to decision-making in exchange for information on improving production (exchange relation 1) that will in turn lead to increased production output (exchange relation 2). This shift in equilibrium is demonstrated by the noncentered positions of the opposing arrows in Figure 2-2. Similarly, managers allow employees greater access to revenues in exchange for these production output improvements (exchange relation 3). It is assumed that gainsharing bonuses will in turn motivate more nonmanagement employees to participate on gainsharing teams and offer more production-related improvement suggestions (exchange relation 4).

In the exchanges that take place under Scanlon-type plans, management expects to obtain from workers information about the production process and improved productivity, whereas the workers expect to be allowed more involvement in the facility's decision making process and to receive higher wages. On the other side of the equation, management expects to lose some authority and facility earnings to workers, who expect to lose some production-related information and production output leverage to management. Both interest groups, by entering into the gainsharing exchange, expect their gains to outweigh their losses.

Importantly, Figure 2-2 shows the first step in this change process is management's willingness to share decision-making power with nonmanagement employees. If nonmanagement employees are not permitted to participate in making decisions, then there will be no suggestions forthcoming, no changes in production process output, and no wage bonuses. Management's essential first step is contrary to its historical interests of minimizing employee wages and access to decisions.

As discussed in Chapter 1, the empirical findings regarding Scanlon-type plans and other participatory management transformations are ambiguous (Hammer 1988; Leana and Florkowski 1992; Wagner 1994). The primary and secondary conflicts of interests help to explain why. Imple-

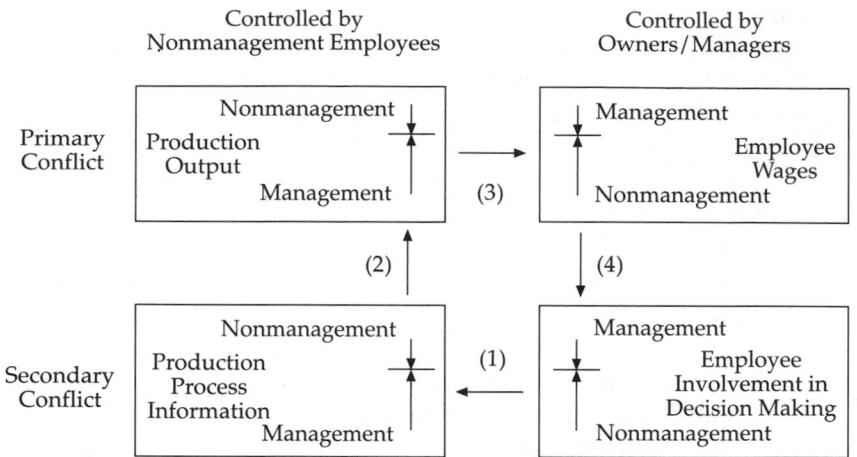

Figure 2-2. Gainsharing solution to conflicts of interest between management and nonmanagement employees

mentation of a plan will not be smooth because both groups are influenced by their conflicting interests. These conflicting interests can be managed better, but they are not likely to disappear with the implementation of gainsharing. Some managers and nonmanagement employees will not want to reduce the power differentials, some will want more modest reductions, and some will want greater reductions. Importantly, management and nonmanagement interest groups are not monolithic entities; there are political coalitions within them. For instance, some participants in the change process may maintain that Scanlon-type gainsharing plans are too democratic, whereas others may assert that the plans are not democratic enough.

A fuller understanding of interest group reactions to Scanlon-type plans can be developed from the political science literature on transforming dictatorships to democracies. Conceptualizing organizations as political systems can enhance our understanding of why individuals, groups, and institutions fail to obtain agreed-upon goals—such as improving facility performance through Scanlon-type gainsharing plans. Facilities that implement an institutionalized suggestion system, department teams whose nonmanagement employees elect representatives to analyze and implement suggestions, and review boards where both management and nonmanagement employees discuss production changes are becoming more democratic. As such, much can be learned by studying what happens when authoritarian political systems attempt to become more democratic.

A very interesting literature highlights the democratic values underlying participatory management plans as the primary reason why facilities should adopt them (Dachler and Wilpert 1978; Dahl 1985; Lindenfeld and Rothschild-Whitt 1982; Pateman 1970). Though I agree with these theorists, I will use democratic theory for descriptive rather than prescriptive purposes, that is, to better understand what happens when organizations adopt democratic mechanisms. We need to step away from the management literature and examine a different literature, the political science literature, which describes solutions to the same problem—conflicts of interest between competing groups.

Political Systems: From Authoritarianism to Democracy

An extensive political science literature describes what happens when authoritarian right- or left-wing governments adopt democratic principles (Baloyra 1987; Diamond, Linz, and Lipset 1989; Di Palma 1990; Karl 1990; Malloy and Seligson 1987; Morlino 1987; O'Donnell, Schmitter, and Whitehead 1986; Przeworski 1986; Weiner and Ozbudun 1987). This transition often resembles a complicated multilayered chess game between the former authoritarian rulers and emerging political leaders who claim to represent the interests of the formerly oppressed polity (O'Donnell and Schmitter 1986; Valenzuela 1989). Although each country's particular transition is unique, three common patterns have emerged from these transitional experiences: the former authoritarian rulers manipulate the transitional process to enhance their own self-interests and/or group interests; power struggles arise among the former authoritarian rulers, among the new political leaders, and between the authoritarian rulers and the new political leaders; and hidden and suppressed social and economic problems surface.

First, the former authoritarian rulers often manipulate the transition by minimizing the diffusion of democratic processes and structures to safeguard their already entrenched interests. They want some pluralism, but they do not want to lose their current power status (Borzutzky 1987; Conaghan 1987; Duncan Baretta and Markoff 1987; Malloy 1987; Vacs 1987).

Second, power struggles arise because of disagreements *within and between* both interest groups over the speed of the transition and its component institutional structures and procedures. Thus, both the former authoritarian rulers and the new political leaders experience factional infighting during the transitional process due to different interests and expectations (Di Palma 1990; Remmer 1991). Typically, neither group is experienced in democratic policies and procedures.

This disunity is particularly obvious among the newly empowered leaders, who typically fall into three categories: opportunists, who fear a coup and often acquiesce in accepting top-down rules restrict democracy; maximalists, who are combative, reject compromises, and are willing to risk the possibility of a coup that could end the transition; and recalcitrants, who recognize the possibility of a coup and confront and compromise only when their participation is guaranteed (O'Donnell and Schmitter 1986; Payne 1991). These leadership patterns can be found among both the former authoritarian rulers and the new political leaders. For instance, Mikhail Gorbachev appears to have been unsuccessful in developing a middle course that was acceptable to the maximalists—who complained that the reforms were developing too slowly—and to the opportunists and the recalcitrants, who complained that the reforms were developing too quickly.

Third, hidden and suppressed social and economic problems surface. The former authoritarian rulers and the new political leaders must appropriately respond to these problems if the transitional process is to continue. For instance, democratization in Russia has forced suppressed social and economic problems, such as crime, pollution, prostitution, and poverty, onto the political agenda. Thus the crafted rather than imposed transitional outcomes greatly depend on how the subgroups associated with both the former authoritarian rulers and the new political leaders respond to the uncertainty that dominates each stage of the transitional process (Di Palma 1990; Karl 1990; Malloy 1987; Przeworski 1986; Weiner and Ozbudun 1987).

Application to Scanlon-Type Gainsharing Plans

Scanlon-type plans represent what Dahl (1989) calls a "middle-range" democratic process. Gainsharing is democratic in that typically a vote is taken among the nonmanagement employees and 75–90 percent must favor implementation for the process to begin, the nonmanagement department team representatives are elected by their peers, any nonmanagement department employee is eligible for the position, and the teams have a budget to implement production changes. Management—the ultimate sovereign—places three important limitations on the democratization process, however. First, only production-related suggestions can be submitted and voted on; suggestions regarding base wages, personnel policies, marketing strategy, and the like are dismissed. Second, expensive production changes (typically those costing more than $400) require final approval from management. Third, elections are limited to the position of department team representative; upper management and supervisors are not elected to their positions. Using the continuum and typology developed by Bernstein (1982) and Logue (1991) for determining the degree of democracy found in organizations, it is reasonable to label Scanlon-type gainsharing plans as "middle-range" democracy.

As shown in Figure 2-3, the patterns of political behaviors that occur when political dictatorships transform into democracies are also likely to occur in organizations that adopt Scanlon-type plans. Most organizations consist of a range of management and nonmanagement employees who are either supportive of, opposed to, or neutral toward organizational change: go-getters, opponents, and fence-sitters, respectively, whose attitudes and behaviors parallel those of the political opportunists, maximalists, and recalcitrants, respectively.

Management and nonmanagement *go-getters* regard Scanlon-type plans as a positive change that is beneficial to the organization and/or themselves. They actively support gainsharing activities and participate in decision-making processes aimed at facility operations. Similar to political opportunists, they are more likely to give each other the benefit of the doubt on sensitive or highly contentious issues. Supportive gainsharing behaviors of go-getters typically include being cooperative and helpful with others, verbally promoting the plan when around others, contributing suggestions, and displaying a positive attitude about work (Hatcher, Ross, and Collins 1991; Ross, Hatcher, and Collins 1992). Nonmanagement go-getters also tend to be those employees who exhibit assisting, or prosocial, behaviors at work, such as helping others who have been absent, volunteering for things that are not required, orienting new people, helping others who have heavy work loads and assisting supervisors with their work (Hatcher, Ross, and Collins 1989). Nonetheless, due to existing power differentials, both management and nonmanagement go-getters will try to manipulate the gainsharing process to guarantee that their group interests are met.

Management and nonmanagement *opponents* are highly skeptical about Scanlon-type gainsharing plans and may sabotage the system. Similar to political maximalists, they may demand that democratic reforms be made either all at once or not at all. Adversarial managers re-

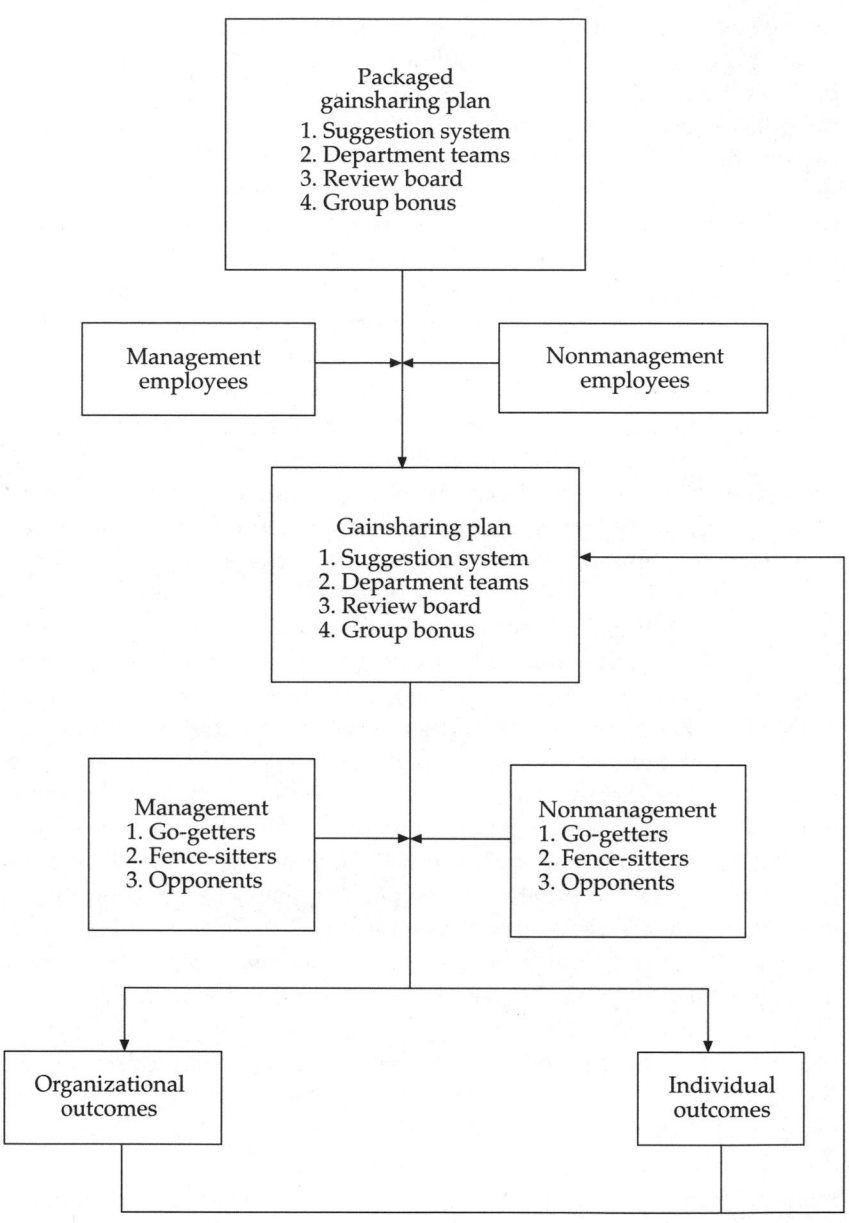

Figure 2-3. Democratizing the workplace

gard employee involvement as a threat to their power and fear gainsharing will increase the power of some nonmanagement employees whom they believe are either untrustworthy or unqualified for this added responsibility. In this sense, adversarial managers espouse Aristotle's objections to political democracy: Democratic reforms are likely to result in mediocrity, rule by the uneducated and unskilled, bureaucracy, instability, and lack of accountability (Ross and Collins 1987). Adversarial nonmanagement employees are highly skeptical of managerial intentions due to their past negative experiences with managers. The destructive gainsharing behaviors of opponents typically include verbally opposing the plan when around others, discouraging the contribution of suggestions by other employees, criticizing other employees who are involved in the plan, hindering the investigation and implementation of gainsharing suggestions, hindering the performance of gainsharing teams, and exhibiting generally negative attitudes toward the plan, management, and the facility (Hatcher, Ross, and Collins 1991; Ross, Hatcher, and Collins 1992). Both management and nonmanagement opponents perceive gainsharing as a threat to dismantling the previously agreed upon boundary lines between the duties of management and nonmanagement employees.

Management and nonmanagement *fence-sitters* are those employees who take a wait-and-see approach toward Scanlon-type gainsharing plans. Similar to political recalcitrants, they do not intentionally undermine the change nor do they exert their effort to make it work. If the system is beneficial to them and the organization, they support it; if not, they let the system fail on its own accord. Fence-sitters may occasionally offer a suggestion that makes their job easier to perform. Go-getters and opponents compete for their allegiance. Go-getters emphasize the positive aspects of gainsharing to encourage the fence-sitters to become more involved and join their coalition; opponents emphasize the negative aspects of gainsharing to convince the fence-sitters to participate and join their coalition. Assuming that involving all facility employees in decision-making processes and sharing the financial gains of their improved production performance with them are highly desirable goals, which this book does assume, then it is also highly desirable that the fence-sitters among the management and nonmanagement employees join forces with the go-getters rather than the opponents.

Below are two "power games" propositions pertaining to the shifting of authority. In labeling these propositions in terms of power games it is important to recall that the concept of *power* is a neutral term describing the authority relationship between two or more people or groups. As described by Machiavelli and experienced in many organizations, power can be obtained, maintained, and distributed in either ethical or unethical ways (Collins 1992):

> *Proposition 1:* Management and nonmanagement employees will likely manipulate the transitional process based on their own self-interests and/or group-interests.
>
> *Proposition 2:* Power struggles will likely arise among and between the go-getters, fence-sitters, and opponents in both management and nonmanagement groups.

After gainsharing is implemented, some hidden and suppressed social and economic problems will demand immediate attention. For instance, nonmanagement employees who are go-getters and fence-sitters may offer production-related suggestions about problems managers were unaware of. Adversarial nonmanagement employees may demand that certain workplace policies be changed immediately.

Last, the long-term stability of gainsharing will be a function of whether management and nonmanagement go-getters, fence-sitters, and opponents believe that gainsharing fulfills their previously unmet needs. Although it is essential for some nonmanagement employees to receive gainsharing bonuses to ensure their participation, other nonmanagement employees will continue to participate due to empowerment issues or if they believe, for instance, that improvements in health and safety conditions are due to the gainsharing system's suggestion and team processes. In other words, gainsharing intervention should not be considered unsuccessful solely on the grounds of a low payout or lack of support from some oppositional managers or nonmanagement employees. Thus, the following two "outcomes" propositions:

> *Proposition 3:* Hidden and suppressed social and economic problems will surface shortly after gainsharing implementation.
>
> *Proposition 4:* Management and nonmanagement employees will likely continue to support gainsharing as long as it fulfills some of their monetary or nonmonetary self-interests and/or group-interests.

As summarized earlier in this chapter in the discussion on workplace conflicts of interest, there is nothing radically new in relying on the concept of self-interest and/or group interests to predict how the implementation process will evolve or how employees will interpret gainsharing outcomes. Instead, the importance of these propositions rests in their potential ability to guide a systematic and evolutionary understanding of gainsharing dynamics. If workplace democracy is inevitable (Slater and Bennis 1990), then evolutionary dynamics require careful attention. What types of manipulations occur (Proposition 1)? What types of power struggles occur (Proposition 2)? What types of social and economic problems surface (Proposition 3)? What types of outcomes are generated (Proposition 4)? For these reasons, several in-depth case studies were conducted to test this theory of gainsharing dynamics.

3 Research Methods
and Facility Profiles

The four propositions formulated in Chapter 2 were derived from a review of the literature, the results of empirical studies, and my field experience with Scanlon-type gainsharing facilities. Conflict of interest theory lacks the empirical foundation for a broad-based aggregate analysis. As argued at the conclusion of Chapter 1, multiple case-study analysis is thus the most appropriate method of data collection to empirically examine this new theory.

Yin (1987: 23) defines case study analysis as "an empirical inquiry that investigates a contemporary phenomenon within its real-life context; when the boundaries between phenomenon and context are not clearly evident; and in which multiple sources are used." Case studies were particularly appealing for this book because the propositions should be examined within the context of business organizations.

Selection of Facilities

Yin (1987) suggests that in undertaking multiple-case studies, "every case should serve a specific purpose within the overall scope of inquiry" (48). For this reason a list of facilities operating under a Scanlon-type gainsharing plan for at least four years was compiled from a leading gainsharing consulting institute. Between the years 1983 and 1987, the consulting institute implemented gainsharing at seventeen manufacturing facilities. In addition to controlling for type of industry (manufacturing), this selection methodology provided important controls for three other rival hypotheses: time period, type of intervention, and intervention agent. First, the analysis was limited to facilities that implemented a plan during a specific four-year period. Thus, all of the facilities were subject to the same national economic and political conditions. Second, the intervention structure, process, and financial bonus system were controlled to the extent that the consulting institute presented the same intervention package to all of the management teams. Third, the intervention agent was controlled to the extent that each management team responded to the same gainsharing consultant.

The seventeen facilities differed according to the following key characteristics: type of ownership, employee representation, number of employees, yearly sales, and reason for implementation. Eleven of the facilities were nonunion, and six were unionized. The six facilities discussed in this book—four nonunion and two union—were chosen from among the seventeen. The two union facilities were not chosen until after I studied the results of the four nonunion field studies.

During November 1989, telephone interviews and surveys were conducted with the gainsharing coordinators of the eleven nonunion facilities. Data were collected in reference to when the gainsharing plan was implemented, why the plan was implemented, number of facility employees, percentage of employees on gainsharing teams, frequency of review board and team meetings, number of customers and suppliers, type of product, facility newsletters, employee attitude surveys, and gainsharing bonus payouts.

Two nonunion facilities were eliminated from consideration because they lacked formal documentation. One facility declined to participate in the study. Of the remaining eight nonunion facilities, there was substantial variance regarding organization size, product, reason for gainsharing implementation, financial status, and size of the gainsharing bonus payouts. Additionally, all of the facilities had key changes in personnel. Each of these factors could present a challenge to the study's findings— that is, the power struggles and gainsharing outcomes could be a function of organizational size, financial status, or changes in facility personnel.

At the same time, these variances could also provide a more comprehensive understanding of gainsharing.Taking this latter approach, I chose the four nonunion facilities based on variances in gainsharing bonus payouts, to gain greater insight into whether organizational changes were a function of employee participation in decision making or in financial improvements. Therefore, Cylinder Lifts was chosen because it had the *lowest* average monthly bonus payout (1.2 percent/$18) among the nonunion facilities that implemented Scanlon-type plans, including no bonus payouts during the twelve months prior to the field study. Foam Seats and Forestland were chosen because they had *modest* average monthly bonus payouts (5.2 percent/$63 and 6.8 percent/$85). Innovations was chosen because it had the *highest* average monthly bonus payout (19.3 percent/$370). In addition, Innovations was listed as one of the one hundred best companies to work for in the United States (Levering, Moskowitz, and Katz 1985). The four nonunion field studies were conducted during 1990.

The two union field studies were conducted during 1992. These facilities were chosen after the four nonunion field studies had been conducted based on how they could further add to an understanding of the gainsharing phenomenon. Innovations-Brotherhood was selected because it belonged to the same publicly owned corporation as Innovations but had a very small average monthly gainsharing bonus payout (0.4 percent/$12). Why would one facility of a corporation operating under a Scanlon-type plan have very large bonuses while another have very small bonuses? In addition, why would union officers praise the plan during the telephone interview if such small bonuses were being earned? Packaging International was chosen because it had abandoned its Scanlon-type plan in April 1991. Gainsharing had improved facility operations through many employee suggestions—over a six-year period, gainsharing teams had accepted 8,114 suggestions from nonmanagement employees, or approximately 6.8 suggestions per employee per year—but the average monthly financial bonuses were small (1.2 percent/$25). Why? With so many employee suggestions, why would management and the union want to abandon the plan? Another interesting feature of Packaging International was its employee-ownership dimension.

At all six facilities, a vote of at least 75 percent approval from the nonmanagement employees was required prior to implementation. Relevant characteristics of all six facilities appear in Table 3-1.

Four of the six manufacturing facilities were publicly owned. Yearly sales ranged from $3 million to $200 million, and the number of employees ranged from 50 to 450. Foam Seats and Innovations had only one customer and operated according to a "just-in-time" system. Average yearly salaries for production employees ranged from $14,600 to $35,400.

At all six facilities, gainsharing was implemented for multiple reasons. Managers were somewhat concerned with the need for greater employee involvement for the benefit of the production employees, but the primary reasons for implementation were typically related to pragmatic

Table 3-1. Profiles of six facilities

	Cylinder Lifts	Foam Seats	Forestland	Innovations	Innovations-Brotherhood	Packaging International
Ownership	Private	Public	Public	Public	Public	Private
Union status	Nonunion	Nonunion	Nonunion	Nonunion	Union	Union
Location	Midwest	East	East	Midwest	Midwest	East
Year opened	1954	1984	1981	1983	1938	1940
Product	Cylinders	Car seats	Hammers	Car axles	Truck clutches	Packaging equipment
Sales/year $	$7.3 million	$40 million	$3 million	$200 million	$84 million	$17 million
Customers	Many	One	Several	One	Several	Many
Employees	100	155	50	145	450	200
Average yearly wages	$18,000	$14,600	$15,000	$23,000	$35,400	$25,000
Implemented	1986	1986	1986	1984	1988	1985
% of employees on teams	40%	14%	100%	100%	100%	40%
No. of suggestions per employee/year	3.7	1.3	0.6	4.9	1.7	6.8
Average monthly bonus %	1.2%	5.2%	6.8%	19.3%	0.4%	1.2%
Average monthly bonus $	$18 (1986–90)	$63 (1986–90)	$85 (1986–90)	$370 (1984–90)	$12 (1988–92)	$25 (1985–91)

production concerns. There was also some variance in the percentage of nonmanagement employees who attended gainsharing team meetings. All employees were on gainsharing teams at Forestland, Innovations, and Innovations-Brotherhood, whereas Cylinder Lifts, Foam Seats, and Packaging International used department representatives to staff the gainsharing teams. As noted earlier, the average monthly bonus paid during the course of gainsharing ranged from 0.4 percent ($12) to 19.3 percent ($370).

Data Collection

Semistructured Interviews

The primary source of data collection for each field study was seventy-four semistructured interviews with key informants. Ten to fourteen semistructured interviews were conducted at each facility. Each interview lasted thirty to forty-five minutes, on facility time, and each interviewee was guaranteed anonymity. All interviewees were asked to describe facility operations prior to gainsharing implementation; the reason for gainsharing implementation; the effectiveness of the gainsharing plan; the evolution of trust or mistrust between management and nonmanagement employees during the gainsharing plan; and employee attitudes toward and reactions to the financial bonuses, suggestion system, team meetings, and other gainsharing outcomes.

To obtain a holistic understanding of each facility's gainsharing evolution, four types of employees were interviewed at each facility: managers, nonmanagement go-getters, nonmanagement fence-sitters, and nonmanagement opponents. Local union officials were interviewed at the two union facilities. All of the interviews were arranged with the help of the gainsharing coordinators.

This interview procedure allowed for cross-verification by those who represented a different role in the facility (i.e., stories told by managers were verified by a nonmanagement employee) *and* the gainsharing coordinator. Gainsharing coordinators, who have a central role to play in gainsharing operations, were interviewed first, at the end of each day, and immediately prior to departure. The gainsharing coordinator was a highly respected employee, even by those who said very few good things about management, at the five facilities that still had a Scanlon-type gainsharing plan. At two of these five facilities—Foam Seats and Innovations-Brotherhood—the gainsharing coordinator was a nonmanagement employee. At Packaging International, I relied on the first gain-sharing coordinator, rather than the second and last gainsharing coordi-nator, because the first coordinator was much more respected by the union employees.

The managers were chosen on the basis of two criteria. First, managers were chosen according to their key positions at different levels of the or-ganization's hierarchy (typically the president, facility manager, con-troller, engineering manager, supervisors). The lower down the manage-rial hierarchy, the more options there were for choosing people to interview. At this point, a second criterion was used—support for gain-sharing. Gainsharing coordinators were asked to list which managers they believed were actively supportive of or vocally opposed to the facil-ity's gainsharing plan. If most of the top managers supported gainshar-ing, then mostly oppositional middle-level managers and supervisors were chosen to complete the management sample.

The nonmanagement employees were chosen to represent go-getters, fence-sitters, or opponents, through a three-step process. First, I counted the number of suggestions per employee in each facility's suggestion log book and grouped nonmanagement employees according to the number of suggestions submitted per year. Second, after I explained the concept of go-getters, fence-sitters, and opponents to the gainsharing coordina-tor, the coordinator chose high suggestion-givers, moderate suggestion-givers, and low suggestion-givers who could best articulate the repre-sentative view of each group. Importantly, nonmanagement employees should not be stereotyped as representing a particular group based solely on the number of submitted suggestions. For instance, some em-ployees may not contribute suggestions because they have routine, me-nial job tasks rather than because they oppose gainsharing (Hatcher, Ross, and Collins 1989, 1991). Similarly, some oppositional nonmanage-ment employees may submit many meaningless suggestions in order to annoy managers. Third, I asked a nonmanagement team representative at each facility to verify the gainsharing coordinator's choice for spokes-person. On two occasions the nonmanagement team representative rec-ommended that a different nonmanagement employee could provide me with a "better" interview, and this recommendation was followed.

The seventy-four interviewees consisted of thirty-nine managers (six per facility), eighteen nonmanagement gainsharing team representatives (two to four per facility), and seventeen other production employees (two to four per facility). Although it would have been desirable to inter-view more nonmanagement employees who were go-getters, fence-sitters, or opponents, the attitudes and behaviors of these groups of employees were asked of all interviewees. The go-getters, many of whom had served as gainsharing team representatives, were particularly helpful in elucidating and verifying the reactions of the other two groups of nonmanagement employees. Prior research has shown that those who become involved in gainsharing mechanisms score relatively high on "prosocial behavior" or "assisting behavior" measures and thus tend to be very well networked within the organization (Hatcher, Ross, and Collins 1989, 1991).

The method by which outcomes were verified depended on the nature of the outcome. For instance, purchases of new tools and machinery were traced directly to the gainsharing suggestion logs and minutes of gainsharing meetings, product quality improvements were traced to facility records, and improved communications were cross-verified through interviews and by observing gainsharing bulletin boards in the facility. Obviously, many factors could influence product quality improvements. If several interviewees—such as the owner, gainsharing coordinator, and nonmanagement employees—credited gainsharing for the product quality award the facility won, I accepted their particular knowledge of the situation. The gainsharing coordinator and facility manager were asked to verify each policy and outcome change and its association with gainsharing.

Gainsharing Evaluation and Attitude Survey

A gainsharing evaluation and attitude survey was administered to all facility employees at the four nonunion facilities during the field study. The survey was not administered at the two union facilities because Packaging International had abandoned gainsharing a year prior to the field study. As requested, Foam Seats and Forestland allowed employees to complete the survey on facility time. At Cylinder Lifts and Innovations, the surveys were distributed at all-employee meetings and returned the following day because of these companies' tight production schedules. All surveys were completed anonymously. The survey return rates were 39 percent for Cylinder Lifts, 85 percent for Foam Seats, 100 percent for Forestland, and 98 percent for Innovations. Managers and nonmanagement go-getters at Cylinder Lifts attributed the low return rates to two factors: approximately 25 percent of the production employees could not read or write; and many opponents and fence-sitters refused to complete the survey on their personal time.

The survey instrument consisted of more than fifty-seven questions on a range of factors. Managers at all four facilities added, but did not delete, survey questions based on other employee feedback information they wanted to obtain. Table 3-2 lists fifteen survey factors, the number of items per factor, the statistical means per facility, and coefficient alphas. Fourteen of the fifteen factors were measured with a 5-point Likert scale (1 = Strongly Disagree, 3 = Undecided, 5 = Strongly Agree). Management style was measured with a 4-point Likert scale (1 = System I [authoritarian]; 4 = System IV [participative]). All but one of the survey factors were created by the the gainsharing consulting institute. The five items for the justice factor were taken from Fryxell and Gordon's (1989) measurement of "belief in a just workplace" (i.e., "Basically, most employees are treated fairly").

Internal reliability was determined by pooling together the 364 survey responses from the four nonunion facilities. This method was chosen to determine if the reliabilities were factor specific rather than facility specific. Coefficient alphas were calculated for the thirteen factors that consisted of more than one survey item. The multi-item factors with the greatest degree of internal reliability, all with coefficient alphas of approximately .80 or greater, were trust, supervisor support, management support, review board meetings, bonus calculation, team representative support, employee support, and team meetings. The four factors that had coefficient alphas of .70 or slightly less, which is usually considered borderline reliability (Kidder and Judd 1986), were justice, identity, suggestion processing, and management style. The cooperation factor, with a coefficient alpha of .58, was unreliable and is not included in the case study discussions.

Statistical means for each factor per facility were calculated by averaging the statistical means per survey item within each factor. Forestland had the strongest support for gainsharing activities from both managers and supervisors. Forestland and Innovations had the strongest nonmanagement employee support for gainsharing activities. Cylinder Lifts had the lowest level of trust in management. The employees at Cylinder Lifts also expressed the least amount of faith in the fairness of the bonus calculation. (In chapters 4–7, the survey results are discussed in greater detail for each of the nonunion facilities.)

The correlation matrix for the survey factors appears in Table 3-3. Any correlation of .20 or greater is statistically significant at the .001 level. Since the three-item "cooperation" factor was unreliable, each item was examined separately. The first cooperation item measured cooperation among managers, the second item measured cooperation among employees, and the third item measured cooperation among departments.

Table 3–2. Survey factors: Statistical means and factor reliabilities

Factor	Survey Items	Cylinder Lifts Mean Score	Foam Seats Mean Score	Forestland Mean Score	Innovations Mean Score	Coefficient Alpha
Management support	3	3.3	3.1	3.8	3.3	.81
Supervisor support	5	3.4	3.1	4.0	3.3	.82
Team representative support	4	3.2	3.1	3.5	3.3	.78
Employee support	4	3.1	3.1	3.6	3.5	.76
Suggestion processing	4	3.3	3.2	3.6	3.2	.68
Team meetings	6	3.5	3.1	3.5	3.1	.76
Review board meetings	6	3.7	3.2	3.6	3.3	.81
Bonus calculation	2	1.8	2.6	3.1	3.4	.80
Facility-wide effort	1	3.2	3.3	3.9	3.7	—
Trust	3	2.4	2.7	3.1	3.0	.91
Cooperation[a]	3	3.3	3.3	3.4	3.1	.58
Employee identity	3	3.3	3.0	3.4	3.3	.68
Employee influence	1	2.4	3.0	3.3	3.3	—
Justice	5	2.9	3.0	3.0	3.0	.70
Management style[b]	6	2.7	2.6	2.9	2.6	.67

[a] Factor found to be unreliable due to a coefficient alpha of .58.

[b] Every factor is measured on a 5-point Likert scale (1=Strongly agree—factor is operating well, 3=Undecided, 5=Strongly disagree), except management style, which was measured with a 4-point scale (1=System I—Authoritarian, 4=System IV—Participative).

Table 3–3. Correlation matrix for survey factors

	1	2	3	4	5	6	7	8	9	10	11	12	13	14	15	16	17
1. Management support	—																
2. Supervisor support	.60	—															
3. Team representative support	.53	.52	—														
4. Employee support	.46	.33	.54	—													
5. Suggestion processing	.48	.48	.51	.46	—												
6. Team meetings	.42	.36	.47	.40	.54	—											
7. Review board meetings	.39	.34	.39	.33	.48	.63	—										
8. Bonus calculation	.39	.29	.36	.46	.36	.33	.31	—									
9. Company-wide effort	.41	.33	.33	.47	.37	.34	.32	.40	—								
10. Trust	.53	.49	.47	.53	.44	.39	.29	.57	.47	—							
11. Management cooperation	.32	.40	.31	.36	.37	.29	.27	.36	.28	.47	—						
12. Employee cooperation	.13	.18	.09	.30	.17	.15	.08	.08	.18	.17	.16	—					
13. Department cooperation	.26	.22	.15	.27	.21	.31	.15	.15	.14	.25	.31	.47	—				
14. Employee identity	.41	.37	.41	.54	.35	.33	.29	.50	.50	.55	.3	.31	.26	—			
15. Employee influence	.33	.33	.27	.36	.33	.30	.22	.37	.42	.51	.28	.20	.21	.46	—		
16. Justice	.44	.42	.39	.37	.39	.32	.21	.40	.42	.64	.37	.17	.20	.38	.48	—	
17. Management style	.50	.50	.43	.44	.45	.44	.39	.38	.39	.60	.41	.16	.30	.43	.52	.56	—

Note: Any correlation of .20 or greater is statistically significant at the .001 level.

The correlation matrix provides a general overview of the relationships among these factors for the four nonunion facilities. Trust in management exhibited the largest number of high correlations. Correlations were .50 or higher for the relationship between trust and (1) management support, (2) employee support, (3) bonus calculation fairness, (4) employee identity, (5) employee influence, (6) justice, and (7) participative management style. Management style also exhibited several relatively high correlations, particularly regarding trust and justice. Those who rated a facility's management style as more participative also rated higher levels of trust in management. Fairness of the bonus calculation also exhibited a relatively high correlation (.57) with trust in management. Whether trust in management is a causal factor cannot be tested with the current database and should be examined in future research.

Other Data Sources

Additional information about each facility's gainsharing experience was gathered from the gainsharing suggestion logs, minutes of gainsharing meetings, facility newsletters, and other relevant facility documents. I attended review board meetings at the five facilities that still had gainsharing plans, as well as facility-wide employee meetings, gainsharing team meetings, and work cell meetings, whenever possible.

PART II

Four Nonunion Facilities

4 Cylinder Lifts: A Privately Owned Nonunion Facility, Small Bonuses

Cylinder Lifts is a privately owned nonunion manufacturing facility located on the outskirts of a midwestern rural community. The facility began operations in 1954 and has had two changes in ownership, with the most recent change occurring in 1974. The production of hydraulic cylinders accounted for 80 percent of its business in 1990. Its five primary markets are automotive wreckers, industrial maintenance equipment, construction equipment, garbage trucks, and aerial lift trucks. As such, fluctuations in sales and profitability are linked with domestic heavy industry sales. In 1989, it had sales of $7.3 million—approximately 4 percent of the market—and profits of $292,000. Cylinder Lifts employs one hundred people and has two production shifts.

The facility has three levels of management. Upper-level management includes the president of Cylinder Lifts (who is the owner and is referred to as the owner throughout this chapter) and the board of directors. Middle-level management includes the facility manager, vice president of marketing/sales, controller, materials manager, and engineering manager, all of whom report directly to the owner. Lower-level management includes the production control manager, quality assurance manager, manufacturing engineer, and four foremen, all of whom report to the facility manager.

The nonmanagement employees earn approximately $18,000 a year. Only 75 percent of the production employees have a high school diploma. Several families have fathers and sons working for Cylinder Lifts. The owner proudly introduced me to one family that had three generations of sons working together in the factory. In general, the production employees are a rather rough-looking group, many of whom go out drinking at a local bar every day after they finish their grueling work shift. During summer months, the factory temperature exceeds 100 degrees.

During the pre-recession 1970s, yearly profits averaged 10.4 percent of sales. Although sales increased from $3.3 to $4.6 million between 1981 through 1985, profits dipped dramatically to 0.7 percent, 2.3 percent, –2.9 percent, 2.0 percent, and 4.2 percent during these recession-plagued years. After attending a speech by a gainsharing consultant in 1985, the owner believed that gainsharing fulfilled several immediate needs: (1) a cost-based incentive system that linked a financial bonus to production performance, (2) an alternative method of pay that could slow down escalating wage rates, and (3) employee participation in the decision-making process.

The owner invited a gainsharing consultant to conduct a gainsharing feasibility survey with employees at his facility. Satisfied with the survey results, he concluded that gainsharing could work at his facility. The owner formed a twelve-person gainsharing steering committee, consisting of himself, six managers, and five nonmanagement employees. The steering committee modified a packaged gainsharing plan, and it was approved by more than 75 percent of the employees. A Scanlon-type gainsharing plan was implemented in March 1986.

Power Games Propositions

Two power games propositions are analyzed below according to management and nonmanagement reactions to three central aspects of Scanlon-type gainsharing plans: the suggestion system, the team structure, and the group-based bonus.

Suggestion System

During four years of gainsharing, production employees implemented 1,478 suggestions. As shown in Table 4-1, the breakdown per year is 192 (1986), 324 (1987), 525 (1988), and 437 (1989), or approximately 3.7 suggestions per employee per year. These numbers are underestimations because production employees made many changes without formally submitting a suggestion.

At the beginning of gainsharing, the owner dismissed the gainsharing consultant's recommendation to employ a full-time gainsharing coordi-

Table 4-1. Cylinder Lifts: Suggestions and bonuses per year

Year	Number of Accepted Suggestions	Bonus as a % of Wages
1986	192	0.6%
1987	324	1.4%
1988	525	2.8%
1989	437	0.0%
Total suggestions	1,478	
Average bonus		1.2%

nator to manage the employee involvement mechanism. Instead, the owner added gainsharing coordination to the *existing* responsibilities of the quality control manager to minimize administrative costs. He distributed some of the quality control manager's nongainsharing responsibilities to other managers after production employees complained that many of their approved suggestions were not being implemented.

The managers most adversarial toward the suggestion system were a small group of supervisors. They maintained that gainsharing eroded their power base in three ways: production employee suggestions they had previously rejected were being implemented by area teams; suggestions that supervisors had previously submitted to upper-level managers but never implemented were being implemented by production employees on area teams; and production employees were taking time away from the production schedule to write suggestions and attend meetings. These supervisors refused to participate in any gainsharing activities and discouraged production employees from participating. Many of them eventually left Cylinder Lifts when the owner did not abandon gainsharing after the first year.

Go-getter production employees continued to provide many suggestions, despite low gainsharing payouts and supervisor resistance, because they enjoyed the challenge of implementing them. Many of these suggestions made their work less stressful. During the second year of gainsharing they began to make changes without formally submitting suggestions; thus, as intended, the barrier represented by the first exchange relation in Figure 2-2 was collapsing. The go-getters also anonymously submitted suggestions on behalf of fence-sitters and opponents who were unwilling to follow up their production-related complaints with written suggestions.

Most fence-sitters typically submitted only one suggestion during the first few months of gainsharing, even though they were aware of many production problems. These were "safe" suggestions, such as the need for a new tool or a minor rearrangement of the work process. They would monitor the monthly team meeting minutes to determine if the suggestion had been discussed and approved for implementation.

Submitting a suggestion was a risky activity for many fence-sitters. It was an act that crossed traditional interest-group barriers because it involved planning rather than just physical labor. They feared that opponents would accuse them of being coopted by management and that go-getters would say the suggestion was stupid. They assumed that there must be something wrong with their suggestion because the issue and solution were so obvious to them that managers must have dismissed the solution for some good reason. Some fence-sitters, who for many years had been hiding the fact that they did not know how to read or write, asked go-getters to submit suggestions for them. Similar risk-related doubts were raised when fence-sitters made their first process change without management approval: Will the supervisor scold them? What will the opponents say? What if the implemented change made things worse?

Most opponents refused to submit any suggestions during the first year of gainsharing. They believed that an inefficient work process was beneficial to them. Working fifty hours a week at low wages as a welder was physically grueling. Thus, they limited their analysis to conflicts of interest over wages and production output, believing that it did not make sense to tell management that an eight-hour task, with minor modifications, could really be performed in five hours. From their perspective, this would result in three more hours of grueling work.

For more than two years, one adversarial production employee observed how go-getters and fence-sitters submitted suggestions that greatly improved their working conditions. Although the production employee expected no action to be taken, he broke ranks with his peer group and submitted a suggestion that simplified his work and saved Cylinder Lifts substantial money. After his suggestion was implemented, he joined the fence-sitter coalition and submitted other suggestions. He modestly encouraged other opponents to submit suggestions that made their work less physically strenuous. His most convincing argument to them was that gainsharing might be eliminated because of the low bonus payouts, so they should submit their suggestions before the opportunity passed. Some opponents submitted suggestions. Others chastised him for acting like management.

Production employee suggestions on the agenda for team meetings that occurred during the February 1990 field study were considered typical. The eight teams reviewed sixty-eight suggestions. Fifty-two were new suggestions submitted during January, and sixteen were suggestions submitted in prior months that required further investigation. Thirty-five suggestions were accepted and scheduled to be implemented. Five suggestions were accepted and put on the review board agenda because their implementation costs exceeded the team's $1,000 discretionary budget. The forty accepted suggestions had estimated costs of $41,781 and estimated savings of $59,881. Twenty-one suggestions were declined. Seven suggestions were tabled for further investigation.

Suggestions accepted by the area teams that fell within their budgetary allocations included making boxes for transporting items, making a gauge to measure the length and squareness of saws, installing lighting in a new storage area, having vendors supply their own yearly shipping records, moving bulletin boards into the lunch room, purchasing a new slide vise, and purchasing a clock, desk, and brooms for the saw department. The five more costly suggestions referred to the review board were to lock the tool room and hire a second-shift attendant because too many tools were missing; develop a five-year plan for the welding department, because rearranging the department every other month caused confusion; purchase a $3,000 drill press that would improve productivity; share scrap savings 50/50 with production employees, because this would motivate them to control an important cost item; and make new pins for the welding department. Suggestions that the area teams rejected included changing material on a machine, putting a scale on top of a cut-off slide, putting a pan under each cylinder fixture, insulating management offices to conserve on heating and air conditioning, using blue computer paper for all gainsharing reports, and purchasing an oil skimmer.

I attended the February 1990 review board meeting where the five referred suggestions were discussed. Below is a brief summary of how discussion on the referred suggestions evolved between management and production employees during the meeting. All of the team representatives were nonmanagement employees. In general, the team representatives had substantial input into the discussion outcomes. Most management discussion contributions pertained to clarifying issues. Each referred suggestion was initially presented by the area team representative where the suggestion originated.

Lock the Tool Room and Hire a Second-Shift Attendant. The problem of missing tools was mostly discussed among the production team representatives. After several minutes of discussion, a production employee noted that the suggestion was a hiring decision and did not fall under the review board's jurisdiction. The facility manager agreed, and the suggestion was dismissed. The facility manager announced that management would most likely hire someone for the job.

Develop a Five-Year Plan for the Welding Area. The suggestion originated from a production team that had trouble locating items in the welding department because the welders were continually rearranging their work area. The welding area team representative said this was necessary because of the new custom orders that were being obtained. A manager argued that a five-year plan would put too many restrictions on the welders. Several other team representatives mentioned that they also had experienced problems with welders because of the changes taking place. The welding representative strongly argued that they needed flexibility. After further discussion among the team representatives, the team representative who had presented the suggestion noted that the suggestion-giver had realized that the suggestion would be impossible to implement—he just wanted to make the problem known to the welders and management. The facility manager called the issue to a vote, and it was defeated, with one in favor and nine opposed.

Purchase a $3,000 Drill Press. The suggestion was first discussed among the team representatives. Then two managers expressed some skepticism about the need for a new drill press. Team representatives took turns explaining bottlenecks in production that occurred in the drilling area. One of the skeptical managers conceded that, in retrospect, a new drill press would greatly improve the production process. A team representative asked whether two or three additional drill presses should be purchased instead of one. This idea was discussed among the team representatives for several minutes. The facility manager noted that the cost would be more than $10,000 and that before such a large expenditure could be made, official cost/benefit calculations should be performed by management. He suggested that if three drill presses were needed, the suggestion should be tabled for further investigation. This was discussed among the managers and team representatives. One team representative argued that at least one drill press was needed immediately. If the suggestion was tabled for further investigation, it would be several months before any drill presses were purchased. He suggested that a vote be taken on the suggestion approved by the area team and that another suggestion be submitted the following month regarding the need for additional drill presses. This idea was discussed in considerable detail. The facility manager, acting as chairperson, ruled that a vote should be taken immediately on the original suggestion of purchasing one new drill press and that if people preferred long-term planning for purchasing multiple drill presses, they should vote against the suggestion. The vote was ten in favor and two opposed.

Share Scrap Savings 50/50. The presentation of this suggestion was followed by questions and answers between managers and team representatives. For the most part, the team representatives favored the suggestion; managers, including the owner, opposed it. The team representatives maintained that scrap was a major cost item. Approving this suggestion would provide an important financial incentive for all production employees to reduce scrap. Managers argued that scrap costs were already part of the gainsharing calculation. A team representative argued that the scrap calculation gets lost in the gainsharing formula and that employees should be directly rewarded for reducing scrap costs. A manager asked the controller if this factor could be independently monitored, and the controller responded that it could be done from an accounting perspective. A team representative suggested that the idea be tabled for further investigation on the condition that it be addressed again at a review board meeting within the next three months. The owner announced that he would personally investigate the suggestion and present a report at the next review board meeting. He also announced that he had already held a meeting with the controller and an outside consultant about revising the gainsharing calculation so that there would be a more tangible linkage between production performance and the gainsharing payout. The facility manager asked if everyone agreed with this temporary solution to the suggestion. There were no objections.

Make New Pins for the Welding Area. This suggestion resulted in another active discussion involving everyone at the meeting. First, team representatives questioned each other about the need for new pins. Then managers joined the discussion, providing both questions and answers. Everyone agreed that the lack of pins was a major problem. Several ideas on how to correct the problem were discussed. The owner provided one idea that several team representatives rejected for being unnecessarily costly. The managers agreed with the team representatives. A vote was taken on the original suggestion. Fifteen were in favor and none opposed. The owner told everyone that the suggestion would be implemented immediately. He also informed everyone that he would submit a

less costly version of his idea to the welding area team for further investigation.

Team Structure

The gainsharing consultant recommended that Cylinder Lifts initially
form eight department teams (one per work area) with four nonmanagement employees per team (two per shift) and establish monthly discretionary budgets of $400 per team to implement suggestions. The owner
argued that these recommendations were too costly and time consum-
ing. Thus, the steering committee approved one gainsharing team with
eight nonmanagement employees (one per work area) and a monthly
discretionary budget of $1,000. The owner also successfully argued for a
seven-member review board consisting of the owner, three managers,
and three team representatives. According to the owner, if a formal vote
was ever taken, then the sound managerial decision would win because
four of the seven votes were controlled by him.

The initial eight team representative elections were all won by nonmanagement go-getters. Fence-sitters maintained that they could best
contribute to gainsharing by focusing on their work tasks rather than
gainsharing responsibilities. Some opponents refused to vote. After several months, the go-getters complained to the owner that there were too
many suggestions for them to analyze. They also argued that the team
meetings were boring. Often, the only person interested in discussing a
suggestion was the nonmanagement employee representing that particular work area.

The owner was pleasantly surprised by interactions at the review
board meetings. The nonmanagement go-getters took management's
concerns into consideration when discussing issues. Sometimes, they offered better solutions than managers. He viewed the nonmanagement
go-getters as constructively feisty rather than destructively adversarial.
According to the owner, he realized that it was unnecessary for him to
dominate discussions at these meetings.

One year after gainsharing implementation, the owner established a
second gainsharing team—one per shift—to reduce the administrative
and implementation overloads. Many of the same problems remained,
however. In March 1988, two years after implementation, the owner established the eight-team structure originally recommended by the gainsharing consultant. As a symbolic gesture, the owner allocated a $1,000
monthly discretionary budget per team. He was pleased with the
changes being made by nonmanagement employees and wanted the

teams to feel unrestrained in their decision-making process. Based on Cylinder Lifts' experience, the owner was confident that very few teams would spend more than $500 a month. According to the owner, he was prepared to decrease the budget allocation if teams actually spent more than that amount.

When the team structure expanded to one per work area, one of the work areas, inspired by several opponents, elected a fence-sitter who obviously lacked the intellectual, verbal, and mathematical skills necessary to be a capable team representative. They did this as a joke and were convinced that management would overturn the team's decision. Although the owner was upset with this particular election result, he honored it. The elected fence-sitter felt ineffective and resigned from the area team after two meetings.

The owner changed the composition of the review board to six management and eleven nonmanagement employees in March 1988 in conjunction with the team structure change. The production employees participating on the area teams and review board believed that they could now actually influence the direction of Cylinder Lifts, particularly when they witnessed the owner change his position on issues because of points raised by team representatives. From management's perspective, the team representatives were presenting, discussing, and solving important organizational problems with minimal managerial input.

Group-Based Bonus

During four years of gainsharing, the average monthly bonus payout was 1.2 percent ($18). As shown in Table 4-2, the breakdown per year is 0.6 percent (1986), 1.4 percent (1987), 2.8 percent (1988), and 0.0 percent (1989). Table 4-2 provides a monthly breakdown of bonus payouts.

Many of the beneficial gainsharing activities described above were offset by the lack of gainsharing bonuses. The production employees expected to earn extra money every month by working hard and administering the gainsharing process. These expectations were not fulfilled. The area teams were operating well, productivity seemed to be better than ever, and Cylinder Lifts was earning monthly profits, but there were very few gainsharing bonuses. According to nonmanagement opponents, this discrepancy verified their initial intuition that management could not be trusted. As noted in Chapter 3, Cylinder Lifts had the lowest scores among the four nonunion facilities for trust in management and fairness of the bonus calculation.

The steering committee approved three bonus-related suggestions

Table 4–2. Cylinder Lifts: Monthly gainsharing bonus payouts (%)

	1986	1987	1988	1989
January	—	0.0	0.0	0.0
February	—	0.0	0.0	0.0
March	1.0	9.2	3.7	0.0
April	0.9	0.0	0.1	0.0
May	0.0	4.1	0.0	0.0
June	0.0	2.3	1.3	0.0
July	0.4	0.0	1.5	0.0
August	2.0	0.0	0.0	0.0
September	0.0	1.6	0.0	0.0
October	0.0	0.0	0.8	0.0
November	0.0	0.0	0.0	0.0
December	2.2	0.0	1.0	0.0
Average monthly bonus % per employee	0.6	1.4	0.7	0.0
Average monthly bonus $ per employee[a]	$9	$21	$11	$0
Reserve pool %	0.0	0.0	2.1	0.0
Year-end reserve pool $ per employee	$0	$0	$378	$0

[a]Average production employee salary: $8.60 an hour, $1,500 a month, or $18,000 a year.

made by the owner prior to gainsharing implementation that allowed him to control and minimize bonus payouts. First, the owner convinced the steering committee that the gainsharing calculation should consist of thirty-four cost factors, many of which were beyond the control of production employees (e.g., advertising, equipment depreciation, and sales commissions), rather than the recommended few cost factors that nonmanagement employees affected directly. Second, only 1985 figures were used to determine the historical base ratio, rather than the recommended three to five prior years' average. The owner argued that including data from the recession years of 1980–84 would make the cost ratios too easy for production employees to surpass.

Third, the owner proposed a 67/33 gainsharing ratio—67 percent of the financial gains would be kept by Cylinder Lifts, with the remaining 33 percent to be shared among the employees—rather than the recommended 50/50 ratio. Of the employee share, 50 percent would be distributed that month and 50 percent allocated to the reserve pool. According to the owner, if the 33 percent employee share was too small, then it could be increased to 50 percent, and employee motivation would improve. But if the initial employee share was 50 percent—and this was very costly—then a reduction to 33 percent could ruin the plan.

Why would the production employees accept these financially detrimental modifications? The go-getters on the gainsharing steering committee considered the group-based bonus an extra financial incentive. From their perspective, gainsharing not only allowed production employees to simplify their job tasks and participate in decision making, but it also provided them with a financial bonus for doing so. Although the owner's suggested modifications would make it more difficult for nonmanagement employees to earn a financial bonus, the go-getters considered these changes equitable because, like wage rates, the financial bonus calculation was a matter of owner discretion. According to the go-getters, it was the owner's money that was being redistributed.

The fence-sitters believed that their interests were being adequately represented by the go-getters on the steering committee. They were not interested in the finer details of the gainsharing bonus. They trusted the go-getters and believed them when told that if they offered good suggestions and continued to work hard, then gainsharing would generate monthly bonuses. From the perspective of the fence-sitters, if the go-getters determined that a gainsharing calculation based on thirty-four cost factors and a 33 percent share was fair, then it was fair.

The opponents maintained that gainsharing was simply the latest effort by the owner to get something from them in exchange for nothing. Gainsharing differed from previous management schemes only in that the go-getter nonmanagement employees rather than managers were manipulating them. The opponents did not dissent at any gainsharing implementation meetings they attended. Rather, these meetings were seen by them as an opportunity to relax in an air-conditioned meeting room away from their physically exhausting, fifty-hour-a-week production tasks.

According to the production employees, they laughed at the two $15 bonuses they earned in the first two months under gainsharing. As shown in Table 4-2, very small bonuses also were earned during two of the next seven months of 1986. At the monthly all-employee meetings the adversarial group scoffed when, as expected, the owner announced that the previous month was profitable but there would be no bonus payout. They would clear their throats and try other ways to make the owner feel uncomfortable whenever he made this public announcement. They challenged the go-getters to find out how the owner was manipulating the financial bonus. The go-getter coalition refused to tell the opponent coalition, because they felt guilty for allowing the owner to modify the bonus payout during the gainsharing plan development process. The opponents told the fence-sitters not to submit suggestions until their improved work methods were rewarded financially. The opponents formed a network of production employees that documented the amount and value of finished goods inventory to see if the numbers provided by management at the gainsharing meetings were legitimate.

According to the owner, he was embarrassed at having to announce each month that Cylinder Lifts was earning 8 percent profit but no gainsharing bonus was generated. The go-getters warned him that the other nonmanagement employees were becoming disillusioned. As a result, after six months of gainsharing, the owner increased the production employee share of the bonus from 33 percent to 50 percent. Simultaneously, he announced the elimination of yearly merit wages for production employees, arguing that the gainsharing bonus would serve as an appropriate substitute. After two years, each employee had earned approximately $340 in gainsharing bonuses, or an average of $14 a month. The owner considered this $34,000 wage expenditure a very worthwhile investment.

The nonmanagement employees continued to complain that the small monthly gainsharing bonuses did not reflect their improved work methods and that the bonus was an inadequate substitute for merit raises. They also were troubled that the rumored elimination of cost-of-living allowances would further devalue their $18,000 annual salaries. In December 1988, the owner eliminated several of the thirty-four cost factors from the gainsharing calculation, thus creating a 2.1 percent year-end reserve pool payout of approximately $378 per employee. The unexpected gainsharing payout surprised the production employees. After receiving the bonus, many of the fence-sitters and opponents submitted suggestions that they had deliberately held back.

At the time of the 1990 field study, nonmanagement employees had not received a gainsharing bonus for more than a year, even though the owner was reporting monthly profits at the all-employee meetings. The owner was considering revising the gainsharing bonus calculation again, but he first wanted to monitor how the loss of another bankrupt customer would affect profits. Approximately 40 percent of the production employees—opponents and fence-sitters—were not actively involved in the gainsharing program, and these employees were not likely to become involved until they perceived more equity in the bonus.

The Outcomes Propositions

There was a strong consensus among management and nonmanagement employees, even those who were still adversarial, that gainsharing was essential to Cylinder Lifts. Both management and nonmanagement employees benefited directly and indirectly from four years of gainsharing.

Benefits

Direct benefits to both management and nonmanagement employees included better production processes, new tools and machinery, increased training and development, improved product quality, group dynamics training, improved communications, and new promotion avenues.

Better Production Processes. During four years of gainsharing, employees implemented 1,478 production-related suggestions. At the February 1990 team meetings, the eight teams reviewed sixty-eight suggestions made by production employees. As noted earlier, the production process suggestions accepted and implemented included making boxes for transporting items, installing lighting in a new storage area, having vendors supply their own yearly shipping records, locking up the tool room to discourage tools from being stolen, and purchasing a $3,000 drill press.

New Tools and Machines. Using their gainsharing team's monthly discretionary budget, production employees purchased many new machines and state-of-the-art tools to improve product quality and reduce production time. According to both management and nonmanagement employees, these purchases would have been postponed indefinitely had the request gone through management channels prior to gainsharing implementation. According to the owner, the suggestions and area team decisions forced management to seriously consider capital equipment improvements that were in the long-term interests of Cylinder Lifts.

Increased Training and Development for Machine Work. As a result of the tool and machine purchases, it became essential for management to develop new training and development courses for production employees. These employees attend the machine seminars at a much higher rate than previously. For instance, prior to gainsharing, many employees learned to read blueprints by working with their peers over the course of several years. Management now provides formal training in this area primarily because the production employees argued that it would help contribute to gainsharing bonuses.

Improved Product Quality. Initial gainsharing improvements in the organization of the production process and the purchase of new machinery enabled Cylinder Lifts to earn the designation of "qualified supplier" from one of its major customers. To earn this rating, the following conditions were met: 100 percent lot acceptance, 99 percent zero defects on piece parts, and 100 percent on-time delivery. The facility extended product warranty statements as a result of the improved product quality.

Group Dynamics Training. The owner initiated a video training course in group dynamics for the production employees. According to the owner, he was disappointed with the awkward group interactions at the initial gainsharing meetings. Neither the production employees nor managers had been trained in leading group discussions or developing a consensus. All department managers and supervisors, and many production employees, have completed the course.

Improved Communications. Bulletin boards are used to manage increases in interdepartmental communications. The monthly facility-wide meetings are used to convey additional information about the organization, such as the likelihood of obtaining a new customer with specialized needs. Team meetings are also used to educate employees about accounting methods, such as keeping track of the cost of quality. In addition, one-on-one communication between production employees and the owner has increased. The owner took some fence-sitters and opponents to other facilities with employee involvement systems so that they could see gainsharing's potential. According to the owner, this process enabled him to learn more about the concerns of nonmanagement employees.

New Promotion Avenues. Managers use gainsharing to evaluate hourly employees as potential supervisors. Several team representatives have been promoted to the level of supervisor based on their involvement in gainsharing.

Direct benefits to management, indirect benefits to nonmanagement employees included significant cost savings, recycling and energy savings, less resistance to production changes, and partnerships established with suppliers.

Significant Cost Savings. Production employees formally submitted 1,793 suggestions and implemented 1,478 of them during the first four years of gainsharing. The owner estimates a resultant net cost saving of more than $300,000. For example, a suggestion to use a lighter material on one product saved Cylinder Lifts $10,000. A suggestion to change from a welded part made at the facility to a stamped part purchased from another facility saved $13,000.

Recycling and Energy Savings. Gainsharing has greatly increased recycling facility-wide. The new machinery has reduced scrap and substantially improved Cylinder Lifts' energy efficiency and recycling abilities.

Less Resistance to Production Changes. According to interviewees, production employees resisted many short-notice production process changes prior to gainsharing implementation. In 1989, however, when Cylinder Lifts was forced to accept new business to increase slumping sales, production employees initiated some changes themselves. Rather than opposing change, they independently implemented suggestions that made it easier to change the process. These suggestions enabled the facility to meet the demands of new custom orders and increase sales without incurring substantial cost increases.

Partnerships Established with Suppliers. Prior to gainsharing, management viewed suppliers in an adversarial manner. The relationship was dominated by the typical conflicts of pricing, timeliness of deliveries, and payment of bills. Several production employees suggested that suppliers visit the facility to become familiar with facility operations. This became a new facility policy. Production employees who work with the supplier's product are encouraged to tell the supplier how their product could be improved. Such suggestions enabled some suppliers to increase their customer base. According to suppliers, this type of information sharing is atypical among their customers.

Direct benefits to nonmanagement employees, indirect benefits to management included easier work tasks, greater voice in decision making, improved health and safety, a basic education course, reduced employee grievances, and new performance evaluation procedures.

Easier Work Tasks. The statement made most often by production employees regarding the benefits of gainsharing is that "it makes my job easier." If they do not like the way the work is processed, they can change it. If factory ventilation is inadequate, they can purchase a fan. If their work is physically stressful, they can purchase a pulley. According to the production employees, some managers cringe at this often-stated benefit, mistaking the term *easier* for *slacking off.*

Greater Voice in Decision Making. Gainsharing gives nonmanagement employees an outlet to express their opinions on facility operations. They fulfill their own work needs with team budgets and no longer have to convince supervisors that what is obviously needed should be purchased or redesigned. This is particularly important with regard to health and safety improvements.

Improved Health and Safety. Team representatives use the gainsharing teams to build coalitions regarding important suggestions, many of which are health and safety related. Although Cylinder Lifts has a safety committee that should receive these requests, production employees found them implemented more quickly if submitted as a gainsharing suggestion.

For instance, an opponent I interviewed twice had hernias from lifting heavy objects at work. He complained to management, but no action was taken. A go-getter encouraged him to submit a gainsharing suggestion to purchase an expensive hoist. Grudgingly, he did. A cost-benefit analysis showed it was less expensive to purchase a hoist than to pay for hernia operations, and the area team approved the suggestion. Because the hoist cost several thousand dollars, the suggestion had to be approved by the review board. According to nonmanagement go-getters, team representatives asked every team to put the suggestion on its agenda and vote on it in preparation for expected management resistance. The following month, the purchase of a hoist appeared on the review board agenda eight different times, and all eight team representatives noted the suggestion had unanimous consent. The hoist was purchased. In addition, teams purchased exhaust fans for better ventilation and rubber mats to cover wet floors. Many adjustments have been made to prevent back problems and other common health ailments.

Basic Education Course. Approximately 25 percent of the production employees, many of them fence-sitters and opponents, do not have a high school degree. After two years of gainsharing, several go-getters informed the owner that some production employees did not submit suggestions or participate on area teams because they were unable to complete the suggestion form, administer team responsibilities such as keeping minutes, or perform more extensive cost/benefit analyses on the suggestions. These employees could articulate problems and solutions, but they did not have the requisite formal reading and writing skills to participate fully in the gainsharing process. According to the owner, he was shocked by the number of illiterate nonmanagement employees. To increase their participation in the suggestion system, the owner obtained the services of a local high school instructor to teach basic reading and math skills.

Reduced Employee Grievances. Grievance-related issues are sometimes submitted as constructive suggestions. Prior to gainsharing, if management was slow in responding to a health and safety issue that entailed rearranging the production process, then several production employees would file a grievance on unsafe working conditions. Under gainsharing, production employees implement these changes themselves. According to several interviewees, management is much more responsive to their claims that particular policies and procedures are unfair.

New Performance Evaluation Procedures. Prior to gainsharing, supervisors completed performance evaluations without any input from the employee being evaluated. In response to a formal employee suggestion, the owner now requires that all employees evaluate their own performance. Also, a line item has been added to performance evaluation forms that rates both managers and production employees in terms of their participation in the gainsharing plan. This policy change has increased gainsharing participation.

Conclusion

As shown in Table 4-3, the gainsharing evaluation and attitude survey conducted during the field study revealed that facility employees have mixed feelings about gainsharing activities and the work climate. It is important to recall that the survey return rate was only 39 percent. The responses are likely to be biased toward go-getter opinions because many opponents and fence-sitters refused to complete the survey on their personal time. On a 1–5 Likert scale, the statistical means are slightly higher than the midpoint (neutral) for the gainsharing support items. Survey respondents rate supervisor support the highest and employee support the lowest. Team meeting activities and review board meetings are rated quite favorably. On the other hand, employees do not

Table 4–3.   Cylinder Lifts: Survey factors

Factor	Statistical Means
Management support	3.3
Supervisor support	3.4
Team representative support	3.2
Employee support	3.1
Suggestion processing	3.2
Team meetings	3.5
Review board meetings	3.7
Bonus calculation	1.8
Facility-wide effort	3.2
Trust	2.4
Employee identity	3.3
Employee influence	2.4
Justice	2.9
Management style[a]	2.7

[a]All factors measured with a 1–5 Likert scale (1=Strongly Disagree, 3=Neutral, 5=Strongly agree), except management style, which was measured with a 1–4 Likert scale.

trust management, have insufficient influence on decisions, and strongly believe that the bonus calculation is unfair. After four years of gainsharing experience, the management style is leaning toward "consultative," which is still a major step away from the goal of participative management style.

The most striking survey findings are the very low statistical means for the fairness of the bonus calculation (1.8), trust (2.4), and employee influence (2.4). Cylinder Lifts is the only facility in the sample whose bonus calculation statistical mean is lower than the trust in management statistical mean. Assuming that the survey results are biased toward the perspective of go-getters, it appears as though their sentiments about the bonus calculation have changed over four years. As noted in the case study discussion, the go-getters on the screening committee initially maintained that it was acceptable for the owner to modify the bonus calculation in a detrimental manner because the money was coming out of his pocket. With the passage of time, the go-getters seem to have adopted the viewpoint of the opponents, and such behavior by the owner is no longer acceptable. The relatively high scores for the team meetings and review board meetings and the low score for employee influence suggests that the go-getters, who tend to participate in these meetings, distinguish between their influence on decisions and the influence of the other production employees.

Last, it is worthwhile to consider these survey results in light of the many benefits to nonmanagement employees described above. Despite these benefits, the survey respondents report a low level of trust in management. After four years of gainsharing, the go-getters have not been coopted by management, even though they actively participated in and supported gainsharing.

Each of the four conflict-of-interest propositions is examined below to aid understanding of the survey results and gainsharing evolution at this privately owned nonunion manufacturing facility.

P1: Manipulating the Transitional Process

The owner was the primary power player during the transitional process. The nonunion production employees began this transition from a very weak position. The owner adopted six strategies at the beginning of the gainsharing intervention that restricted the degree of employee involvement in decision making and the amount of the group-based financial bonus. Contrary to the gainsharing consultant's recommendations, the owner (1) added gainsharing responsibilities to the quality control manager's existing full-time job responsibilities rather than reducing the manager's other responsibilities or employing a full-time gainsharing coordinator; (2) formed one gainsharing team with one representative from each of the eight work areas rather than one gainsharing team for each work area; (3) assigned more management employees than nonmanagement employees to the review board rather than the reverse; (4) included thirty-four factors in the gainsharing calculation, some of which were not affected by nonmanagement employees, rather than a few factors that were affected directly by nonmanagement employees; (5) developed the historical standard based on the previous year's cost figures rather than cost figures from the previous three to five years; and (6) shared the financial gains with the employees based on a 33/67 ratio rather than a 50/50 ratio. These strategies were pursued to control review board decisions, limit gainsharing's administrative costs, and restrict bonus payouts. Nonmanagement go-getters realized that the owner was manipulating the transition, but they did not object because they were grateful for the opportunity to become involved in the decision making process. In addition, they maintained that this manipulation was fair because the owner was risking his capital.

P2: Interest-Group Power Struggles

Based on information gathered during the semistructured interviews, no manager was categorized as a go-getter. Some managers acted like go-getters when pushed by the owner, but the production employees were skeptical about mangers' enthusiasm. Most managers were fence-sitters and took a wait-and-see attitude toward gainsharing. They interpreted gainsharing as the latest fad that the owner was experimenting with.

An adversarial group of managers consisted of supervisors who believed that gainsharing eroded their power. They actively discouraged production employees from submitting suggestions and attending gainsharing meetings. They scolded workers who wrote suggestions on facility time and threatened to file a complaint against them. Eventually, these supervisors became fence-sitters, or they left Cylinder Lifts.

The go-getters among the nonmanagement employees were assigned to the initial gainsharing steering committee and were elected by their peers to be team representatives. Even though financial bonuses were minimal, they continued to participate in gainsharing activities because they could change their work processes. They submitted suggestions on behalf of the fence-sitters and opponents, partly to show them that gainsharing benefited them, partly to help generate a bonus, and partly out of prosocial sentiments toward their peers.

Most nonmanagement employees were fence-sitters. Throughout the plan's evolution, members of this coalition were caught in the middle, between go-getters and opponents. They preferred that the go-getters become team representatives, submitted a "safe" suggestion, and then observed carefully how the teams responded to the suggestion. After the first large year-end bonus payout, many fence-sitters felt guilty about withholding suggestions, so they submitted them.

A small but very vocal group of production employees were opponents. They did not want to participate in gainsharing activities and refused to vote during the first few elections. They sought to embarrass the owner, team leaders, and fence-sitters. They formed a network of contacts that documented whether the amount of shipments reported by management matched the inventory sheets. Also, they deliberately elected an unqualified person as a team representative.

All three groups of nonmanagement employees are still evident during the fifth year of gainsharing. The go-getters are a little discouraged, but they still want gainsharing to work. They do not want management to go back to the old way of doing things. The fence-sitters are more aligned with opponents than with go-getters. Both fence-sitters and opponents maintain that management has not yet earned their trust because the bonus payouts are either rare or small, even though Cylinder Lifts is profitable. Fence-sitters limit their participation to an occasional suggestion that makes their work easier. Opponents—unable or unwilling to overcome their traditional interests—refuse to do even that.

P3: Hidden and Suppressed Problems Surface

A variety of hidden and suppressed problems have surfaced as a result of the 1,478 accepted suggestions. Most suggestions were to correct production inefficiencies. Problems that surfaced as a result of gainsharing implementation included the following: some production employees could not read or write; employees needed new tools and machines; health and safety issues were not being adequately addressed by the safety committee; there was inadequate communication among departments; and management and nonmanagement employees were not trained in group dynamics. The owner's favorable responses to these previously hidden and suppressed problems were greatly influenced by his desire for the gainsharing plan to improve production output at minimal financial cost to himself.

P4: Fulfilled Monetary and Nonmonetary Interests

The owner and managers are looking forward to many more years of gainsharing despite the low level of trust that still characterizes the work climate. Managers had expected gainsharing to improve the level of trust, but many are convinced that just the opposite has happened— trust has declined. Nonetheless, managers claim that gainsharing suggestions have had a very positive impact on the efficiency and effectiveness of the production process. In addition to substantial cost savings, many of the suggestions have improved the production process and contributed to a better-quality product.

Despite the low bonus payouts, nonmanagement go-getters, fence-sitters, and opponents also want gainsharing to continue. Most nonmanagement employees, including the opponents, see gainsharing as a way to address their grievances, improve health and safety conditions, and obtain better tools and machinery. Gainsharing is also credited for having improved the yearly job evaluation process. Importantly, many nonmanagement employees note that managers have become more sensitive to claims that a particular policy is unfair to production employees. For instance, according to production employees, managers are more willing to accept complaints about assigning too much overtime. In particular, they maintain that the owner's increased social interaction with them through gainsharing activities has made him more sensitive to their concerns about the fairness of the bonus calculation. Production employees also note that the owner has become more uncomfortable with his monthly announcements that no bonuses will be paid, even though Cylinder Lifts is highly profitable.

Summary

Cylinder Lifts has had difficulties with several conflicts-of-interest exchange relationships, as diagrammed in Figure 2-2. The owner allowed greater employee involvement by creating department teams, allocating them a monthly budget, and permitting nonmanagement employees to meet with suppliers. On the other hand, he initially restricted employee involvement by creating only one gainsharing team for the entire facility, rather than one per work area. In addition, some managers accused workers of "slacking off" when they discussed production problems. One year later, the owner created a second gainsharing team. Two years after implementation, the owner found it necessary to establish the eight-team structure originally recommended by the gainsharing consultant.

As a result of greater employee involvement, accepted suggestions increased from 210 in 1986, to 360 in 1987, 654 in 1988, and 569 in 1989. Importantly, nonmanagement employees have also made many production improvement changes without submitting formal suggestions. Adversarial nonmanagement employees refuse to participate in the decision-making process, however, and some are deliberately working inefficiently because financial bonuses are not forthcoming.

The weakest link in the exchange relationships is employee wages. The owner initially restricted bonus payouts by choosing a very broad-based calculation, keeping 67 percent of the financial gains and using only one year for a historical average. After six months of gainsharing, he increased the employee share from 33 percent to 50 percent, as initially recommended by the gainsharing consultant. Two years after gainsharing implementation, the owner eliminated several of the thirty-four cost factors from the gainsharing calculation, but the calculation still included factors that production employees did not affect.

All of the production employees believe that their improved work efforts are not rewarded appropriately. Despite the 1,478 accepted suggestions for improving the production process, the employees have earned an average monthly gainsharing bonus of only 1.2 percent. Assuming an average yearly salary of $18,000, this amounts to $216 a year ($18 a month) per employee. As a result of the unfair bonus calculation, fence-sitters and opponents are restricting the degree to which they participate in employee involvement mechanisms and production process improvements. Even the go-getters struggle with the owner's manipulation of the bonus because they have to continually explain to other nonmanagement employees why profits increase without any corresponding increase in gainsharing bonuses.

5 Foam Seats: A Publicly Owned Nonunion Facility, Modest Bonuses

Foam Seats is a publicly owned nonunion facility located in an eastern suburban industrial park. It is a subsidiary of a multibillion-dollar corporation. The facilty began operations in July 1984 with the sole purpose of building automotive seats on a just-in-time system for a customer located thirty miles away. Purchase orders arrive on a computer readout in the morning, and the appropriate number of foam molds are made, upholstered, and assembled to seat frames. Final delivery is made within two days of the purchase order. Two hours after shipping, the seats are installed by the customer's employees in new vehicles. The customer had previously built its own seats, but during the early 1980s it decided to contract out to reduce costs. As a result, more than three hundred union employees' jobs were eliminated at the customer's production facility. In 1989, Foam Seats had sales of approximately $40 million a year to the customer and employed 155 people on two production shifts. Nonmanagement employees earned approximately $15,000 a year. Foam Seat employees produced approximately 2,500 seats a day and more than 3 million seats during its first five and a half years of operation.

Foam Seats has three levels of management. Upper-level management consists of the facility manager, who reports to corporate headquarters. The facility manager travels extensively because he is in charge of managing two facilities that are more than 250 miles apart. Middle-level management includes the production manager, employee relations manager, facility engineer, materials manager, facility accountant, quality control manager, and foam coordinator, all of whom report directly to the facility manager. Lower-level management includes day and night shift supervisors, who report to the production manager.

Production employees are organized on production teams based on the type of seat they build. For example, the bench seat team consists of thirteen production employees. The production team leaders report to their shift supervisors. Many production employees are hired right out of high school. While I was administering the gainsharing evaluation and attitude survey, a police car drove by, and two production employees jumped out of their chairs to hide in the factory. While everyone laughed, a nearby production employee assured me that they most likely were wanted for different crimes, not the same crime. Production employee turnover is relatively high. Management expects production employees to quit after several years because of the strenuous physical work. No production employee is expected to retire from the facility. Some production employees believe that management is not concerned with reducing the physical stress associated with production work; doing so would result in higher wages and potential pension costs. If production employees do not quit, then management typically fires those at the top of the wage scale because they can no longer meet the physical demands of the job. At the time of the field study, the oldest production employee was forty-five years old and took pride in still being able to keep up with the "young kids." Management expected him to quit within five years.

Several factors contributed to the implementation of a Scanlon-type gainsharing plan in February 1986. Because the facility had production teams, the facility manager wanted to install a group-based financial incentive system that would foster group cohesiveness. In addition, corporate headquarters expected a union organizing effort in retaliation for the role Foam Seats played in eliminating three hundred union jobs at the customer's facility. Corporate officials saw gainsharing as an anti-union strategy whereby production employees would fund their own wage increases through production improvements. The facility manager believed that he would lose his job if a union was formed at the facility.

After hearing a gainsharing consultant make a presentation at corporate headquarters, the facility manager invited the consultant to conduct a gainsharing feasibility survey with his employees. Impressed by the survey results, he concluded that gainsharing would fit well with his facility's operations. He met with the gainsharing consultant, several managers from corporate headquarters, and several managers from his facility to determine how the gainsharing plan should be designed. A gainsharing steering committee that included three nonmanagement go-getters was formed to make final plans. The facility manager dominated the steering committee meetings. A modified gainsharing plan was approved by more than 75 percent of the employees, and it was implemented in February 1986.

Power Game Propositions

The two power games propositions are analyzed below according to management and nonmanagement reactions to four central aspects of Scanlon-type gainsharing plans: the gainsharing coordinator, the suggestion system, the team structure, and the group-based bonus.

Gainsharing Coordinator

The facility manager dismissed the gainsharing consultant's recommendation to employ a full-time gainsharing coordinator because it would be too costly. Instead, the facility manager added gainsharing responsibilities to the regular duties of the employee relations manager. When the employee relations manager left Foam Seats shortly thereafter for other reasons, the facility manager assigned a production employee as gainsharing coordinator on a part-time basis. The facility manager chose a production employee he trusted, unaware that this person was disliked by many production employees. Gainsharing responsibilities were added to the production employee's regular forty-hour work week duties. By working twenty hours a week overtime to fulfill his gainsharing responsibilities, production employees' resentment toward him increased on two counts: they were envious of his guaranteed twenty hours of overtime every week, and since the gainsharing bonus was based on a percentage of an employee's monthly wage, the gainsharing coordinator was eligible to receive a much higher bonus payout than the other production employees.

In May 1988, more than two years after gainsharing implementation, two production employees submitted a gainsharing suggestion requesting that there be a full-time gainsharing coordinator and that the job be separate from any other managerial or production responsibilities. At the following review board meeting, the facility manager suggested that the incumbent part-time coordinator be relieved of his production responsibilities and made a full-time gainsharing coordinator. Several team representatives objected because many production employees were not pleased with the incumbent coordinator: some did not like him;

some thought he was on a "power trip"; and some thought that he was too close to management. They suggested that a facility-wide election be held to determine the new full-time gainsharing coordinator. The facility manager assumed that the part-time coordinator would be elected to the position and agreed reluctantly to the election.

Two production employees submitted their names for the gainsharing coordinator position: the incumbent part-time coordinator and one of the production employees who had submitted the suggestion that gainsharing required a full-time coordinator. The challenger was a team representative who had submitted many useful production suggestions yet was perceived by most managers, including the facility manager, as an opponent. He was a member of a vocal, adversarial group of production employees who were continually critical of management on the production floor and during all-employee meetings. When I administered the gainsharing evaluation and attitude survey, this group of employees refused to participate and heckled those who did. Although the challenger acted like an opponent at employee meetings, he acted like a go-getter when independent of his work group. Importantly, though disliked by managers, he was well liked by most of the other production workers. He submitted constructive suggestions that impressed the go-getters and made taunting suggestions that impressed the opponents. He saw the position of gainsharing coordinator as one of the only avenues open to him for career advancement within Foam Seats, particularly since he was an African-American, and there were no African-American managers.

The gainsharing coordinator election reintroduced excitement to gainsharing activities. Many managers, who had by this time withdrawn from gainsharing activities, campaigned on behalf of the part-time coordinator. Many production employees, including the opponents, campaigned on behalf of the challenger. The challenger won the election, 60 percent to 40 percent. Managers were apprehensive about the outcome of the election. The facility manager told each manager not to undermine the new gainsharing coordinator. The new gainsharing coordinator immediately encouraged both nonmanagement fence-sitters and opponents to give gainsharing a second chance. One year later, he was the only person to run for the gainsharing coordinator position.

Suggestion System

During four years of gainsharing, production employees implemented 776 suggestions. As shown in Table 5-1, the breakdown per year

Table 5–1.   Foam Seats: Suggestions and bonuses per year

Year	Number of Accepted Suggestions	Bonus as a % of Wages
1986	250	7.0%
1987	200	3.5%
1988	153	6.1%
1989	173	4.2%
Total suggestions	776	
Average bonus		5.2%

is 250 (1986), 200 (1987), 153 (1988), and 173 (1989), or approximately 1.3 suggestions per employee per year. These numbers are underestimations because production employees made many changes without submitting formal suggestions.

The initial waves of suggestions were from go-getters and team representatives. Many of the approved suggestions entailed action by the maintenance department. When the maintenance department responded slowly, the opponents told others that the gainsharing plan was a sham. For instance, every team submitted a suggestion for better lighting in its work area. With each passing week that new lighting fixtures were not installed, opponents and fence-sitters would joke about the lack of management commitment to change: "Look, they think it's too expensive to tell maintenance workers to change the lights we already bought!" In addition, production teams implemented the least expensive suggestions first because these suggestions did not require review board approval. This led opponents to conclude that management only wanted "cheap ideas." These viewpoints were further substantiated in the minds of the opponents by the much smaller than expected bonus payouts.

In October 1987, the review board developed a "suggestion of the month," "employee of the month," and "employee of the year" reward system to encourage more suggestions. Each gainsharing team voted for the best suggestion submitted by a department member. The gainsharing coordinator presented these suggestions at the review board meeting, and a vote was taken to determine the suggestion of the month. The author of the suggestion was awarded employee of the month status, which included having his or her name listed on a plaque, use of the parking space nearest the front door, and automatic nomination for employee of the year. At the end of the year, a card with each employee of the month's name was placed in a barrel. The person whose card was drawn from the barrel won a choice between a vacation trip to the Bahamas or two $1,000 savings bonds. This reward system was appealing to both go-getters and fence-sitters, as suggestions from the three most active teams increased from eight in October to twenty in November. Fence-sitters assumed that go-getters had better-quality suggestions and would win the monthly awards.

I attended the March 1990 review board meeting. Thirteen people were in attendance: six managers, six team representatives, and the gainsharing coordinator. According to the facility manager, the attendance among managers was higher than usual because of my presence at the meeting. Thirteen suggestions that teams had accepted for implementation were taped to the walls of the conference room for everyone to read. Polaroid snapshots of each implemented suggestion, taken by the gainsharing coordinator for visual effect, were posted next to the suggestion.

Six issues were discussed in detail during the one-hour meeting: current business, nominating a customer's employee idea for suggestion of the month, paving the road by the receiving dock, freezing the reserve pool, installing a "cost of tools" bulletin board, and the gainsharing bonus. Much of the discussion was a dialogue between the facility manager and the gainsharing coordinator. Team representatives were intimidated by the facility manager and expected the gainsharing coordinator to speak for them. The other managers were also intimidated by the facility manager, and they mostly listened to the discussion. The most intense discussion regarded the facility manager's desire to nominate a customer's employee idea for suggestion of the month.

Current Business. The facility manager announced that January was a terrible sales month. It was the first time in the history of the facility that production had to be stopped because of low customer sales. Foam Seat's only customer closed its assembly facility for three weeks in January because of an oversupply of product. The facility manager announced that business was improving, and there would be "good" overtime on Saturday. Good overtime was the result of more sales, whereas "bad" overtime was the result of low production efficiency. The gainsharing coordinator asked about the customer's long-term production plans. The facility manager responded that the customer only provided short-term, three-month forecasting.

Nominating a Customer's Employee Idea for Suggestion of the Month. The facility manager announced that an employee of the customer had recently corrected a machine problem at the customer's facility that would result in fewer product returns. This saved Foam Seats about ten damaged seats a month, which amounted to a financial savings of approximately $4,000 a year. The facility manager thought that it would be appropriate to consider this as suggestion of the month. Doing so would also improve employee relations with the customer. The gainsharing coordinator suggested that sending a thank-you card on behalf of all facility employees would be a sufficient sign of gratitude. He asked rhetorically whether the customer was going to offer a $4,000 credit for 120 seats their machines had damaged over the past year. The facility manager pointed out that the customer's employee did not have to fix the machine causing the damage. The gainsharing coordinator noted that an employee winning the suggestion of the month award was also given the employee of the month award. The employee then automatically qualified for the randomly selected employee of the year award. He asked if Foam Seats would be willing to send the customer's employee to the Bahamas, and if so, how employee morale at Foam Seats would be affected.

The facility manager asked for input from others at the meeting. The production manager said that he and other managers knew that part of the defective product problem was caused by resentful customer employees retaliating for Foam Seats having replaced three hundred union jobs. Several team representatives argued that giving the award to an employee of the customer after a month in which the customer forced Foam Seats to ask its employees to go on layoffs would deteriorate morale further. The facility manager concluded that it would be appropriate to send a thank-you card.

Paving the Road by the Receiving Dock. Several production employees submitted suggestions that the road leading to the receiving area should be paved. The gainsharing coordinator noted that delivery trucks get stuck in the mud on rainy days. The facility manager argued that paving the road could be a major expense and should be examined in greater detail. A team representative argued that the production employees could do the paving themselves if business remained slow. The facility manager responded that if the road was repaired, it should be done in a professional manner. The gainsharing coordinator said that some production employees had this professional talent. The discussion concluded with the facility manager's promise to examine the cost of paving.

Freezing the Reserve Pool. The facility manager gave a short presentation on the background of the suggestion to freeze the reserve pool for the month of January because the customer stopped production. He had discussed the issue with managers at corporate headquarters, and they were hesitant initially. Headquarters argued that the purpose of the reserve pool was to cover bad months. Since January was a bad month, the reserve pool was fulfilling its stated purpose. The facility manager told headquarters that January had extenuating circumstances beyond any employee's control in that the customer closed its assembly facility for three out of the four weeks. He argued that gainsharing could be ruined for the entire year if January's bad results were included in the reserve pool. Headquarters eventually agreed with the facility manager. The gainsharing coordinator asked if the reserve pool would be frozen for February as well, since the customer was closed for one week. The facility manager reported that the agreement with headquarters was that the reserve pool could be frozen only if the customer was closed for two weeks or more in a given month. Therefore, the February reserve pool would not be frozen.

"Cost of Tools" Bulletin Board. The gainsharing coordinator reported that there had been an increase in tools being abused, lost, or stolen. There was a short discussion between the facility manager and a team representative on how costly this problem could get, since the facility had more than $1 million in tools inventory. The team representative suggested, and the facility manager agreed, that a sheet with the cost of each tool should be posted on a bulletin board.

Gainsharing Bonus. The facility accountant reported that in a normal month, about 50,000 seats are delivered to the customer. In February only 33,000 seats were delivered because of the one week of lost production; therefore, labor costs were $9,000 over budget. The accountant showed a slide that listed other items in the bonus calculation that were over budget, pointing out that despite the low sales, if there had not been a lost-time accident, a bonus would have been earned for the month. The gainsharing coordinator was offended by this perspective and argued that it was inappropriate to blame the failure to earn a bonus on the lost-time accident since it was only one of many factors that affected the bonus. As an example, he indicated that the telephone budget item, which the production employees could not affect, was also over budget. The employees would have earned a bonus if managers had not made so many telephone calls during the month of February. The gainsharing coordinator asked why the phone bill was so high. The facility manager said that he would review the telephone issue.

Team Structure

Because Foam Seats already had production teams, the gainsharing consultant recommended that each production team per shift be transformed into a gainsharing team that met on facility time. This change would have resulted in sixteen gainsharing teams, since each shift had a seat department with several production teams, a foam department with several production teams, a shipping department, a maintenance department, and an office department. The facility manager argued that this recommendation would be too costly. Instead, he created five gainsharing teams (one per department) consisting of one or two people per shift. In addition, the facility manager assigned a supervisor to serve as chairperson of the gainsharing team meetings. The seven supervisors were fence-sitters and opponents. A simple majority vote was required to approve a suggestion. Each gainsharing team had a monthly discretionary budget of $400, and any suggestion costing more than $5,000 required corporate approval.

The initial review board consisted of five nonmanagement employees and five management employees. Each of the five gainsharing teams chose one team representative to serve on the review board. The five management members were the facility manager, facility accountant, production manager, facility engineer, and the gainsharing coordinator (the employee relations manager).

The facility manager also rejected the consultant's meeting time recommendation and scheduled team meetings after working hours so that they would not disrupt production activities. The meeting schedule was detrimental to gainsharing for two reasons. First, production employees wanted to go home and relax after eight to ten hours of physically exhausting work. Second, this meeting schedule discouraged women production employees from running for team representative because they had to arrange extra daycare hours.

The four election cycles paralleled the evolution of general attitudes toward gainsharing. For the 1986 election, each employee nominated three department team members. The employee whose name appeared on the most ballots became a team representative. Go-getters campaigned during production team meetings. As expected, all of the informal leaders of the production teams were elected. Four of the initial fourteen team representatives (two teams had two representatives per shift) were women. In 1987, there was no campaigning or voting; those who wanted to be team representatives simply signed up for the position. There were no disputes about who should sign up. In 1988, the facility manager and part-time gainsharing coordinator had to recruit production employees to sign up to be team representatives. In 1989, the new full-time gainsharing coordinator simply reappointed all of the team representatives to another one-year term. Several team representatives refused to serve another term. The coordinator then had to recruit new team representatives to take their place.

After a few months of gainsharing, supervisors who were fence-sitters and opponents stopped attending gainsharing team meetings. The supervisors saw gainsharing as more work, meetings, and paperwork initiated by nonmanagement employees. In addition, they believed that many of the suggestions were critical of their management skills and that their time would be better spent on other production tasks. An example of the type of suggestion that they would cringe at when read at a gainsharing meeting is: "The two lifts, one in the tour package area, the other in the warehouse, are presently not being used. Foam Seats spent around $20,000 to install the lifts. Was this a good investment?"

Supervisors often felt embarrassed when excellent suggestions were read during team meetings because they had not thought of the idea. The situation was worse at review board meetings, because they feared that the facility manager would assume that they were not doing a good job. Supervisors and other managers also resented the facility manager's effort to get them to submit suggestions to demonstrate their support for gainsharing. They felt that their loyalty to the facility was being questioned. From their perspective, it was demeaning for a manager to submit a suggestion when he already had the authority to make the necessary change or tell the facility manager directly what changes were needed.

Supervisors' withdrawal from gainsharing activities surprised the nonmanagement go-getters, because the gainsharing bonus was the only financial bonus incentive supervisors had. It also disrupted team meetings, because nonmanagement production employees, who were untrained in facilitating meetings, were forced to take the role of chairperson. Similarly, some upper-level managers stopped attending review board meetings. Production go-getters wanted managers to attend these meetings to discuss issues they raised. Several go-getters claimed that if managers were not present to answer questions then that meant they did not really care about the success or failure of gainsharing. Opponents interpreted these events as a management ploy to undermine the opportunity for production employees to earn a bonus based on the improvements they were making. Without management support, suggestions would only be partly implemented, thus restricting the financial benefits of the suggestions.

With the withdrawal of management participation, the nonmanagement team representatives felt isolated. In addition, female team representatives faced a conflict between paying extra for daycare to attend team meetings that managers were ignoring or going home after a physically exhausting work day. They resigned their positions. When the bonus payouts declined during the second year of gainsharing from 7 percent to 3.5 percent for the year, fewer suggestions were submitted. Many go-getters lost interest in taking on additional gainsharing responsibilities. With fewer suggestions and smaller bonuses, some team representatives concluded that it was not worth the extra efforts to solicit and analyze suggestions.

The gainsharing plan team structure was somewhat rejuvenated when the new full-time coordinator was elected in 1988. To develop a better sense of community among the team representatives, he combined all of the gainsharing teams into one team. He believed that the newly integrated effort would foster new excitement about participation the gainsharing process, but this did not happen. The bonuses were still minimal, as were the number of suggestions.

Furthermore, the gainsharing coordinator had to cajole nonmanagement employees into becoming team representatives. It was very difficult to replace a go-getter who resigned. The attitude of the others was that if the go-getter did not believe that the gainsharing teams were worthwhile, why should anyone else. Managers were not attending meetings, and the facility manager was missing review board meetings because he was managing a second manufacturing facility approximately 250 miles away. Facility employees attributed his absence from review board meetings as a lack of commitment to the gainsharing plan. At the team meeting I attended, only seven of the fourteen team representatives were in attendance: five were women and two were men. Two of the women were newly selected and attending their first-ever team meeting. Although invited, no managers attended the meeting.

Group-Based Bonus

During four years of gainsharing, the average monthly bonus payout was 5.2 percent ($63). As shown in Table 5-1, the breakdown per year is 7.0 percent (1986), 3.5 percent (1987), 6.1 percent (1988), and 4.2 percent (1989). Table 5-2 provides a monthly breakdown of bonus payouts.

The historical cost standard for calculating the financial bonus was based on two ratios consisting of eighteen cost factors averaged over the

Table 5–2. Foam Seats: Monthly gainsharing bonus payouts (%)

	1986	1987	1988	1989
January	—	2.1	5.7	1.5
February	4.1	0.0	6.7	6.1
March	4.9	2.1	6.3	5.4
April	6.4	0.7	8.1	4.9
May	6.1	5.1	6.9	2.1
June	6.7	2.3	5.1	1.0
July	6.3	2.4	4.2	3.7
August	5.6	0.0	0.0	0.0
September	1.1	1.3	0.0	3.1
October	5.3	5.9	2.6	4.6
November	3.3	4.9	2.0	3.4
December	5.4	7.6	5.6	2.4
Average monthly bonus % per employee	5.0	2.9	4.4	3.2
Average monthly bonus $ per employee[a]	$61	$35	$54	$39
Reserve pool %	2.0	0.6	1.7	1.0
Year-end reserve pool $ per employee	$292	$88	$249	$146

[a]Average production employee salary: $7 an hour, $1,218 a month, or $14,616 a year.

previous three years, and one cost factor that was deducted directly from the bonus. The facility manager constructed the financial bonus to encourage employees to improve six cost factors: production labor costs, support labor costs, use of scrap, overtime, other expenses (consisting of fifteen items), and product returns. The first two factors were grouped into one calculation, the "people pool ratio," which compared actual labor costs to standard labor costs. The second gainsharing calculation, the "other cost pool ratio," compared the next three factors—scrap costs, overtime costs, and other expenses—with standard labor costs. The other expenses factor consisted of fifteen cost items, including facility and machinery repairs, product materials, perishable tools, general supplies, outside janitors, and telephone costs. Finally, there was a deduction from the bonus for defective returns: a 100 percent cost deduction for each of the first forty seats returned by the customer every month and a 200 percent cost deduction for each of the next forty seats returned. Typical product return problems included deformed seats, seats with excessive foam, and seats damaged during shipping. Production employees insisted that the third type of damaged goods was often the result of sabotage by resentful union workers at the customer's facility.

The cost savings were shared 50/50 between Foam Seats and its employees. Of the employee share, 70 percent was distributed that month, and 30 percent allocated to the year-end reserve pool. At the end of the fiscal year, positive year-end reserve pool accumulations would be distributed, or negative year-end reserve pool balances would be absorbed by Foam Seats. Everyone employed by the facility was eligible for the financial bonus.

The facility manager emphasized the financial benefits of gainsharing when selling the idea to production employees. Gainsharing was a way to make extra money while working fewer hours. From the perspective of nonmanagement employees, this meant that gainsharing bonuses should be equivalent to reductions in overtime wages. Prior to gainsharing, some production employees had been earning $300 a month in overtime. If overtime decreased but there was no financial bonus, then gainsharing resulted in lower wages. Go-getters, fence-sitters, and opponents therefore focused their attention on the financial bonus.

During the first year of gainsharing, the bonus payout seemed reasonable. Thereafter, the payouts were smaller, although at monthly review board meetings, the facility manager or accountant consistently announced larger profits. Fence-sitters and some go-getters felt that the decline in the size of bonuses substantiated the view expressed by the opponents, namely, that gainsharing was simply a new form of management manipulation. For instance, in 1987, there was a $25 bonus in January, no bonus in February, and a $25 bonus in March. Opponents told fence-sitters that they were foolish to work more efficiently when the monthly bonus was equivalent to only two hours of overtime per month. The opponents also argued that by improving productivity every month, it would become even harder to earn a gainsharing bonus in the future because they were creating historical standards that would be more difficult to surpass.

Most production employees, particularly the opponents and fence-sitters, associated the gainsharing bonus with the number of seats shipped to the customer minus returned seats. It did not make sense to them that productivity improved and product returns decreased, yet employees were receiving very low bonus payouts. For several months, the opponents requested that shipping department employees document when production goals were achieved in comparison to previous bonus months. For instance, if the same number of employees produced the same number of seats a few days earlier than a previous bonus month, and if returns were consistent, then they thought they should earn a proportionately higher bonus the forthcoming month. But rarely was this the case. Fence-sitters and opponents concluded that management was manipulating the calculation.

Several items included in the calculation, such as telephone costs, were beyond the control of production employees. The facility manager defended including these cost items in the calculation because managers (who also participated in the gainsharing bonus plan) needed an incentive to limit these expenses. According to nonmanagement opponents, managers were not trying to control these costs because they had already given up on gainsharing. Therefore, managers were sabotaging nonmanagement efforts to earn a financial bonus by improving the production process. In addition, opponents believed that the financial gains of production improvements were being used by management to fund other cost factors in the bonus calculation, such as repairing the roof.

During the field study, even management employees mentioned that the facility manager "had to allow" higher gainsharing bonuses, suggesting that they believed the facility manager was manipulating the bonus calculations. Several nonmanagement interviewees simply said, "Give more bonus and we'll give more suggestions!" From the perspective of many opponents and fence-sitters, management knew that more suggestions would be forthcoming if a higher bonus were allowed. Since management was not paying a higher bonus and not attending gainsharing meetings, then they must not really have wanted employee suggestions.

The gainsharing coordinator maintained that Foam Seats would have better results if only factors specific to production employees were included in the bonus calculation. These factors could include such highly valued managerial concerns as reworked parts, absenteeism, lost-time accidents, excess scrap, nonproduction hours, and other efficiencies. If efficiencies were high and the amount of rework, absenteeism, lost-time accidents, scrap, and nonproduction hours were low, then the production employees should earn a gainsharing bonus. Opponents favored adopting a profit-sharing plan rather than gainsharing because the facility manager announced that facility profits increased every month that production employees improved the production process. Therefore, the opponents argued, profit sharing was a more appropriate measure of their productivity improvements.

The Outcomes Propositions

There was a strong consensus among management and nonmanagement employees that gainsharing greatly improved facility operations.

Both management and nonmanagement employees benefited directly and indirectly from four years of gainsharing.

Benefits

Direct benefits to both management and nonmanagement employees included better production processes, improved product quality, and improved communications.

Better Production Processes. Employees implemented 776 suggestions during four years of gainsharing. As noted earlier, many other production process changes made by production employees without submitting formal suggestions. Many production employees are holding back further suggestions, however, until management demonstrates good faith in support of the gainsharing system.

Improved Product Quality. Managers attribute improvements in product quality and customer satisfaction to gainsharing implementation. Foam Seats received numerous commendations from the customer soon after gainsharing implementation. The facility has received a "gold medal achievement award" for meeting supplier requirements of "zero follow-up." In 1988, it received a "mark of excellence award," an honor bestowed on only twenty-two of the customer's sixteen hundred suppliers. This award enables the facility to certify its own parts rather than having a representative from the customer visit the facility to do so. The facility also won a "targets for excellence award" from the customer based on successful production audits. Finally, the number of automobile seats rejected by the customer every month declined from sixty-four to forty-eight.

Improved Communications. In June 1988, the gainsharing coordinator published the facility's first monthly newsletter. It contains information on business, production, product quality, gainsharing bonuses, employee birthdays, perfect attendance records, and other sundry items. Another avenue of improved communication is the installation of an anonymous suggestion box. Some production employees are afraid to speak out at gainsharing meetings for fear of how the facility manager or production manager might react. An employee suggested that one production employee serve as a point person, one whom everyone could approach with anonymous complaints. The facility manager argued that employees could approach either the gainsharing coordinator or employee relations manager. As a compromise, the facility manager has installed a suggestion box for exmployees to anonymously submit suggestions that express critical viewpoints. There are many other examples of improved communications, including the "cost of tools" bulletin board, which informs production employees about the costs associated with misplaced or stolen tools.

Direct benefits to management and indirect benefits to nonmanagement employees included significant cost savings, less resistance to production changes, and feedback on supplier products.

Significant Cost Savings. Foam Seats has saved more than $1 million during four years of gainsharing. Scrap accounts for the most savings, at $628,527. After considering facility costs of $486,560 in employee bonuses, a net savings of $540,313 was achieved. The people pool ratio stabilized during four years of gainsharing as production labor costs rose slightly and the support labor costs decreased slightly. The facility manager regards this achievement as a substantial one, because it enables Foam Seats to keep its prices steady. The other cost pool total has decreased significantly, from 60 percent to 43.9 percent, indicating improvements in these areas. On closer inspection, overtime costs increased slightly, and other expenses decreased slightly. Reductions in scrap costs, from 23.7 percent to 7.7 percent, account for most of the decrease. All interviewees noted that production employees are much more cost conscious because of gainsharing.

Less Resistance to Production Changes. Changes in production, particularly changes initiated by production employees, occur with less employee resistance. The job rotation suggestion (discussed in detail below) is one example. Management had ordered employees to perform the undesirable work assignment, and the result was high turnover. Under gainsharing, the production team determined how the undesirable work assignment could be rotated. Similarly, a production employee suggested that Foam Seats purchase a trash compactor to recycle cardboard. According to managers, if management had established a new recycling policy, some employees would have changed their behavior, but many others would not. Because the compactor was suggested by a production employee and the employee took responsibility to monitor the recycling and educate other nonmanagement employees about the benefits of recycling, workers' behavior changed quickly.

Feedback on Supplier Products. Production employees make product quality improvement suggestions to suppliers. In addition, production employees have requested that management end relations with suppliers of low-quality products. Unfortunately, two major suppliers who were slow to adopt employee suggestions were not eliminated because they are part of Foam Seats' corporate system, thus frustrating the production employees.

Direct benefits to nonmanagement employees and indirect benefits to management included improved health and safety, job rotation, voluntary layoffs, clothing allowance, employee uniforms, joining a credit union, and the opportunity to state grievances.

Improved Health and Safety. Foam Seats has a safety committee, but its budget is limited. Safety-related ideas often got lost in the facility's bureaucracy. Nonmanagement employees now submit health and safety suggestions to the gainsharing teams because they have a discretionary monthly budget. An example of a prominent safety suggestion is the installation of a guardrail and stairs for a maintenance platform. Whenever there was a maintenance problem in the area, the maintenance worker had been lifted up to the platform on a forklift. Two maintenance workers were seriously injured in falls from the platform. After the second maintenance worker was injured, a gainsharing team considered submitting a suggestion to build stairs and a guardrail, but the unpredictable fate of the suggestion would rest with the review board because of the high cost. To increase the likelihood of success, the gainsharing team decided to split the suggestion in half. First, a production employee submitted a suggestion to install a guardrail around the platform. The cost fell within the team's discretionary monthly budget. At the review board meeting, production employees actively lobbied for the suggestion to win suggestion of the month. After the guardrail was installed, the new employee of the month submitted a suggestion that stairs be built leading to the platform, at a cost of $5,000. The suggestion was approved and implemented by the review board.

Other health and safety suggestions passed by the gainsharing teams include the purchase of appropriate worktables to reduce backaches, eliminating glue fumes from the ventilation system, providing fire-drill training, rotating materials so that workers' arms can get a variety of movements during the day, removing excessive pieces of cardboard from the production floor, reducing noise, installing fans, purchasing safety clothes, installing emergency lighting, covering exposed pipes, doing hand exercises, installing safety straps for maintenance workers, putting guardrails around electrical power areas, and installing better lighting outside the building for the evening shift employees.

At the time of the field study, the facility manager decided to use the gainsharing calculation to reduce lost-time accidents. The work is tedious, and accidents do occur. Production employees with minor injuries were using lost-time accidents as a reason not to come to work, although there were other job tasks they could perform. The facility manager hopes that this new bonus factor will raise additional safety issues at the team meetings. Opponents see this new bonus factor as a management ploy to extract more work out of them through peer pressure when they are hampered physically.

Job Rotation. When the facility began operations, management intended to implement job rotation for most jobs but did not follow up on this intention. In many instances, managers believe that job rotation can hurt overall productivity rates because workers need time to become familiar with new job tasks. Whenever job rotation slows down, production employees submit suggestions requesting it because they believe that job rotation keeps them alert, thus limiting accidents caused by boredom on the production line.

An employee suggestion on job rotation solved a production problem. No one wanted to perform one essential job task because of its menial and repetitive nature. Anyone employed to perform the task typically quit after a short period or requested a different job assignment. An employee in the work cell suggested that each person in the cell perform the tedious task one day a week. On that day, the designated employee is allowed to arrive at work later than the other employees as a reward for performing the task.

Voluntary Layoffs. In early December 1989, car dealers stopped ordering the customer's product, and production slowed down. Management found out in mid-December that the customer intended to close its production facilities for three weeks in January. The facility manager called a meeting with members of the initial gainsharing steering committee to inform them of the business problem and its major impact on the gainsharing calculation. Foam Seats had never had a layoff, and the facility manager wanted feedback from some go-getters on how the problem could be managed.

The steering committee made two recommendations: obtain permission from corporate headquarters to freeze the gainsharing calculation for the month of January, and experiment with a voluntary layoff policy rather than the mandatory layoff policy followd by the customer. Some managers objected to the second recommendation on the grounds that nobody would request a voluntary layoff. Nonmanagement go-getters argued that many production employees would welcome the opportunity to take an unscheduled break from work, spend time with their families, and collect unemployment benefits. When presented to the employees, approximately half chose voluntary layoff. According to management, in the short term, Foam Seats lost $100,000 by having employees work for three weeks, mainly doing cross-training and odd jobs around the facility. But over the long term, they expect to benefit from building morale and trust. When I conducted the semistructured interviews, every employee mentioned the voluntary layoff as a policy that developed because of the trust the facility manager had fostered for nonmanagement go-getters during four years of gainsharing.

Clothing Allowance. A production employee suggested that Foam Seats provide a clothing allowance for people who were ruining their clothes on the production line. The facility manager decided that it would be too expensive to provide a clothing allowance for all production employees. Nonetheless, he felt that it was reasonable to provide a clothing allowance for one particular work cell, which had the most soiled and tattered clothes.

Employee Uniforms. Some production employees complained about one work cell receiving a clothing allowance but not others. The full-time gainsharing coordinator told the facility manager that providing uniforms might offset this problem. Production employees were approached about receiving laundry discounts on company uniforms—a shirt and pants combination—but opponents rejected the idea of wearing a company uniform, and others followed their lead. Several uniforms were purchased by Foam Seats and worn by the gainsharing coordinator and the employee relations manager. Shortly thereafter, several production employees asked about the cost—they were free except for a $2 a week cleaning fee—and whether they could have one. Soon other production employees began wearing the uniforms.

Credit Union. A production employee who had been a member of a credit union through his previous job suggested that Foam Seats join a credit union. The employee provided all the necessary materials, and the facility joined. At the time of the field study, more than half the production employees were members.

Opportunity to State Grievances. According to the production employees, gainsharing allows them to voice their frustrations about their strenuous jobs. They do not like performing this type of work and see their job as an interim step until they can find a better job. The suggestion system and the facility-wide meetings give them a forum to express their displeasure with working conditions.

Conclusion

As shown in Table 5-3, the gainsharing evaluation and attitude survey conducted during the field study revealed that facility employees believe gainsharing activities have obtained a middle-of-the-road existence. On a 1–5 Likert scale, the statistical means are all at or near the midpoint (neutral) of 3.0. In general, managers, supervisors, team representatives, and nonmanagement employees are neither very strong supporters nor opponents of gainsharing. Employee identity, employee influence, and organizational justice also have middle-of-the-road status. On the other hand, the employees do not trust management and believe that the bonus calculation is unfair. After four years of gainsharing expe-

Table 5-3.   Foam Seats: Survey factors

Factor	Statistical Means
Management support	3.1
Supervisor support	3.1
Team representative support	3.1
Employee support	3.1
Suggestion processing	3.2
Team meetings	3.1
Review board meetings	3.2
Bonus calculation	2.6
Facility-wide effort	3.3
Trust	2.7
Employee identity	3.0
Employee influence	3.0
Justice	3.0
Management style[a]	2.6

[a]All factors measured with a 1–5 Likert scale (1=Strongly Disagree, 3=Neutral, 5=Strongly agree), except management style, which was measured with a 1–4 Likert scale.

rience, the management style is between "benevolent authoritative" and "consultative"—far from the goal of participative management style.

The most striking survey findings are the low statistical means for the four support factors (all 3.1), team meetings (3.1), review board meetings (3.2), bonus calculation (2.6), and trust in management (2.7). The survey respondents do not see support for gainsharing from any of the facility's key constituencies. This can be attributed to the checkered history experienced by the gainsharing teams. First, supervisors stopped attending the gainsharing team meetings. Then managers stopped attending the review board meetings. The review board meetings were dominated by arguments between the facility manager and the gainsharing coordinator. At the review board meeting I attended, managers were placing blame for the low bonus payouts on nonmanagement employees, and nonmanagement employees blamed managers. During the field study, managers noted that the facility manager should pay out bonuses more often. Their comments suggest that even other managers believe that the facility manager is manipulating the gainsharing bonus. Such obvious financial manipulations at Foam Seats damages trust as well as gainsharing support.

Each of the four conflict-of-interest propositions is examined below as an aid to understanding the survey results and gainsharing evolution at this publicly owned nonunion manufacturing facility.

P1: Manipulating the Transitional Process

The facility manager was the primary power player during the transitional period. The nonunion production employees began this transition from a very weak bargaining position. The facility manager adopted five strategies at the beginning of the gainsharing intervention that restricted the degree of employee involvement in decision making and the amount of the group-based financial bonus. Contrary to the gainsharing consultant's recommendations, the facility manager (1) added gainsharing responsibilities to the employee relations manager's existing full-time duties rather than employ a full-time coordinator, (2) created five gainsharing teams (one per department that combined both shifts) rather than sixteen gainsharing teams (one per shift per department), (3) assigned a supervisor to chair each gainsharing team meeting rather than allow nonmanagement employees to elect a peer, (4) scheduled gainsharing meetings after work rather than during regular working hours, and (5) included eighteen factors in the gainsharing calculation, some of which were not affected by nonmanagement employees, rather than a few factors that were directly affected by nonmanagement employees. These strategies were pursued to limit gainsharing's administrative costs and bonus payouts. The gainsharing steering committee members, all of whom were assigned by the facility manager, did not question these decisions.

P2: Interest-Group Power Struggles

Based on information gathered during the semistructured interviews, no manager was categorized as a go-getter. Gainsharing implementation was the facility manager's idea, and no other manager claimed ownership. Managers and supervisors were fence-sitters or adversarial. The facility manager assigned them to the review board or to facilitate the gainsharing team meetings. After a few months, supervisors stopped attending team meetings because gainsharing had become an unwelcome burden involving extra work, meetings, and paperwork. Supervisors interpreted gainsharing suggestions as critical of their performance abilities. High-quality suggestions made managers feel that they were inadequately performing their job duties. When such suggestions were read at review board meetings, they feared the wrath of the facility manager for not thinking of the idea themselves. In addition, several very critical suggestions were submitted by nonmanagement opponents. Attempts by the facility manager to force managers to participate were met with resentment. As a result, managers developed a list of excuses to justify not attending gainsharing team meetings and review board meetings.

Determining who should be the gainsharing coordinator resulted in many interest-group power games. Initially, the facility manager assigned the coordinator job to the employee relations manager, to minimize costs and ensure management control. When the employee relations manager left Foam Seats, the facility manager chose a production employee he trusted but was disliked by production employees for being "too close" to management. Then a suggestion for a new full-time coordinator was submitted by a team representative whom many in management considered adversarial because of his confrontations with managers. The facility manager agreed to the election primarily because he expected his handpicked incumbent to win. He was wrong. Following the election, the facility manager asked each manager not to sabotage the newly elected gainsharing coordinator.

The most influential nonmanagement employees after four years of gainsharing are the opponents. At the beginning of gainsharing they heckled management during all-employee meetings, offered very critical suggestions to gainsharing teams, and emphasized that management only wanted "cheap" suggestions. By the second year of gainsharing, many fence-sitters were persuaded by the opponents that management was manipulating the gainsharing bonus. Nonmanagement employees received higher wages by working overtime prior to gainsharing than they received by working more efficiently under gainsharing. Gainsharing bonuses did not replace this wage gap. An employee of the month award system encouraged both go-getters and fence-sitters to submit more suggestions. Nonetheless, at the time of the field study, the dominant view among nonmanagement employees was that the financial benefits of improved production performance were being used by management to subsidize facility repairs rather than be distributed as a bonus. Both management and nonmanagement employees believe that the facility manager restricted payouts by manipulating the financial bonus calculation.

Last, power struggles were quite evident at review board meetings. Managers had to be coerced to attend. Suggestion discussions were primarily limited to two opinions—that of the facility manager and the gainsharing coordinator. Everyone else remained quiet unless directly called upon. It was common for management and nonmanagement employees to blame each other for low bonus payouts. At the review board meeting I attended, the facility accountant attributed the lack of a bonus that month on a nonmanagement employee's lost-time accident; in response, the gainsharing coordinator quickly placed the blame on a particularly high monthly telephone bill.

P3: Hidden and Suppressed Problems Surface

Hidden and suppressed problems have surfaced as a result of the 776 accepted suggestions. Most of the suggestions corrected production inefficiencies. Another major problem that surfaced as a result of gainsharing implementation was health and safety. Although a health and safety committee existed, production employees had not submitted issues to this committee because it lacked the appropriate authority and funding to make the changes requested. A hidden or suppressed problem discussed during the review board meeting I attended was the need to pave the road leading up to the receiving dock. Apparently, managers ignored or discounted the problem of vendors getting stuck in the mud until a gainsharing suggestion was submitted.

The gainsharing suggestion system and team meetings have been used to address other types of problems as well. For instance, nonmanagement opponents use these outlets to express their strong dislike for existing working conditions. Their jobs are physically strenuous, a point made clear in the wording of suggestions and comments at meetings. According to some nonmanagement employees, the suggestion system solves only a very small number of working-condition problems. Nonetheless, production employees continually submit working condition suggestions to keep the issue on the monthly review board agenda, thus making the issue harder for managers to ignore.

P4: Fulfilled Monetary and Nonmonetary Interests

The facility manager is looking forward to many more years of gainsharing, despite growing opposition on the part of nonmanagement employees and lack of management support. Gainsharing generated many suggestions that improved production, improved product quality, and reduced costs. There is better communication between and within departments. He believes that these factors will continue to improve because the full-time gainsharing coordinator, who has the respect of nonmanagement opponents, will improve the gainsharing system. In addition, Foam Seats's high employee turnover rate means that both go-getters and opponents quit their jobs on a regular basis. The facility manager believes that gainsharing can be sustained through more careful screening of job applicants and employing more go-getters and fewer opponents.

Despite the low bonus payouts, nonmanagement go-getters, fence-sitters, and opponents also want gainsharing to continue. They, too, have benefited from improvements in the production process and in product quality. Many production employees want to make a high-quality product and minimize production problems. Gainsharing suggestions have improved health and safety and job rotation. Gainsharing interactions have resulted in a clothing allowance, employee uniforms, and voluntary layoffs. From the perspective of opponents, gainsharing allows them an opportunity to state their many grievances.

Summary

Foam Seats has had difficulties with all four conflict-of-interest exchange relationships (see Figure 2-2). Although gainsharing, by design, increases employee involvement in decision making, the facility manager restricted the degree to which employees participate significantly. Instead of transforming each production team into a gainsharing team, the facility manager chose to create only five gainsharing teams that included both shifts. As a result, only 14 percent of the employees were on gainsharing teams. The gainsharing meeting times—after normal working hours—were particularly troublesome for women employees who relied on daycare.

In addition, accepted suggestions decreased from 250 in 1986 to 153 in 1988. With the election of a full-time gainsharing coordinator, suggestion acceptances increased to 173 in 1989. At the time of the field study, it was well known that nonmanagement employees were restricting the number of suggestions submitted. Many nonmanagement employees believe that management only wants "cheap" suggestions that fall within the gainsharing team's discretionary budget. There have been constructive changes in the production process, but for the most part, the production experience is still dominated by mistrust.

Although employees submitted 173 suggestions in 1989, and these suggestions improved production output, some opponents and fence-sitters believe that it is in their interest to restrict their production output because managers are not attending gainsharing meetings and also because gainsharing bonuses are not high enough to replace lost overtime wages. Many management and nonmanagement employees believe that the bonus calculation is unfair: production employees have improved their performance, the facility is winning quality awards, and profits are announced on a monthly basis, but the gainsharing bonuses are minimal. A growing number of employees believe that more money can be earned through less efficient work methods and increased overtime. Some production employees had earned several hundred dollars a month in overtime prior to gainsharing, whereas they now earn only $40 a month from their gainsharing bonus. Both managers and nonmanagement employees maintain that the facility manager is restricting the bonus payouts. As a result, even go-getters have had to be coerced to become team representatives and submit suggestions.

6 Forestland: A Publicly Owned Nonunion Facility, Modest Bonuses

Forestland is a publicly owned, nonunion facility located in a small community situated on the edge of a northeastern mountain range. It is a subsidiary of a multibillion-dollar international corporation. Forestland had been an independent sawmill until it was purchased by the corporation in 1946. In 1981, the corporation consolidated the sawmill with its wood-working operations and relocated both groups of employees to the facility's current location. There are two primary buildings, the sawmill and the wood products manufacturing building, and a lumber yard. The facility was built in 1981 with an elaborate waste-recovery system that uses sawdust and wood shavings to supply its energy needs.

In 1989, Forestland had sales of approximately $3 million a year. Saws, scratch awls, and wooden handles for screwdrivers, all manufactured for the parent corporation, account for 75 percent of the facility's sales. Forestland's other major product is the sale of waste byproducts, such as tree bark for landscaping, wood chips for paper mills, and dust and grit for floor-sweeping compounds.

The business is seasonal. Most work is performed in the summer, fall, and early winter months to fulfill the high demand for saws and hammers in the fall. In November and December, the facility typically operates twenty-four hours a day, six to seven days a week, to finish yearly orders. Forestland employs fifty people—70 percent of them male, on two production shifts, with the second shift a skeleton crew of just three to five employees. Nonmanagement employees earn approximately $15,000 a year. They produce approximately thirty thousand saw handles a week.

Forestland has three levels of management. Upper-level management consists of the facility manager, who reports to corporate headquarters. Middle-level management includes the production manager, facility engineer, controller, and quality manager, all of whom report directly to the facility manager. Lower-level management consists of the production supervisor, who reports to the production manager.

The production employees, like many citizens of the state, pride themselves on their individualism, ruggedness, and willingness to confront people. They distrust political authorities, and this attitude adds to the normal distrust production employees have toward management. Working in the sawmill or manufacturing department is a physically demanding job. For the most part, production employees want to be left alone to perform their job tasks. One employee has been with the facility forty years, three for more than twenty years, and six for more than ten years. There are clear divisions among managers, sawmill employees, who cut the wood, and manufacturing employees, who assemble the product. As noted above, the sawmill and manufacturing employees work in different buildings.

The facility manager was motivated by several concerns when he decided to implement a Scanlon-type gainsharing plan in January 1986. He believed that gainsharing could serve as an anti-union strategy that would give production employees an institutional voice. It was well known among managers of nonunion facilities that corporate headquarters demoted managers whose facilities became unionized. The facility manager had operated both union and nonunion facilities, and he believed that it was essential for nonunion employees to have a voice in facility decisions. In addition, every year some production employees complained that their efficiency-related suggestions were ignored by managers. He believed gainsharing was likely to succeed because the employees had responded well to corporate-sponsored suggestion contests and a team-based quality productivity improvement program that were not institutionalized. Gainsharing also provided an opportunity to bridge the antagonistic work cultures of the sawmill and manufacturing departments.

When the corporation began a decentralization phase during the mid-1980s, the facility manager maintained that the time was right to try gainsharing. He invited a consultant to conduct a gainsharing feasibility survey with facility employees. He was satisfied with the results and concluded that gainsharing could be successful at his facility. In fall 1985, the facility manager created a gainsharing steering committee consisting of four managers and eight production employees to determine how gainsharing should be implemented. A modified gainsharing plan was

approved by more than 75 percent of the employees, and it was implemented in January 1986.

Power Games Propositions

The two power games propositions are analyzed below according to
management and nonmanagement reactions to three central aspects of
Scanlon-type gainsharing plans: the suggestion system, the team structure, and the group-based bonus.

Suggestion System

During four years of gainsharing, production employees implemented 121 suggestions. As shown in Table 6-1, the breakdown per year
is 43 (1986), 29 (1987), 26 (1988) and 23 (1989), or approximately 0.6 suggestions per employee per year. Management considers the total number
of suggestions artificially low because many suggestions are implemented directly by employees. The facility manager believes that completing a formal suggestion form is often an unnecessary bureaucratic
precedure.

Managers optimistically publicized the potential of gainsharing prior
to implementation. All five managers, in addition to the facility manager, were go-getters. From their perspective, they were uninformed
about too many production activities. Employee involvement made theoretical sense to them, but they were not sure how production employees would respond. As noted earlier, many of these employees took
pride in being rugged individualists. Some had previously mentioned a
desire for more influence on how the production process was organized,
but these go-getters were a distinct minority. Most production employ-

Table 6–1. Forestland: Suggestions and bonuses per year

Year	Number of Accepted Suggestions	Bonus as a % of Wages
1986	43	4.2%
1987	29	7.1%
1988	26	9.0%
1989	23	7.0%
Total suggestions	121	
Average bonus		6.8%

ees were content with their job duties and did not want any major changes. Older production employees were skeptical of gainsharing and viewed it as a fad, like many other management promotions that had come and gone during their industrial careers.

When gainsharing was introduced, only a few production employees were excited by the change. The first problem that arose with gainsharing implementation was managing opponents, who antagonized both management and nonmanagement employees. Nine of the fifty employees were considered oppositional about everything, not just gainsharing.

The most adversarial production employee upset all the other production employees in two instances during Forestland's gainsharing experience. Two months after gainsharing began, she submitted a suggestion complaining that others were taking too many bathroom breaks. After she submitted the suggestion, but before it was presented at the team meeting, the production manager recommended that she soften the suggestion's tone and emphasize the underlying issue, which was that every minute on the production floor was important. The opponent then calculated that Forestland could save $10,872 a year if each person spent ten minutes more working. When the suggestion was presented at a team meeting, the other departmental employees who already knew about the contents of the suggestion, were disturbed that gainsharing was being used to monitor them in this way. A heated argument ensued between the oppositional employee and the other team members.

The same production employee also submitted a suggestion in opposition to wage increases given to a group of laborers who had been paid below the regional wage average. She argued that wage increases had a negative impact on the bonus calculation. Her suggestion was rejected.

I attended the February 1990 review board meeting. At the meeting were three managers and the five nonmanagement team representatives. The personnel administrator, who worked out of corporate headquarters, was the only person absent from the meeting. Each team representative presented a brief report on the most recent team meeting. Seven issues were addressed in detail during the ninety minute meeting: installation of a production line mirror, vacation eligibility, time clock policy, an electrical power problem, a new product, current business, and recycling. The discussions were quite interactive and informative for both management and nonmanagement employees.

Production Line Mirror. A team representative reported that a suggestion to install a mirror in a strategic production location to improve product quality had been declined. The suggestion attempted to solve a quality problem attributed to workers being unable to see underneath the product as it was being manufactured. A manager asked the team representative to explain why the suggestion had been declined by the team. The team representative noted that when this suggestion was tested, it had resulted in an unanticipated safety hazard. He informed the review board that during the following month the team would explore alternative solutions.

Vacation Eligibility. A team representative reported that for the fifth or sixth time during the past year, someone at the team meeting had said that the arbitrary cutoff date used to determine vacation eligibility was unfair. It benefited some employees at the expense of others. Team members believed that vacation eligibility should be based on the anniversary date of employment. After minor discussion, the facility manager noted that he would examine the current vacation policy and try to develop a system that was more fair.

Time Clock Policy. A team representative reported that production employees in his area were confused about the time clock policy. Usually, production employees arrived early to work, punched the time clock, had a cup of coffee, and then went to the production floor when scheduled. A production employee had been reprimanded recently for punching in more than six minutes before she was scheduled to work. The facility manager noted that although punching the time clock appeared to be a meaningless formality, if a government labor committee performed an audit matching time clock slips with wage hours, Forestland would be fined for not paying employees an extra ten or fifteen minutes every day. Several team representatives argued that the government policy was foolish and another example of unnecessary government intrusion. The team representative provided several examples of why it was not practical to obey the law. The facility manager reiterated that it was the law and asked team representatives to inform team members about the importance of complying with this policy.

Electrical Power Problem. A team representative noted that production employees were concerned about power outages because of a recent snowstorm. Emergency power was not coming on until after the regular power went out completely. With unpredictable power shortages, a worker could get severely hurt if the electricity went off and on while the worker was in the middle of a production task, such as sawing wood. There was much discussion among managers and team representatives on how the power shortages caused various production problems. Possible solutions for each problem were discussed. The facility manager ended the discussion by stating that he would pressure the utility company to cut down trees around the power lines, because they often fell on the lines and were the source of many power outages.

New Product. A manager explained that he was in the process of developing a new product at the facility. The facility would need $2.5 million from corporate headquarters to develop it further. Team representatives asked how these costs would affect the gainsharing bonus. After the controller explained that it would have no effect on the bonus calculation, a team representative asked about the budget approval process at corporate headquarters. The facility manager explained in detail how budget decisions were made and the type of politicking he had to do before requesting additional funds from corporate headquarters.

Current Business. A team representative asked the facility manager how was business. The facility manager said business was terrible because of the recession. Nonetheless, there would be no layoffs in the foreseeable future. Other team representatives asked about potential new business and how business this year compared to previous years. Several managers provided explanations. The facility manager noted that at this time of year business was always slow and that it should improve by the beginning of summer. In addition, there would be substantial overtime again in the fall. A discussion followed, initiated by team representatives, on how work could be organized so that overtime could be minimized in the fall.

Recycling. A team representative asked what management was doing about the recycling issues being discussed in the local media. The facility manager explained that Forestland already recycled glass and aluminum, but he had not fully developed a paper recycling policy. A team representative suggested that Forestland could burn excess paper for fuel, like some people did at home. The facility manager said that this was illegal, unless Forestland obtained a state license. A team representative asked if homeowners needed a state license, and if so, most of his neighbors were in violation of the law. This comment led to another discussion about intrusive government policies. A manager volunteered that he was looking into the issue and wanted to develop a policy before any new laws were passed. A team representative argued that Forestland would be better off by just waiting and simply adopting the standards of the new law. The facility manager responded that the new environmental regulation would most likely be very flexible, so Forestland could get a head start and not worry about the issue later.

Team Structure

As recommended by the gainsharing consultant, the facility manager put all fifty employees on one of the five gainsharing department teams. One team slot was set aside for a manager, and the five managers rotated attendance at the monthly team meetings. Each gainsharing team had a monthly discretionary budget of $400, and any suggestion costing more than $5,000 required corporate approval. Each team elected one nonmanagement member to serve on the review board. In addition to five nonmanagement employees, the review board included the facility manager, engineer, personnel administrator, and controller, who also served as the gainsharing coordinator.

Initially, the facility manager attended every team meeting. But every time a major decision had to be reached, team members would turn to the facility manager for his opinion. He found it difficult not to present his views and, against his better judgement, would make the decision for the team. As a result of this often-repeated experience, the facility manager stopped attending team meetings so that the nonmanagement team members would exercise more authority over the team's decisions. Another early change was in the meeting schedule for the office team. The team had only four members, and they found their monthly meetings unproductive. With the facility manager's permission, the office team voted to meet quarterly and attend the meetings of other gainsharing teams during the other months.

Production employees in the sawmill were expected to oppose gainsharing because of their independent nature and lack of education. Instead, the sawmill team was the most impressive and productive team in terms of the number of suggestions offered and implemented. Unexpectedly, there were three go-getters among the eleven sawmill production employees. Managers enjoyed attending these team meetings because they often had active and dramatic discussions.

When gainsharing was first implemented, three older sawmill team members took responsibility for the team's success and rotated the focal positions of chairperson, recorder, and review board representative, with the full consent of the other team members. These three production employees had never had an opportunity to work under a participatory management system, and they wanted to make the most of their experience. When it became apparent that gainsharing was not just a fad and that the meetings would continue for several more years, they refused to volunteer for the three team positions in order to force other sawmill production employees to become more active. Beginning in 1989, sawmill team members agreed to rotate the chairperson position based on the alphabetical order of members' names so that everyone would have an opportunity to run the team meeting.

Management viewed gainsharing team meetings as learning opportunities. No topic was off-limits for discussion. The production manager attended all team meetings to hear the concerns employees had about production. Other managers attended one team meeting a month as a source for new ideas, viewing the team discussions as idea incubators. From their perspective, although the nonmanagement employees on a team might reject a suggestion, production employees' views could inspire a solution to another problem on the manager's agenda.

Sometimes, when teams had a good idea requiring further exploration, management formed a task force. For instance, the facility always had a yield problem (the percentage of wood wasted between the beginning and end of the production process). After several teams raised this issue, management formed a yield task team that addressed the problem successfully by integrating production employees from different teams.

Three team-related issues continually arose: some fence-sitters and opponents did not want to attend team meetings, some fence-sitters and opponents would not speak at meetings, and some opponents used the meetings to antagonize managers.

First, in every year of the plan a fence-sitter or opponent submitted a suggestion that production employees should not be forced to attend team meetings if they would rather work on production. The review board rejected this suggestion every time it was offered. The facility manager maintained that it was good for team and department cohesiveness to have everyone attend the meetings. Some teams had become stagnant, and he wanted production employees to take responsibility for reinvigorating their meetings rather than give up on them.

Second, some fence-sitters and opponents wanted to attend the team meetings to be well informed, but they would not contribute to any discussions. They were content to sit in the background and listen to discussions. Management, thinking about the sawmill team's unexpected success in involving everyone, wondered how to develop the same dynamic for other teams. At the time of the field study, no patterned solution to the problem had been developed.

Third, some opponents used the gainsharing team meetings to antagonize management. Sometimes a key issue would be raised that required the input of opponents. They deliberately refused to say anything as a way of making a statement against the manager in attendance. When asked directly to reply to the issue being discussed, the opponent would just shrug his or her shoulders. Other times, opponents would say things just to irritate the manager and to show the other team members that they could get away with being disrespectful. These opponents acted out their dislike for particular managers at the expense of the team. Sometimes go-getter nonmanagement employees told managers to discipline a disruptive opponent. Managers typically ignored the problem, however, because they were unsure about how to handle the situation without causing greater opposition from the adversarial employee.

Group-Based Bonus

During four years of gainsharing, the average monthly bonus payout was 6.8 percent ($85). As shown in Table 6-1, the breakdown per year is 4.2 percent (1986), 7.1 percent (1987), 9.0 percent (1988), and 7.0 percent (1989). Table 6-2 provides a monthly breakdown of bonus payouts.

The historical cost standard used for calculating the financial bonus was based on four ratios consisting of six cost factors averaged over the previous three years. The *productivity ratio* compared actual hours worked with earned direct labor hours. The *scrap ratio* compared actual scrap dollars with standard labor dollars of production. The *yield ratio* compared the amount of board feet received with the amount of board feet in the finished product. The *yearly supplies, services, and utilities ratio* compared the actual expenses for supplies, services, and utilities with the total standard labor cost of sales. The cost savings were shared 50/50 between Forestland and its employees. Of the employee share, 50 percent was distributed that month, and 50 percent was allocated to the reserve pool. The employees' year-end bonus was limited to 15 percent of Forestland's total payroll as a precaution against excessive bonus payouts. Everyone employed by the facility was eligible for the financial bonus.

Production employees on the steering committee surprised management by arguing that the gainsharing bonus calculation was unfair to Forestland. The initial bonus plan eliminated the reserve pool deficit at the end of each year—a common feature of Scanlon-type plans. Some of the younger go-getters complained that this showed a lack of confidence in them, because they expected to surpass the historical standards. In addition, it was wrong for Forestland to have to absorb reserve pool

Table 6–2. Forestland: Monthly gainsharing bonus payouts (%)

	1986	1987	1988	1989
January	4.7	4.9	0.5	—
February	3.6	6.7	0.6	1.2
March	0.0	4.6	0.0	0.3
April	4.3	4.6	3.2	2.6
May	2.0	4.4	1.5	3.3
June	4.7	6.6	5.6	2.4
July	7.4	6.9	0.0	3.9
August	3.7	9.4	1.9	3.2
September	2.7	3.8	9.6	3.4
October	4.2	2.5	6.8	4.7
November	3.0	3.1	2.8	5.5
December	7.5	1.0	1.5	2.6
Average monthly bonus % per employee	4.0	4.8	2.9	2.8
Average monthly bonus $ per employee[a]	$50	$60	$36	$35
Reserve pool %	0.2	2.3	6.1	4.2
Year-end reserve pool $ per employee	$30	$345	$915	$630

[a]Average production employee salary: $7 an hour, $1,250 a month, or $15,000 a year.

deficits caused by employees' inability to surpass historical standards. They proposed that the reserve pool deficit be carried over from one year to the next. Management countered by offering that Forestland absorb 50 percent of the deficit and carry over 50 percent of the deficit for the following year. There was never a deficit in the reserve pool at the end of a year during the facility's first four years of gainsharing.

Management made it more difficult for production employees to earn a bonus, however, by arguing successfully for a weighted average historical standard where the previous year counted for three-sixths of the historical base calculation, two years prior counted for two-sixths, and three years prior counted for one-sixth. Although this method of bonus calculation had been mentioned by the gainsharing consultant, he had proposed initially that each year in the historical base period should count equally.

Management, in turn, compromised on two bonus issues after gainsharing was implemented: the electricity calculation and the supplies and services calculation. First, during 1986, the public utility hiked Forestland's electricity rate to 9 percent. Since fluctuations in the price of electricity were beyond production employees' control, management decided to change the electricity measurement from dollars to kilowatt usage.

Second, in 1987, the reserve pool slowly increased during the course of the year. Toward the end of the year, management decided to pave the driveway—a very costly expense that was fully deducted from the supplies and services pool. Many production employees complained about the way this expense was handled. Opponents interpreted this action as evidence of management trickery. Managers were surprised by how closely everyone had been following the growth of the reserve pool. They did not anticipate that this allocation would cause a problem. The review board decided to obtain input from each team about how the issue should be handled in the future. The alternatives were that Forestland could either eliminate the supplies and services pool or cap expenditures for items included in the pool. Production employees wanted to keep the supplies and services pool because the pool still had a surplus, even though the paving costs had reduced it substantially. They suggested that a $5,000 cap be placed on any expenditure. This solution was accepted by the review board.

Some mistrust about the bonus calculation developed when Forestland hired a new controller in January 1988. No bonus checks were distributed during his first three months at Forestland. The payouts for January and February (about $6 per person) had been so small that he set them aside for distribution during a month with a higher payout. In March, no bonus was earned. This was the longest period in Forestland's gainsharing experience without a bonus payout. Opponents spread rumors on the production floor that the new controller was manipulating the bonus calculation and could not be trusted. Although bonuses were earned in future months, the opponents continually doubted the integrity of the controller whenever there was a questionable deduction.

At the time of the field study there were three primary concerns about the gainsharing bonus: opponents' belief that the historical standard was becoming too difficult to surpass; the impact of higher wage rates assigned to a particular labor grade; and the reaction of corporate headquarters to the bonus size.

First, opponents argued that the size of the monthly bonuses was decreasing (from $60 a month in 1987 to $35 a month in 1989) because (a) productivity was improving each year, hence the historical standard was becoming harder to surpass; (b) management was manipulating factors in the reserve pool (such as roof repairs); and (c) the new controller could not be trusted. Management explained that Scanlon-type gainsharing plans typically use a rotating historical standard to encourage continuous improvements. Opponents responded that production employees would soon run out of improvement ideas and not earn any gainsharing bonus. Go-getters from the sawmill team were not concerned with this issue, however, believing instead that production improvements were endless. But other teams that were struggling or stagnant believed that they may have run out of good ideas and would no longer be able to improve on the previous year's performance.

Second, the wage increases given to upper labor grade production employees accentuated problems associated with federal law governing gainsharing bonus payouts. The law requires that gainsharing bonuses be distributed as an across-the-board percentage. For instance, in June 1989 there was a 2.4 percent gainsharing bonus for all employees. An employee earning $1,200 a month received a $29 bonus, whereas someone earning $1,400 a month received a $34 bonus. The lower-paid production employees maintained that everyone should receive an equal monetary amount, not an equal percentage. The inequity of this type of bonus distribution resurfaced when a select group of the more highly paid production employees received wage increases of 6 percent to 20 percent.

Last, managers at corporate headquarters were concerned about the size of the gainsharing bonus. Every few months, someone from headquarters would question the bonus payouts. From the corporate perspective, the facility was "giving away" $200,000 by paying gainsharing bonuses. The facility manager argued that production employees earned the money and that their efforts resulted in substantial cost savings. Managers at corporate headquarters would next ask why the facility engineer could not implement the efficiency suggestions and why other managers could not motivate employees to surpass historical standards without receiving a gainsharing bonus. According to the facility manager, at this point in the discussion it would become obvious that the corporate managers asking these questions had been away from facility management too long and that there was no way he could win the argument. From his perspective, corporate headquarters was momentarily tolerating the bonus payouts.

The Outcomes Propositions

There was a strong consensus among management and nonmanagement employees that gainsharing greatly improved facility operations.

Both management and nonmanagement employees benefited directly and indirectly from four years of gainsharing.

Benefits

Direct benefits to both management and nonmanagement employees included better production processes, maintenance of high product quality, and (3) improved communications.

Better Production Processes. Employees implemented 121 suggestions over four years. As noted earlier, employees made many other production process changes without submitting formal suggestions. Examples of production process suggestions adopted in 1989 include purchasing a remote-controlled device for alerting the sawer to problems with the load of cut wood, using strappings made of plastic rather than steel ($800 annual savings), and reusing stain in the tumble room. Since 1986, employees have broken the record seven times for the number of saw handles shipped per week per employee—an increase from 31,892 in October 1986 to 50,692 in September 1988.

Maintenance of High Product Quality. The facility is considered the highest-quality supplier in the corporation's tools division, having won its first supplier certification award a year prior to gainsharing implementation. The facility has received quality awards every year since. In 1989 only one shipment had an obvious quality problem. According to management, gainsharing is responsible for maintaining—not obtaining—high product quality at the facility. Besides continuous quality improvements, managers claim that gainsharing increases employee respect for the customer. Before gainsharing, production employees' attitudes toward customer requests had been, "Those bastards want something." The general attitude toward broken material was, "It's management's problem." Production employees have become more service and quality oriented because customer sales and returns affect the gainsharing bonus.

Improved Communications. According to nonmanagement employees, before gainsharing, they dreaded seeing a manager on the production floor. Management stated continually that they wanted employee input, but production employees did not believe them. Since gainsharing, nonmanagement employees demand that managers spend more time on the production floor to respond to immediate problems they want to change. In addition, the team meetings are treated as a forum to express a wide variety of concerns. Many of the barriers between sawmill and manufacturing employees have been reduced significantly through gainsharing interactions.

Direct benefits to management and indirect benefits to nonmanagement employees included significant costs savings, less resistance to production changes, and improved supplier relations.

Significant Cost Savings. Management approximated that gainsharing resulted in a four-year savings of $471,100. Part of this savings is attributable to new machinery and other capital improvements. According to management, it is very difficult to attribute an absolute dollar value to gainsharing because other changes occur simultaneously. Nonetheless, according to the facility manager, "everyone is a cost accountant" because of the gainsharing calculation.

Management developed the gainsharing financial bonus to improve four production factors: productivity, amount of scrap produced, yield, and supplies and services. During four years of gainsharing, productivity and scrap costs have decreased by $91,000, and supplies and services costs have stabilized. The productivity pool measures the ratio of actual hours worked in comparison to direct labor hours. Management's goal is to increase direct labor hours, thus reducing the ratio. In 1985, actual hours worked were more than double (2.19) the amount of direct labor hours. In 1989, it was slightly less than double (1.98) the amount of direct labor hours. Therefore, more working hours are now charged to direct labor accounts, and fewer hours are charged to indirect labor accounts. According to managers, production employees now complain about downtime rather than take advantage of it. The scrap pool measures scrap dollars in comparison to standard labor dollars of production. The scrap ratio has decreased from 28.4 percent to 16.5 percent. The supplies and services ratio, also a percentage of direct labor dollars, has stabilized at 13.5 percent.

Five of the seven yield pools have improved since gainsharing was implemented. Yield compares the amount of board feet received to the amount of board feet contained in the finished product. The ideal standard is 100 percent; that is, every inch of board received is transformed into a finished product delivered to the customer. Sawmill yield has decreased rather than increased. Management attributes this change to the development of new products and the use of different types of wood.

They maintain that the sawmill yield would have been much lower without the gainsharing goal.

Less Resistance to Production Changes. Management claims that changes in the production process are more readily accepted by production employees because of the yearly bonus. Some of the cost savings are not apparent in financial calculations. For instance, in 1989, management had been considering a large capital expenditure in the rack area. The area team worked on the problem and developed an alternative strategy that required only minor modifications to the production process and no capital expenditure. The facility manager maintains that this type of production behavior was not evident prior to gainsharing. Production employees are more likely to ensure an improvement is implemented if they are the originators of the suggestion.

Improved Supplier Relations. Gainsharing has brought production employees in closer contact with suppliers. Prior to gainsharing, suppliers would approach management with ideas on how they could better meet management's needs. Production employees were not interested in giving feedback to suppliers, although they tended to complain whenever supplier-related changes occurred. After gainsharing implementation, management had suppliers approach production employees with their ideas, since any change suggested by suppliers was likely to have some effect on the gainsharing bonus. Production employees tend to provide forthright feedback and constructive recommendations on how suppliers can better serve the facility.

Direct benefits to nonmanagement employees and indirect benefits to management included easier work tasks, improved health and safety, new grievance procedures, a basic education course, alternatives to layoffs, payday changes, recreational activities, and job rotation.

Easier Work Tasks. Production employees implement their own efficiency-related suggestions. Before gainsharing, they simply complained among themselves that managers had deliberately designed their jobs to be strenuous. Rather than allowing an unnecessary work task to continue or stating that management is responsible for improving the work task, production employees make the change in how they perform their jobs.

Improved Health and Safety. In May 1989, health and safety was formally made part of every gainsharing team's monthly agenda because of the large volume of suggestions in this area. Each team regularly discusses safety tips, such as how to use the fire extinguisher, what to do during a fire, and how to clean up hazardous work areas. Many health and safety improvements, such as the purchase of adjustable chairs for the sanders to reduce backaches, are paid out of team budgets.

Some production employees use the suggestion system to obtain health treatments that are not covered by their insurance policies or require a substantial deductible. Based on an employee suggestion, Forestland provides a health awareness program that examines a person's overall lifestyle. The facility manager had concluded that these illness-prevention suggestions resulted from an inadequate corporate health plan, which had a deductible equivalent to two weeks' pay. Employees would visit a physician only under extreme conditions. After consulting with local doctors and corporate administrators about the problem, the facility manager arranged for every employee to receive a complete physical at Forestland's expense every other year. The facility manager developed a similar arrangement for family counseling, which also had been rarely used by those who needed it because of the high deductible.

New Grievance Procedures. Before gainsharing was implemented, each production employee met with the facility manager once a year to discuss grievances. Many production employees were intimidated by the facility manager, and although they had grievances, they would not express them during these one-on-one meetings. Management now uses team and review board meetings to address employee grievances. Typically, these grievances are initially raised during the team meetings and are anonymously presented at the review board meetings.

A Basic Education Course. In early 1989, managers had been surprised when a very capable production employee received her GED, not realizing that she lacked a high school diploma. After reviewing the personnel files, management became alarmed that there were other production employees without a high school diploma. They believed that this deficit explained the low level of gainsharing involvement on the part of some production employees. In June 1989, management began an adult basic education program at the facility. The state government provided the instructor, and Forestland provided space and materials. The class meets in the cafeteria once a week, after the first shift is finished. Several employees and their family members have completed the program.

Alternatives to Layoffs. Management had always attempted not to lay off production employees during the slow periods, usually the winter months. The facility manager believes that this policy creates a more committed workforce. The problem, however, is that management struggles to find things for production employees to do when they are not needed for their usual production tasks. Since gainsharing was implemented, production employees take responsibility for determining production-related activities they can perform, because nonproduction hours have a negative impact on the gainsharing productivity pool.

Payday Changes. Forestland had distributed paychecks on Friday afternoons. Second-shift employees complained about this policy because their work schedule prevented them from depositing their pay on Friday afternoon. An employee suggestion requesting a different payday forced management to investigate other alternatives, and payday is now on Thursdays.

Recreational Activities. A manager submitted a gainsharing suggestion to purchase a ping-pong table. Although this purchase was within the team's budget, some management and nonmanagement employees questioned its relevancy to gainsharing concerns. The manager justified the ping-pong table on the grounds that it would increase social interactions between management and nonmanagement employees. The table was purchased and set up in a vacant area. Both management and nonmanagement employees form teams and compete during lunchtime.

Job Rotation. Before gainsharing, management had on several occasions considered cross-training for the purpose of job rotation. In mid-1988, a production employee's suggestion made the issue public, and it was addressed at several team meetings. Production employees complained about the repetitive nature of their work. Management remained reluctant to institute job rotation, believing that it would be more detrimental than beneficial to productivity. Production employees have argued that Forestland should experiment with job rotation during the next production slowdown. At the time of the field study, management was examining the details of implementing this suggestion.

Conclusion

As shown in Table 6-3, the gainsharing evaluation and attitude survey conducted during the field study reveals that facility employees believe gainsharing activities are performing well, with the exception of the bonus calculation. On a 1–5 Likert scale, the statistical means are relatively favorable on facility operations. Supervisors and management are supportive of gainsharing activities. There is a strong commitment to gainsharing throughout the facility. In the aggregate, employees believe that the bonus is neither fair nor unfair. After four years of gainsharing experience, the management style is "consultative"—one step short of the desired participative management style.

The most striking survey findings are the relatively high scores for gainsharing support from managers (3.8) and supervisors (4.0). These high scores can be attributed to the way the facility manager encourages other managers and supervisors to treat team meetings as idea incubators. Managers use these meetings to learn something from the production employees and to apply this new knowledge to other work-related issues. Despite having nine of fifty employees (18 percent) categorized as oppositional, employee support, team meetings, and review board meetings are rated relatively high compared to the other four nonunion facilities. The reason for these results could be that the facility manager encourages employees to use the team meetings and the suggestion system to express and deal with their work-related grievances.

Nonetheless, the trust in management score is only 3.1. This low score is probably related to employees questioning the fairness of the bonus

Table 6–3. Forestland: Survey factors

Factor	Statistical Means
Management support	3.8
Supervisor support	4.0
Team representative support	3.5
Employee support	3.6
Suggestion processing	3.6
Team meetings	3.5
Review board meetings	3.6
Bonus calculation	3.1
Facility-wide effort	3.9
Trust	3.1
Employee identity	3.4
Employee influence	3.3
Justice	3.1
Management syle[a]	2.9

[a]All factors measured with a 1–5 Likert scale (1=Strongly disagree, 3=Neutral, 5=Strongly agree), except management syle, which was measured with a 1–4 Likert scale.

calculation (3.1). Four events at Forestland lend credence to the negative views expressed by oppositional employees about the bonus calculation. First, a large unexpected cost item (paving the driveway) reduced the year-end reserve pool drastically. Second, the facility manager told production employees that he had to justify the financial bonus at corporate headquarters. Third, for several months, there were no or low bonuses paid after a new controller was hired. Fourth, it seemed more difficult to earn monthly bonuses with each succeeding year of gainsharing.

Each of the four conflict-of-interest propositions is examined below to aid an understanding of the survey results and the evolution of gainsharing at this publicly owned nonunion manufacturing facility.

P1: Manipulating the Transitional Process

The facility manager was the primary power player during the transitional period. The nonunion production employees began this transition from a very weak bargaining position. The facility manager adopted two strategies at the start of the gainsharing program that restricted the amount of the group-based financial bonus. First, concerned that corporate headquarters would not accept large bonus payouts, he placed a cap on employee bonuses at 15 percent of yearly salaries. Second, he convinced the steering committee to accept a weighted calculation for the historical base period, with the most prior year counting for one-half of the standard. At many gainsharing facilities, all years in the historical base period count equally. Assuming continuous improvement, the weighted calculation creates a higher historical standard every year. With each passing year, this bonus calculation strategy became a more important point of contention among the opponents. Importantly, the facility manager did not make any changes to the original gainsharing plan that would restrict employee participation. As recommended by the consultant, all facility employees were assigned to a department-based gainsharing team.

Interestingly, nonmanagement go-getters on the steering committee suggested that the rules regarding the year-end reserve pool be changed in a way that made it more difficult for them to earn year-end bonuses. They believed that it was unfair for Forestland to absorb year-end reserve pool deficits. According to these go-getters, eliminating negative year-end reserve pool totals demonstrates a lack of faith in their ability to improve facility performance. The facility manager, in turn, successfully suggested a compromise position whereby Forestland would absorb 50 percent of year-end reserve pool deficits. Here were nonmanagement employees, motivated by the concept of fairness, trying to make it more difficult for themselves to earn a bonus, and the facility manager was limiting the degree to which they could.

P2: Interest Group Power Struggles

Based on information gathered during the semistructured interviews, all of the managers were categorized as go-getters. Gainsharing implementation was the facility manager's idea, and the rest of the managers welcomed the challenge. They want gainsharing to succeed. Gainsharing team meetings and review bard meetings are seen as a tremendous opportunity to learn about production process issues faced by nonmanagement employees.

The facility manager responded favorably to several key power issues. First, he stopped attending team meetings because production employees were relying on him to make decisions or solve problems for them. The facility manager wanted the nonmanagement teams to take ownership of their suggestions. Second, when electricity prices increased, the facility manager created a more equitable method for determining nonmanagement employees' improvements regarding the use of electricity. Third, when production employees expressed concern about the negative impact that paving the driveway had on the supplies and services pool, the facility manager requested that all gainsharing teams discuss solutions to the problem. As suggested by the teams, he placed a cap on these expenditures. Nonetheless, at the time of the field study, the facility manager was still receiving criticism about what employees perceived was a biased weighting scheme.

Except for a few opponents, nonmanagement employees have responded favorably to several key power issues. Based on many years of managing sawmill employees, managers expected the sawmill team to be the most troublesome. Instead, they were the most productive. Three sawmill employees unexpectedly became gainsharing go-getters and took responsibility for improving sawmill operations and managing the sawmill gainsharing team. During the third year of gainsharing, they decided to rotate the team chairperson position among all sawmill employees so that everyone would participate in team activities. Similarly, the four-member office team decided not to exploit unproductive team meeting time and requested that they be permitted to attend other team meetings to learn about what was going on in other departments. These positive employee attitudes have enabled management to form interdepartmental task teams to examine specific production problems.

A favorable power game has developed between the sawmill and manufacturing departments as a result of gainsharing. From production employees' perspective, gainsharing provides an opportunity to take greater responsibility for their work area, a financial incentive to make necessary production changes, and a public forum where their work achievements are recognized. For instance, if the sawmill improves its yield, everyone in the facility is aware of the department's performance when the yield figures are presented at review board and facility-wide meetings. If yield losses increase and are not corrected immediately, this too becomes public knowledge when the monthly figures are presented. The sawmill employees want manufacturing employees and management to know that they are fulfilling their end of the gainsharing bargain. The same sentiments are expressed by manufacturing employees.

Unlike the events at Cylinder Lifts and Foam Seats, nonmanagement opponents—not management—want to restrict the degree of employee participation. They do not want to be forced to attend team meetings or to respond to gainsharing issues directed at them. The review board consistently rejects this attempt to restrict participation. Opponents exhibit their dislike for gainsharing by antagonizing both management and nonmanagement employees at team meetings. Some opponents also deliberately submit suggestions to agitate someone. When no bonuses were distributed during the first three months' employment of a newly hired controller, the opponents accused the controller of manipulating the bonus and attacked his credibility. Fortunately for gainsharing, the opponents are not organized. The examples mentioned above involve individual rebellions, not concerted efforts.

Finally, corporate headquarters is an important power player and can take actions detrimental to gainsharing. Every year, corporate managers ask the facility manager to defend the gainsharing bonus system. According to the facility manager, he can lobby successfully on behalf of gainsharing because the total bonus amounts are reasonable. He believes that corporate managers will not tolerate high bonuses, even if production employees have appropriately earned them.

P3: Hidden and Suppressed Problems Surface

Hidden and suppressed problems have surfaced as a result of the 121 accepted suggestions. Most suggestions correct production inefficiencies. Other problems that have surfaced as a result of gainsharing implementation include the illiteracy of some production employees, and health and safety hazards. In the past, some ill production employees had come to work anyway because they could not afford to pay the insurance deductible on their health policies.

Each month, a different set of problems arises. At the meetings I attended, production employees discussed problems associated with vacation eligibility, the time clock policy, extensive overtime in the fall, and the danger of electrical power outages.

P4: Fulfilled Monetary and Nonmonetary Interests

The managers are looking forward to many more years of gainsharing. Gainsharing has generated suggestions that improved the production process, improved product quality, and reduced costs. Before gainsharing, production employees looked forward to downtime as an unanticipated break period, refused to help employees from other departments, and interpreted help from others as an insult to their working ability. All of this changed as a result of gainsharing. The problem of antagonistic work cultures between sawmill and manufacturing employees has also declined through constructive interactions on gainsharing teams and interdepartmental task teams. In addition, production employees demand that managers spend more time on the production floor when problems occur.

Nonmanagement go-getters, fence-sitters, and opponents also want gainsharing to continue. They, too, have benefited from improvements in the production process and product quality. Before gainsharing was implemented, management had viewed production employees as strong individualists with antimanagement sentiments; thus management did not trust that production employee initiatives were in the best interests of Forestland. With the gainsharing bonus as a control mechanism, managers are more willing to give them autonomy.

Summary

Forestland has had minor difficulties with two of the conflict-of-interest exchange relationships diagrammed in Figure 2-2. The facility manager structured gainsharing to maximize employee involvement. Formally, 121 suggestions have been accepted by the gainsharing teams. As noted earlier, this number is artificially low because the facility manager believes that completing a formal suggestion form is an unnecessary bureaucratic requirement. In addition, managers attending the gainsharing meetings learn about production problems and apply this information to other departments without documenting any of it.

Nonetheless, some employees still want little to do with acting and thinking like managers on the production floor. If they want to take on managerial responsibilities, they reason, then they can go to college and become managers. They choose not to. They prefer to perform production work without any managerial concerns. They justify their contribution to the gainsharing bonus checks in terms of their contribution to the quantity of production output.

Second, concern is growing among nonmanagement fence-sitters and opponents about the gainsharing bonus. They believe that with each passing year, it is getting too difficult to earn a bonus. In 1989, the average monthly bonus declined to $35, compared to $50 and $60 a month in the first two years of gainsharing. On the other hand, the year-end bonuses have increased from $30 in 1986 to $915 in 1988 and $630 in 1989. For the time being, the many production changes, sincere interactions at gainsharing team meetings, and the year-end bonuses have swayed the fence-sitters to join forces with the go-getters.

7 Innovations: A Publicly Owned Nonunion Facility, Large Bonuses

Innovations is a publicly owned nonunion final assembly facility located on the outskirts of a midwestern suburb. It is a subsidiary of a Fortune 200 corporation that is highly praised in the business press for its human resource innovations. The corporation controls 35 percent of its domestic market. The facility began operations in April 1983 with the sole purpose of assembling axles and transmissions on a just-in-time system, with no finished goods inventory, for a large automotive facility fifty miles away. The customer previously assembled its own axles, but as part of an early 1980s massive downsizing plan, it eliminated these jobs from its union facility and contracted out to Innovations. Many of the services the corporation provided to the customer, such as drive shafts and clutches, were centralized at the new facility. As a result of the agreement, the customer was guaranteed a high-quality supplier, and Innovations was guaranteed a steady customer during the recession.

The assembly facility was designed to be innovative—no supervisors, no time clocks, no time cards, one job classification (quality technician), salaried wages for production employees (though employees could earn overtime wages), self-managed work cells, and extensive job rotation. In 1989, the facility had sales of approximately $200 million a year and employed 145 people on three production shifts. Nonmanagement employees earn approximately $23,000 a year, a salary that is among the top 10 percent for jobs at area manufacturing facilities. The facility pays high wages to attract the best employees. Typically, production employees assemble 20,000 drive shafts, 13,000 axles, 5,000 clutches, and 2,000 transmissions a month.

Innovations has two levels of management. Upper-level management consists of the facility manager, who reports to corporate headquarters. Lower-level management, all of whom report to the facility manager, includes the manufacturing manager, five area managers, controller, night shift supervisor, quality control manager, facilities manager, personnel manager, and excellence-in-manufacturing manager. Innovations operates without any production floor supervisors. Production employees report directly to an area manager. At the time of the field study, the current facility manager was the second to be employed since gainsharing was implemented.

When the facility began operations in 1983, many of the newly hired production employees had been previously laid off because of the recession. According to corporate policy, new jobs were first offered to employees laid off from its other facilities. Nonetheless, the selection criteria were quite high because of the facility's innovative self-management concept. All production employees are responsible for managing the twenty-five square feet around them. Applicants were evaluated in terms of personal initiative and team-oriented attitudes.

Though grateful for being rehired, many new employees had previously worked in union facilities and were quite critical of management. Some had to travel long distances, whereas others had moved their families. They did not expect much more from their factory job than a steady paycheck. Some employees maintained ill feelings toward the corporation for being laid-off from what they assumed to have been a secure job. Despite the corporation's reputation in the general media as an excellent company to work for, many production employees rejected this image as inflated, particularly after being laid off.

The facility manager responsible for implementing gainsharing in March 1984 was motivated by multiple concerns. The corporate philosophy encouraged employee involvement. For instance, corporate headquarters evaluated facility managers on their ability to involve employees in the decision-making process, a system of management that was also viewed by the corporation as an anti-union strategy. The facility manager, who had successfully managed a Scanlon-type plan at another corporate facility, believed that gainsharing was essential for managing facilities that operate without floor supervisors. Another major contributing factor to his decision was the corporation's eight-year partnership agreement with its only customer. The agreement required a 5 percent reduction in prices during each of the first two years, a 10 percent reduction in prices the third year, and a 1 percent reduction in price for each of the next five years, at a time when manufacturing costs were rising throughout the industry. Finally, two major U.S. competitors and several Japanese companies were threatening to break into the corporation's domestic truck market.

The facility manager invited a consultant to conduct a gainsharing feasibility survey with employees at his facility. He was satisfied with the results and concluded that gainsharing could be successful. The facility manager created a steering committee consisting of six managers and five production employees to determine how gainsharing should be implemented in March 1984. In February 1984, more than 80 percent of the production employees voted in favor of gainsharing, and it was implemented in March.

Power Games Propositions

The two power games propositions are analyzed below according to management and nonmanagement reactions to three central aspects of Scanlon-type gainsharing plans: the suggestion system, the team structure, and the group-based bonus.

Suggestion System

During six years of gainsharing, production employees implemented 4,238 suggestions. As shown in Table 7-1, the breakdown per year is 115 (1984), 170 (1985), 206 (1986), 214 (1987), 1,462 (1988), and 2,071 (1989), or approximately 4.9 suggestions per employee per year.

The facility manager dismissed the gainsharing consultant's recommendation to employ a full-time gainsharing coordinator as being too costly. Instead, he added gainsharing responsibilities to the regular du-

Table 7–1.   Innovations: Suggestions and bonuses per year

Year	Number of Accepted Suggestions	Bonus as a % of Wages
1984	115	12.0%
1985	170	14.5%
1986	206	24.0%
1987	214	22.1%
1988	1,462	22.3%
1989	2,071	20.7%
Total suggestions	4,238	
Average bonus		19.3%

ties of the employee relations manager. Much was being expected of all managers, because Innovations had to reduce costs significantly. The gainsharing coordinator, who was well liked by production employees, took responsibility for attending meetings and delegated much of the paperwork to his staff assistant.

The first round of suggestions was submitted by go-getters. They saw gainsharing as an opportunity to take greater responsibility for their work and to develop management skills. Managers were surprised that several of the older employees whom they had predicted would be oppositional to gainsharing were go-getters instead. According to these production employees, they were very sensitive about the need to reduce production costs immediately because they had been laid off prior to gainsharing.

Nonetheless, many employees were fence-sitters when gainsharing began. Their reluctance was a result of three factors. First, many of them had worked in union shops, so they were skeptical about management's true intentions regarding gainsharing. From their perspective, they had experienced too much hypocrisy to give managers the benefit of doubt. Second, fence-sitters believed that management had complete knowledge about production problems. It was a new experience for them to observe management's surprised reaction to production problems that team representatives presented at gainsharing meetings. Third, both go-getters and fence-sitters were concerned that their production improvement suggestions might result in layoffs for those whose jobs were redesigned. As noted earlier, most of the production employees had been previously laid off, and they did not want to offer a suggestion that could mean layoffs for other production employees. The facility manager promised that no full-time employee would be dismissed as a result of productivity gains. The facility manager said he would reassign the person to a more needed task.

Many fence-sitters aligned themselves with the go-getters early in the gainsharing experience. During the first few months, some obvious improvements in the production process generated monthly bonuses of $150 to $200. Even in July, when the entire facility closes for a two-week summer vacation, employees earned a 5.8 percent bonus. Fence-sitters realized that their ideas were meaningful and could contribute to everyone earning a monthly bonus.

When employees began earning bonuses immediately, go-getters took an active role in lobbying fence-sitters and opponents to participate in gainsharing. Go-getters appealed to their self-interest (you can make your job easier, you can earn a bigger bonus) and guilt (how can you collect the bonus when you know you are withholding suggestions). For example, one fence-sitter resisted overtures to submit improvement-oriented suggestions for three years. Then a go-getter submitted a suggestion with him that made his work less stressful physically. After the suggestion was implemented, the fence-sitter submitted twenty suggestions over the next few months.

Nonmanagement go-getters also had the full cooperation of their area managers. The facility manager was able to persuade area managers to become go-getters based on his previous positive experience managing a Scanlon-type gainsharing facility. In addition, managers were well aware of the pressure and the difficulty of ensuring that the facility stay nonunion, because many of the production employees had previously belonged to a union.

Despite the efforts of management and nonmanagement go-getters, suggestions were being implemented too slowly. Employees submitted suggestions and closely followed how long it took for a suggestion to get on a team meeting agenda, on the review board agenda, and then implemented. This typically long period discouraged fence-sitters. Sometimes, go-getters from several teams had to facilitate the quick passage of a prominent suggestion. For instance, when an extra forklift was needed, three teams put in the request during the same month so that when the review board met, all three team presentations included a discussion about the immediate need for another forklift. One area manager established weekly gainsharing meetings so that employees could implement suggestions as soon as possible, rather than waiting a month.

According to go-getters, their greatest challenge was to overrule management production process changes. Occasionally, manager's made decisions that go-getters believed were detrimental to the production process. If, after a few weeks, it appeared as though the managerial decision had not improved production efficiency, a production employee submitted a suggestion without stating directly that it would reverse a change made recently by a manager. Some managers would get quite upset when they learned that production employees had changed one of their planned interventions. Other managers maintained that they were overextended and appreciated production employees' willingness to take the risk of changing their direct interventions. Even after six years of gainsharing, some managers struggled with production employees changing their production process plans. If a production change was expected to upset managers yet needed to be made prior to the next review board meeting, production employees would make the change and lobby other teams to include the issue on their respective agendas. This demonstrated broad-based support for the suggestion.

Management turnover was quite high at production facilities owned by the corporation. Managers were transferred from one facility to another to apply knowledge they had gained at their previous facility or to learn new skills as they moved up the managerial hierarchy. In 1987, corporate headquarters changed facility managers. Although facility employees were consistently earning large gainsharing bonuses for improved production performance, the new facility manager was concerned that the number of suggestions had plateaued at about two hundred a year. Through discussions with several staff managers, the facility manager found that production employees were becoming increasingly frustrated with their efforts to find large cost savings and that many small improvements were being overlooked.

Beginning March 1, 1988, the facility manager challenged each gainsharing team with a 100/100/100 plan: obtain one hundred suggestions costing less than $100 each to implement during the next one hundred days. Any team that achieved this goal would earn a $50 bonus for each person the team represented. One team achieved the goal in less than one hundred days. The facility manager extended the deadline for another two months, and three of the other four teams achieved the goal. This plan increased employee participation in the gainsharing process significantly. Innovations had averaged 30 suggestions a month for January and February. From March through June, the average was 193 suggestions a month. The least-active team went from 1 suggestion in January and February, to 20 in March, 36 in April, and 25 in May. After the contest ended, the team once again averaged 1 suggestion a month. Importantly, the contest helped some production employees establish a habit of submitting "small suggestions" that could be implemented immediately.

As is noted below in the discussion on team structure, the new facility manager also created four area cell teams to serve as a buffer between the gainsharing teams and the review board. He also merged gainsharing with an excellence-in-manufacturing (EIM) program that was promoted by corporate headquarters, discussed in detail below. As a result, there was an explosion in the total number of accepted suggestions, from 214 in 1987, to 1,462 in 1988, and 2,071 in 1989.

I attended the weekly half-hour EIM/gainsharing meeting of the rear-axle team during the April 1990 field study. The six production employees listed current production problems, discussed possible solutions to

these problems, and submitted their solutions as gainsharing suggestions. The facility manager joined the meeting after the employees had
ranked their concerns in order of priority during the first five minutes.
He listened to their proposed solutions. The team members were surprised that the facility manager was unaware of problems between a
supplier and the facility's warehouse. During the past four days, some of
the supplier's product had too much oil on it, making assembly more
difficult. The manager accepted the team's recommendations, one of
which was for him to call the supplier and complain.

I also attended the April 1990 review board meeting. Team representatives provided a summary of their area cell team meetings. The area cell
teams had reached a consensus on every suggestion except two—the
need for designated visitor parking and job rotation of the senior technician position.

Visitor Parking. According to the facility's egalitarian parking policy,
any person could park in any parking space. There were no reserved
spaces for management staff or visitors. A team representative asserted
that everyone wanted to keep the policy for facility employees, but several people thought that it did not extend proper respect to visitors.
Several visitors had been offended because they expected to find a reserved visitor section near the facility's front door. Instead, they had to
locate an available spot where the production employees parked, often
far from the front door. A substantial amount of discussion ensued, involving everyone in attendance. The facility manager said he had never
heard anyone complain about the problem. The team representatives informed him otherwise, noting that visitors were more willing to express
their concerns to production employees than to facility management.
Several solutions were proposed, but no consensus could be reached.
The facility manager argued that because the issue was not related to
gainsharing or safety, the suggestion should be submitted to facility security, which was in charge of monitoring parking. Security staff would
conduct an informal survey to determine the extent to which visitor
parking really was a problem.

Job Rotation for the Senior Technician Position. Every job task in the production area was available for job rotation except that of the senior technician. Although the facility had only one job classification—quality
technician—this particular job task was the closest the facility came to
having a second job classification. Two team representatives argued that
it should also be rotated. One team representative disagreed, and he was

supported by the facility manager. The job task required extensive training and was a special, earned position. A compromise was achieved when a team representative suggested that each area cell team should discuss whether alternates for the senior technician job could be trained.

Team Structure

In 1984, Innovations had sixteen work cells. Most of them operated during the first shift. The gainsharing consultant recommended that each work cell be transformed into a gainsharing team that met on facility time. The facility manager argued that this recommendation would be too costly. Based on his previous gainsharing experience, he believed that one gainsharing team per department was sufficient. As a result, five gainsharing teams were formed. Three teams represented the first-shift production employees (one per department—rear axles, front axles, and drive shafts), one team represented the second-shift production employees, and one team represented the office employees. Each team consisted of two elected representatives and one management representative assigned by the facility manager. Each gainsharing team had a monthly discretionary budget of $400. Any suggestion costing more than $5,000 required corporate approval.

The first elections were quite exciting for the production employees. Because of the strict hiring criteria, there were more go-getters than available positions. Some go-getters ran very extensive campaigns. They had not experienced this opportunity at their previous places of employment and wanted to make the most of it. Fence-sitters and opponents did not step forward to be considered for election.

The initial review board consisted of five nonmanagement employees and ten managers. Each of the five gainsharing teams chose one team representative to serve on the review board. The ten management members were the facility manager, manufacturing manager, controller, night shift supervisor, quality control manager, facilities manager, three area managers, and the personnel manager/gainsharing coordinator. This arrangement created a very intimidating situation for the outnumbered nonmanagement team representatives. Initial review board meetings were dominated by the facility manager and two other managers who worked closely with him. In order to create an environment in which nonmanagement team representatives could realize they had significant influence, all review board decisions required a consensus rather than a simple majority vote. In addition, the team representatives presented every suggestion that was discussed at their team meetings.

As noted earlier, corporate headquarters changed facility managers in 1987. In addition to creating the 100/100/100 suggestion contest, the new facility manager created area cell teams. From his perspective, the monthly review board meetings, which lasted between two and three hours, were too time-consuming. He blamed the length of the meetings on the inability of the five gainsharing teams to achieve adequate levels of consensus on many suggestions. Typically, each of the five teams presented four to five suggestions for review board discussion. The ensuing attempts at consensus building were sometimes quite lengthy. As a result, the new facility manager created four area cell teams to serve as a buffer between the production department gainsharing teams and the review board. These area cell teams consisted of a team representative and several managers who were assigned the responsibility of reviewing and implementing employee suggestions. Typically, these were suggestions that cost more than $400 to implement or entailed interdepartmental communication. This change in the team structure pushed the decision-making process down one level of management and involved only those with direct knowledge of the issues being discussed.

In 1988 a staff manager attended seminars sponsored by corporate headquarters on the new, EIM system of management. EIM consisted of weekly work cell meetings at which everyone brainstormed how to solve production problems and continually improve performance. EIM training had two important features. First, all facility employees were to be trained in team-building activities. Second, all facility employees were to be taught how to perform a parieto analysis for their job responsibilities. Basically, the EIM philosophy was that 80 percent of a production area's problems could be attributed to 20 percent of the work area. The challenge for work cell members was to determine what 20 percent of the work area was generating 80 percent of the problems. Once those problems were eradicated, then the process began all over again—determine what 20 percent of the work area caused 80 percent of the current problems. This was the practical ramification of the continuous improvement concept. EIM objectives included: zero inventory, zero set-up time changeovers, zero scrap/rework, zero unplanned downtime, 100 percent participation, 100 percent safety, and a 100 percent through-time ratio.

In November 1988, the facility manager decided to incrementally merge EIM and gainsharing, with the EIM manager serving as a new gainsharing coordinator. According to the facility manager, EIM was a matter of going back to the gainsharing consultant's original recommendation of one gainsharing team per work cell, increasing gainsharing meetings from once a month to once a week, and focusing on small, incremental suggestions. Gainsharing complemented EIM in that it provided a financial incentive for making continuous improvements.

The new gainsharing coordinator began one-week in-house EIM training seminars with quality technicians from two work cells. At the end of the week, the sixteen graduates were assigned to permanent EIM/gainsharing teams of eight members each. Every week thereafter, sixteen more employees were trained, and two new EIM/gainsharing teams were created. When half of the 150 employees had been trained, a schism developed between those who were attending weekly EIM/gainsharing meetings and those who were not. After two-thirds of the employees had gone through the training process, everyone (including those still not trained) was put on an EIM/gainsharing team. By the end of 1988, seventeen EIM/gainsharing teams—eight rear-axle teams, three front-axle teams, five drive-shaft teams, and one office team—had been created, with six to seven production employees per team.

Because the gainsharing teams had expanded from five to seventeen teams, the facility manager also restructured the area cell teams. Each EIM/gainsharing team voted for two nonmanagement employees to be on its respective area cell team. Two area cell teams were created for the rear-axle department because of its large size. For example, one rear-axle area cell team had eight nonmanagement employees (two from each of the four teams), whereas the front-axle area cell team had six nonmanagement employees (two from each of the three teams). In addition, the facility manager assigned the area manager, process manager, quality engineer, and materials manager to each of the five area cell teams.

Last, the review board was expanded from five to ten nonmanagement employees. Each of the five area cell teams elected two nonmanagement employees to serve in this capacity.

Both management staff and production employees believed that the changes associated with EIM greatly assisted gainsharing, and vice versa. The facility was considered one of the corporation's most successful EIM projects. Management attributed this success to three years of gainsharing meetings and bonuses. Production employees struggled with personality clashes in the first few EIM/gainsharing meetings. The weekly meetings forced them to trust each other. For example, when only a few production employees were meeting once a month to discuss gainsharing suggestions, some fence-sitters would not submit their ideas for fear of criticism. After several weeks of EIM/gainsharing meetings, fence-sitters were forced to voice their opinions and began to play an important role in the process.

During the field study, interviewees characterized three types of production employees attending EIM/gainsharing meetings: the "dreamer," who cannot figure out how to implement his or her dreams; the "implementer," who cannot come up with ideas but knows how to put them into practice; and (3) the "communicator," who bridges the other two types. All three types of employees needed to be patient with each other. The result of these changes in team structure was a group of employees who were constantly thinking about how to improve the production process. Fence-sitters who were giving one or two good suggestions a year started giving one or two good suggestions a week.

At the time of the field study, production employees highlighted several problems with the EIM/gainsharing teams: individual recognition was being overlooked, managerial expectations for personal development and change were too high, and nonmanagement opponents needed to be disciplined.

First, management used gainsharing activities to increase team identity and minimize individualism. For instance, management praised teams when suggestions were signed by every team member under the assumption that each member played an active role in formulating the suggestion. Some EIM/gainsharing teams had achieved this desirable state of affairs. Some had not. For the latter, go-getters felt pressured to put everyone's name on suggestions even though only one person was responsible. This was cause for resentment, because they wanted to be individually recognized for their contributions and be acknowledged at the monthly facility-wide meetings.

Second, several fence-sitters complained that management expectations were too high regarding their ability to be ideal gainsharing participants. Management wanted them to quickly become fully cooperative individuals who took leading roles at EIM/gainsharing meetings, discussed every suggestion in an intelligent manner, and served as catalysts on the production floor. These people did not like being compared to go-getters, for whom such attributes seemed to come easily. They wanted to be praised for increasing their monthly suggestions from one to two, rather than criticized because someone else was offering ten suggestions. They wanted to be evaluated according to their unique progress and not in terms of their current distance from an ideal standard.

Third, a discipline problem had arisen. Some opponents were slacking off on the production floor or at team meetings because of the latitude they had been given by management. When asked information questions at EIM/gainsharing meetings, the opponent would respond: "This isn't my thing; I just want to go back on the production floor and work."

If an opponent's idea was rejected, he or she blamed the rejection on politics. Go-getters teased opponents about their attitude problem, but they did not want to be responsible for disciplining them. Go-getters feared retaliation from opponents if it was their responsibility to discipline opponents. Go-getters asked managers to discipline opponents who exhibited adversarial behavior at the weekly EIM/gainsharing team meetings for an extended period of time. Management, however, feared that taking strong disciplinary action against an opponent would increase the likelihood of union organizing activities within the facility. At the time of the field study, management hoped that production employees would discipline each other, even though go-getters refused to do so.

Group-Based Bonus

During six years of gainsharing, the average monthly bonus payout was 19.3 percent ($370). As shown in Table 7-1, the breakdown per year is 12.0 percent (1984), 14.5 percent (1985), 24.0 percent (1986), 22.1 percent (1987), 22.3 percent (1988), and 20.7 percent (1989). Table 7-2 provides a monthly breakdown of bonus payouts.

The historical cost standard used for calculating the financial bonus was based on two cost factors: the ratio of payroll costs to sales, and product returns that were the fault of facility employees. Payroll costs included direct labor salaries, indirect labor salaries, overtime premiums, absenteeism, rework, and related items. The screening committee wanted to emphasize product quality, not just quantity, so they also created a product returns bonus factor. Cost savings were shared 75/25: 75 percent for the employees and 25 percent for Innovations. Of the employee share, 75 percent was to be distributed that month and 25 percent allocated to the year-end reserve pool. If the reserve pool was negative at the time that a bonus was earned, then 50 percent rather than 25 percent of the bonus was to be allocated to the year-end reserve pool until it was positive again. Everyone employed by the facility was eligible for the financial bonus.

The facility implemented gainsharing in 1984, only a year after it began operations. This short labor history proved problematic in determining the historical standard for the bonus calculation. The one-year standard would be too easy for production employees to surpass because of the learning curve associated with starting a new production facility. The facility manager sought permission from the steering committee to allow frequent reevaluations and modifications of the bonus calculation. The go-getters accepted this request because it seemed reasonable.

Table 7–2. Innovations: Monthly gainsharing bonus payouts (%)

	1984	1985	1986	1987	1988	1989
January	—	15.9	18.4	20.3	17.6	15.9
February	—	7.8	12.3	13.4	19.1	9.6
March	5.6%	15.6	20.6	15.4	21.8	20.0
April	7.9	16.2	20.3	15.2	16.8	17.1
May	9.7	17.2	25.8	14.9	18.2	18.7
June	8.9	8.8	20.9	21.3	16.1	18.3
July	5.8	7.0	9.7	2.2	9.5	5.1
August	17.1	8.7	20.6	17.2	21.9	10.3
September	7.2	9.5	22.3	21.2	14.5	20.1
October	10.1	8.5	15.3	19.7	15.9	17.9
November	10.3	8.0	19.5	16.1	20.6	17.4
December	7.8	7.3	10.7	21.5	8.4	17.4
Average monthly bonus % per employee	9.0	10.9	18.0	16.5	16.7	15.7
Average monthly bonus $ per employee[a]	$172	$209	$345	$316	$320	300
Reserve pool %	3.0	3.6	6.0	5.6	5.6	5.0
Year-end reserve pool $ per employee	$689	$827	$1,378	$1,286	$1,286	$1,150

[a] Average production employee salary: $11 an hour, $1,914 a month, or $22,968 a year.

The unexpectedly high early bonus payouts caused excitement among the production employees, convincing some fence-sitters to get involved in the gainsharing process. Some fence-sitters expressed feelings of guilt when they received the first few gainsharing bonuses while they were still wondering whether to become involved. They were also surprised by the amount of financial information management was sharing with them when presenting the bonus calculation at the monthly facility-wide meetings.

Although production employees earned high bonuses, there was some dissatisfaction among fence-sitters and opponents about the bonus calculation. Most production employees believed that the bonus reflected their production effort, but they disliked it being distributed as a percentage of monthly wages rather than as a flat monetary amount. Management provided two reasons for not distributing the bonus on an equal monetary basis: federal law mandated that earnings from group-based bonus plans involving management and nonmanagement employees be distributed as an equal percentage rather than an equal monetary amount, and distributing an equal amount to each employee would be detrimental to those employees who put in an extra effort toward earning the bonus by working overtime. Production employees argued that the law was unfair in this case, because most of the savings came from their efforts, not from management. In addition, it was unfair to use a percentage calculation because managers had higher salaries. At this point in the disagreement, management usually reiterated the law.

At the time of the field study, the facility manager had resisted yearly overtures from corporate headquarters to reduce the bonus payouts by changing the gainsharing calculation. He maintained that changing the calculation because it resulted in bonuses that were "too high" would ruin managerial credibility and provide a further rationale for production employees to seek union representation. Nonetheless, every year someone at corporate headquarters complained about paying 20 percent monthly bonuses to production employees through gainsharing.

The facility manager notified production employees of this potential problem and asked EIM/gainsharing teams to provide some reasonable solutions. According to the facility manager, if production employees did not solve the high bonus problem during his tenure at the facility, the next facility manager would be forced to take drastic action. A production employee suggested that a cap be placed on the gainsharing bonus at 20 percent. Whenever the bonus exceeded 20 percent, the residual should be split evenly between Innovations and employees' base salary. Production employees' share of gains greater than 20 percent would then count as a yearly merit raise. At the time of the field study, the facility controller was analyzing the implications of this suggestion.

The Outcomes Propositions

There was a strong consensus among management and nonmanagement employees that gainsharing greatly improved facility operations. Both management and nonmanagement employees benefited directly and indirectly from four years of gainsharing.

Benefits

Direct benefits to both management and nonmanagement employees included better production processes, high product quality, and improved communications.

Better Production Processes. Employees implemented 4,238 suggestions over six years. Examples of efficiency-related suggestions include moving materials that employees had previously had to walk around, repairing machines, replacing worn-out tools, purchasing additional hoist lines to reduce direct labor time wasted while waiting for the one hoist line to become available, installing a roller conveyor for bearings and seals at hub stations, using dowels instead of bolts to keep an often-relocated machine in place, and using a Lotus software package for bookkeeping.

High Product Quality. After gainsharing implementation, the customer awarded the facility the title of certified parts supplier for its drive shafts. As a result, the customer no longer inspects the product upon delivery. Benefits to the facility from this award include corporate recognition from the customer and preferred supplier status for similar business applications.

Improved Communications. Constant employee interaction within and among work cells during weekly EIM/gainsharing meetings and monthly review board and facility-wide meetings improved communications greatly. The facility now has a "Great Wall of Information" consisting of fourteen bulletin boards that display EIM/gainsharing suggestions,

EIM/gainsharing team communications, newsletters, safety issues, productivity numbers, and supply costs.

In addition, the second facility manager initiated communication feedback sessions with groups of production employees. At team meetings, employees had complained that management was more "distant" after the formation of EIM/gainsharing teams. In the process of delegating responsibilities to production employees, managers were seen less often on the production floor. Production employees wanted to meet more often with managers about production problems. The facility manager requested that each team provide a list of complaints that they wanted him to address at subsequent team meetings. This response evolved into a policy whereby the facility manager has lunch once a month with each team to discuss employee complaints and production problems.

Direct benefits to management and indirect benefits to nonmanagement employees included significant cost savings, improved customer relations, and improved supplier relations.

Significant Cost Savings. During the first three years of gainsharing, direct labor efficiency increased 45 percent and scrap and rework costs were reduced by 50 percent. From 1988 to 1990, the facility achieved average gross payroll savings of $1,246,355 a year (net $311,589). Pieces produced per labor hour increased from 2.8 in June 1989, when Innovations began tracking this factor, to 3.8 in February 1990. Gainsharing suggestions in one area eliminated 42,000 square feet of production space. As a result, management created an in-house warehouse that saved the facility $15,000 monthly. Product returns declined substantially. When Innovations' sole customer threatened to purchase some supplies from a competitor, nonmanagement employees used gainsharing team meetings to brainstorm ideas that led to a substantial reduction in product price.

Some of these improvements may be the result of Innovations' EIM program rather than gainsharing. Managers claim, however, that it is impossible to distinguish between EIM and gainsharing improvements. For example, the facility manager maintains that production employees would not have determined how to eliminate 42,000 square feet of production space without having a financial stake in the cost savings.

Improved Customer Relations. Management attributes the facility's perfect just-in-time delivery record to the gainsharing plan. Production employees are very receptive to emergency delivery issues because they affect the gainsharing bonus. In the mid-1980s, the customer would call the facility if a product had not been delivered within twenty-four hours of the customer's production schedule. Because of the confidence developed over time, in 1990 the customer waited until four hours before delivery was scheduled before calling. The facility manager also extended Innovations' EIM/gainsharing training workshops to the customer.

Improved Supplier Relations. Management tried to develop partnerships with suppliers. The facility manager provided suppliers training in statistical process control and invited them to attend EIM/gainsharing training sessions. Production employees have submitted several vendor-related suggestions that improved their service. Vendors were surprised to receive product improvement input from a customer's production employees. Nonetheless, many suppliers have not felt the competitive pressure to adopt the facility's production policies.

Direct benefits to nonmanagement employees and indirect benefits to management included easier work tasks, improved health and safety, higher wages, job rotation, and training and development.

Easier Work Tasks. Many production employees claimed that "if your job is a pain, you have nobody to blame but yourself." If production employees did not want to walk all the way across the facility to get supplies, or hurt their backs from lifting a heavy object ten times a day, they submitted gainsharing suggestions to change the process. As noted earlier, production employees had assumed falsely that management deliberately designed the production process to make work difficult. Under gainsharing, they realized that managers were unaware of the physically stressful aspects of their job. Now they can redesign their job process.

Improved Health and Safety. Gainsharing team meetings have been used to discuss and implement many health and safety improvements. Typical suggestions include putting safety bars under racks to prevent large items from falling on people's feet, putting beepers on all floor vehicles, installing first-aid boxes in centrally located positions, and attaching dust collectors to the lathes. A gainsharing suggestion led to the formation of a safety committee consisting of two production employees from each shift. This committee surveyed the facility for safety hazards and implemented safety-related suggestions in an expeditious manner.

Higher Wages. The gainsharing bonus was a substantial monetary addition to yearly wages. For instance, in 1989 the average production employee received a $300 gainsharing bonus every month and $1,150 year-end reserve pool bonus. Production employees have submitted suggestions on how to solve problems associated with yearly wage increases in a more competitive market and an escalating increase in the gainsharing bonus.

Job Rotation. Production employees submit suggestions to increase job rotation whenever management slows it down. They believe that job rotation increases their production efficiency. In one work area, production employees reduced job rotation when a quality problem arose because nobody was mastering the job task.

Training and Development. Production employees often submit suggestions requesting additional training and development, such as reviewing just-in-time educational tapes. The employees also receive additional EIM/gainsharing training on how to reach consensus at meetings and how to develop and implement incremental suggestions.

Conclusion

As shown in Table 7-3, the gainsharing evaluation and attitude survey conducted during the field study reveals that facility employees have moderate feelings about gainsharing activities. On a 1–5 Likert scale, the statistical means are primarily between 3.0 and 3.5, or just slightly above the midpoint. The lowest scores are for trust, team meetings, and justice. The highest scores are for facility-wide effort, employee support, and fairness of the bonus calculation. After six years of gainsharing experience, the management style is between "benevolent authoritative" and "consultative,"—far from the goal of participatory management style.

Why the moderate scores for a facility where employees are earning gainsharing bonuses approximately equivalent to 20 percent of their monthly wages? The moderate score for the bonus calculation was attributed to two factors: some production employees still do not understand how the bonus is calculated, and many production employees believe that everyone should earn the same monetary bonus, rather than the same percentage of bonus. The moderate scores pertaining to gainsharing activities were attributed to confusion surrounding the new EIM/gainsharing team structure. The moderate scores regarding trust and justice were attributed to growing disciplinary problems. Some op-

Table 7–3.   Innovations: Survey factors

Factor	Statistical Means
Management support	3.3
Supervisor support	3.3
Team representative support	3.3
Employee support	3.5
Suggestion processing	3.2
Team meetings	3.1
Review board meetings	3.3
Bonus calculation	3.4
Facility-wide effort	3.7
Trust	3.0
Employee identity	3.3
Employee influence	3.3
Justice	3.1
Management style[a]	2.6

[a]All factors measured with a 1–5 Likert scale
(1=Strongly disagree, 3=Neutral, 5=Strongly
agree), except management style, which was
measured with a 1–4 Likert scale.

ponents are getting away with abusing the time allocated to team meetings. In addition, go-getters maintained that managers are not spending enough time on the production floor.

Each of the four conflict-of-interest propositions is examined below to aid understanding of the survey results and the evolution of gainsharing at this publicly owned nonunion manufacturing facility.

P1: Manipulating the Transitional Process

The facility manager was the primary power player during the transitional period. Nonunion production employees began this transition from a very weak bargaining position. The facility manager adopted three strategies at the beginning of the gainsharing intervention that restricted the degree of employee involvement in decision making. Contrary to the gainsharing consultant's recommendations, the facility manager added gainsharing responsibilities to the personnel manager's existing full-time duties rather than employ a full-time coordinator; created five gainsharing teams (one per department) rather than fifteen gainsharing teams (one per work cell); and assigned twice as many managers as nonmanagement employees to the review board. The gainsharing steering committee members, all of whom were assigned by the facility manager, did not question these decisions. Previously, the facility manager had managed another corporate facility with a Scanlon-type gainsharing plan, and they trusted his experience.

The facility manager made a decision very favorable to nonmanagement employees regarding the gainsharing bonus distribution, however. He rejected the gainsharing consultant's recommendation of a 50/50 split in favor of a 75/25 split, with employees receiving the larger share, because this bonus ratio had been at his former gainsharing facility. Nonmanagement steering committee members believed that the facility manager was quite reasonable in requesting that the historical standard be adjusted on a regular basis because of the facility's short labor history.

P2: Interest Group Power Struggles

Based on information gathered during the semistructured interviews, all of the managers were categorized as go-getters. Gainsharing implementation was the facility manager's idea, and he successfully persuaded all of the other managers to give it their best effort. Their favorable response was attributed to the facility manager's previous success in managing a gainsharing facility, the natural fit between gainsharing and the facility's innovative self-management concept, and corporate pressure to stay nonunion. One manager went a step further regarding employee involvement by adopting a weekly rather than monthly gainsharing meeting schedule.

The biggest struggle for go-getter managers pertained to production employees modifying management-originated production process changes. Although some managers were grateful that the production employees made these necessary changes, other managers were upset when these changes were made without their input.

The second facility manager, who arrived during the fourth year of gainsharing, responded very favorably to several key power issues. First, he challenged the gainsharing teams to develop one hundred suggestions for less than $100 each in one hundred days. This challenge focused employees' attention on small suggestions that were being overlooked. Although the contest was successful, suggestion contributions declined to their pre-contest level when it ended. Second, he created area cell teams to manage the suggestion implementation process more efficiently. Third, he merged EIM with gainsharing. From a few nonmanagement employees meeting every month, gainsharing meetings changed to all of these employees meeting once a week. Condensing the meetings from monthly to weekly increased the rate of fence-sitter suggestions from every other month to every other week. Fourth, he made gainsharing coordination the full-time duty of the EIM manager rather than an extra duty of the personnel manager. Fifth, he restructured area cell teams following the EIM/gainsharing merger and put more production employees on them. Sixth, he also put more production employees on the review board.

With the exception of a few opponents, nonmanagement employees responded favorably to several key power issues. Go-getters were elected to the initial team representative positions. Some older employees, whom managers expected to be oppositional, became go-getters because they wanted to prevent layoffs. Go-getters and fence-sitters accepted the facility manager's promise of no layoffs resulting from gainsharing production improvement suggestions. Go-getters lobbied fence-sitters and opponents to coauthor suggestions that made their work easier and appealed to their sense of guilt for receiving relatively large monthly bonuses without participating in the gainsharing process. These early bonuses convinced many fence-sitters to align themselves with go-getters. In addition, fence-sitters witnessed go-getters from different teams plotting to get essential suggestions, such as purchasing a new forklift, quickly through the gainsharing decision-making process. The biggest obstacle for fence-sitters was realizing that managers were really unaware of production inefficiencies.

Despite significant improvements in the production process and large monthly gainsharing bonus payouts, the facility still had some fence-sitters and opponents after six years of gainsharing. These production employees defined their job duties narrowly, to working hard on a production task. They did not want to participate at team meetings or understand how the bonuses were calculated. Their job was to put in eight hours of stressful physical labor. No more, no less. Though they spoke favorably of the second facility manager, they believed that he was expecting them to change their personal characteristics too much and too fast. In addition, opponents rejected all the arguments for distributing the gainsharing bonus as an equal percentage of salaries. This method gave managers (who had the highest salaries) the largest bonuses, even though production employees were the ones making the favorable production changes.

There was also significant resistance by many go-getters and fence-sitters to submitting team-authored suggestions. They wanted to receive individual recognition for ideas they originated, even if some members of their EIM/gainsharing team helped them formulate the final suggestion. They wanted to hear the facility manager announce at all-employee meetings that "Joe Smith" had submitted ten suggestions. They did not want managers to attribute their unique efforts to the entire team, particularly if not all team members were active participants. Nonmanagement go-getters also resisted management attempts to get them to discipline their oppositional coworkers.

Finally, corporate headquarters was an important power player that could take actions detrimental to gainsharing. Corporate managers were becoming more critical of the 20 percent employee bonuses earned between 1986 and 1989. The facility manager was experiencing pressure to reduce the bonus payouts.

P3: Hidden and Suppressed Problems Surface

A variety of hidden and suppressed problems surfaced as a result of the 4,238 accepted suggestions. Most of the suggestions corrected production inefficiencies. Unlike the other three facilities, Innovations had only two levels of management, having eliminated one level of supervisors, and was guided by a self-management concept. Production employees were continually surprised by management's ignorance about daily production problems. For instance, at the EIM/gainsharing team meeting I attended, production employees were obviously shocked that the facility manager did not know that there was too much oil on a recently received batch of supplies. They had been complaining for four days about how difficult it was to assemble the new supplies and simply assumed that someone had told the facility manager about the problem. Nobody had. The facility manager immediately called the supplier to fix the problem.

Similar to Cylinder Lifts, Foam Seats, and Timberlands, a major hidden or suppressed problem that surfaced as a result of gainsharing implementation was health and safety. A gainsharing suggestion led to the formation of a safety committee. Every week and month, a different set of hidden problems was discussed at EIM/Gainsharing team and review board meetings. At the review board meeting I attended, production employees informed managers about the ill feelings that some visitors felt because there were no specially marked visitor parking spaces. Managers also became aware that some production employees were resentful that the senior technician position was not open for job rotation.

P4: Fulfilled Monetary and Nonmonetary Interests

Managers look forward to many more years of gainsharing. Gainsharing suggestions have reduced payroll costs and improved production and product quality. Innovations' product market was becoming more competitive, and it had to achieve the severe price reductions demanded by its only customer. At the time of the field study, these price goals were being accomplished.

Nonmanagement go-getters, fence-sitters, and opponents also want gainsharing to continue. They are earning approximately $300 a month in extra wages plus a $1,200 year-end reserve pool bonus. Similar to managers, they have benefited from improvements in the production process and product quality. Most important, gainsharing suggestions have made their work less stressful. In addition, gainsharing suggestions have improved health and safety, increased job rotation, and resulted in more training and development.

Summary

At the time of the field study, Innovations had a minor difficulty with one of the conflict-of-interest exchange relationships diagrammed in Figure 2-2. Initially, the first facility manager restricted the degree to which employees could participate by limiting the number of gainsharing teams and nonmanagement employees on the review board. The second facility manager restructured gainsharing, however, to maximize employee involvement. Four years after gainsharing intervention, all employees were placed on EIM/gainsharing teams that met weekly to discuss continuous improvements. Formally, more than four thousand suggestions have been accepted by gainsharing teams. Nonmanagement employees have improved production output, and in turn, they receive relatively large gainsharing bonuses.

The minor difficulty pertains to fence-sitters and opponents who do not want to participate at EIM/gainsharing meetings. Managers believe that go-getter nonmanagement employees should persuade fence-sitters and opponents to become active gainsharing participants. Go-getters believe that managers have to discipline some opponents, particularly those who are perceived as not carrying their fair share of the production burdens.

PART III

Two Union Facilities

8 Innovations-Brotherhood:
A Publicly Owned Union Facility,
Very Small Bonuses

Innovations-Brotherhood is a publicly owned union facility located in a midwestern rural community. It was established in 1938 and was purchased by a publicly held corporation in 1947. It is a subsidiary of a Fortune 200 corporation, the same one that owns the nonunion Innovations, examined in Chapter 7. The corporation is highly praised in the business press for its human resource innovations. When gainsharing was implemented in July 1988, the corporation controlled 95 percent of the domestic market and 35 percent of the international market for manufacturing a particular type of truck clutch. With increased competition, its North American market share declined steadily to a 1992 level of 80 percent. The facility produces approximately four hundred clutches a day for several major customers. The facility has yearly gross sales of approximately $84 million.

Innovations-Brotherhood employs 450 people on three production shifts. Nonmanagement employees are members of the United Auto Workers. Elections are held every three years for union officers. The union employees earn approximately $17 an hour and $35,360 a year. The facility pays high wages to attract the best workers. These wages are the highest in the local labor market.

In 1984, a major business periodical selected this facility as one of the ten best-managed factories in the United Sates. Innovations-Brotherhood has three levels of management. Upper-level management consists of the facility manager, who reports to corporate headquarters. Middle-level management includes four manufacturing department managers, the quality manager, information systems manager, engineering manager, materials manager, purchasing manager, controller, and human resources manager. Lower-level management consists of work-cell managers. At the time of the field study, the current facility manager was the second to be employed since gainsharing was implemented. Corporate divisional headquarters is also located at the facility.

Gainsharing implementation in July 1988 was an outgrowth of several prior events. During the mid-1980s, Innovations-Brotherhood's virtual monopoly on North American sales was threatened by the entry of two large competitors. Simultaneously, a major customer demanded a 5 percent price reduction over five years to reduce the cost of its trucks. As at Innovations, facility management had to develop a strategy to cut costs.

In 1985, a new facility manager arrived with three primary agenda items to reduce nonwage costs: adopt a JIT inventory system to reduce inventory costs; transform existing quality circles into work cells to improve product quality; and switch the bonus system from a forty-year-old piece-rate incentive system to a group-based gainsharing bonus. The three ideas, listed from low to high according to management's perception of union resistance, represented radical change. Adopting a JIT inventory system and work cells would dramatically change work processes for the union employees. Gainsharing would also change decision-making processes and the union members' compensation scheme. Management argued that these changes would allow the same number of union members to produce 25 percent more truck clutches. Because Innovations-Brotherhood would probably continue to lose market share, however, union officers believed that these improvements would result in a workforce reduction of 25 percent.

The adoption of a JIT inventory system required very little union assistance and was accomplished in early 1986. In December 1987 and January 1988, management moved 450 new machines into the building to form work cells. Small cells of union members were responsible for organizing themselves to produce an entire product, from start to finish. The adoption of gainsharing followed a more complicated path.

Several of the parent company's facilities besides Innovations had Scanlon-type plans. The facility manager at Innovations-Brotherhood invited a consultant to conduct a gainsharing feasibility survey with employees. He was satisfied with the results and concluded that gainsharing could be successful. During summer 1987, the facility manager created a gainsharing steering committee consisting of four managers and four union members to further consider the feasibility of implementing a gainsharing plan that could be linked to the soon-to-be-formed work cells. An affirmative vote by 75 percent of the employees was required to adopt the plan for a one-year trial. In April 1988, only 64 percent of the union employees voted in favor of the plan. A second vote was taken on July 8, and 78 percent supported implementation, to begin retroactively on July 1, 1988.

Power Games Propositions

The two power games propositions are analyzed below according to management and nonmanagement reactions to four central aspects of Scanlon-type plans: the gainsharing implementation vote, the suggestion system, team structure, and the group-based bonus.

Gainsharing Implementation Vote

Union officers and management employees agreed to two separate votes on changes to the compensation system. One vote was to decide whether the piece-rate incentive system should be abandoned, and the other was on the adoption of gainsharing. Each required a different voting criterion. The issue of abandoning piece-rate incentives would be decided by a simple majority vote, whereas the adoption of gainsharing would require approval by 75 percent of the voters. Both union officers and management believed that overwhelming support from union members was needed for gainsharing to succeed. If the first issue passed but the second failed, the union could suggest an alternative team decision-making process and financial bonus system. To obtain the 75 percent majority vote, the steering committee believed it was necessary to educate union members about gainsharing. A task force consisting of twenty-five union members and five managers was created to discuss the gainsharing plan line by line. The task force visited several gainsharing facilities, including Innovations.

On April 18, 1988, the first issue passed as 60 percent of the union members voted in favor of switching from the piece-rate to the day-rate incentive. Gainsharing failed, however, because the majority vote was not large enough—218 in favor (63.5 percent) and 125 opposed. Even though the vote in support of gainsharing was insufficient, union members who voted against gainsharing were surprised that they were in the minority. They had expected most union members to oppose gainsharing. Some union members thought that the 63 percent vote should be sufficient to implement gainsharing, but the facility manager disagreed. He believed that taking another vote in a few months would allow the union to become more active either in support of gainsharing or in offering an alternative plan.

Shortly after the April vote, the steering committee met to discuss why 36 percent of the union members opposed gainsharing. The list of reasons included the following: some union members did not trust management, particularly the facility manager; some questioned the fairness of the bonus calculation; some preferred a different individual incentive system because they thought other union members would not work hard under a group bonus plan; some resented union members lobbying on management's behalf; and some believed that gainsharing would mean that union members would be coopted by "hanging out too much with a bad crowd" (i.e., management).

The steering committee decided that more education about gainsharing was needed. Some union members were surprised that the steering committee did not give up after the first vote. This convinced them that management was very serious about wanting to implement gainsharing. Pro-gainsharing union members emphasized that even if gainsharing was a management sham, the plan had a clause wherein the union could back out of the agreement after giving sixty-days' notice. After further discussions, many union members became convinced that gainsharing would increase their wages. A second vote was taken on July 8, 1988, that would make the plan effective retroactive to July 1. The vote was 78 percent in favor of implementing gainsharing.

Suggestion System

As recommended by the gainsharing consultant, the facility manager agreed to have two gainsharing coordinators: one appointed by the union and the other by management. Whereas nonunion facilities usually have only one gainsharing coordinator, most union facilities have two coordinators to oversee daily operations. Typically, this is because neither side initially fully trusts the other (Ross and Collins 1987). The union-appointed gainsharing coordinator is often in a particularly delicate position. Management may never fully accept the person because he or she is a union member, and union members may reject the person for working "too closely" with management. Union officers chose an electrician who, in addition to being an eighteen-year member, had been a manager for a one-year trial early in his career at Innovations-Brotherhood. Although he could have accepted a permanent position in management, he preferred the lifestyle of an electrician. The facility manager chose the quality circle manager to be the other gainsharing coordinator, because he had worked well with the electrician in the past.

The gainsharing coordinators estimated that production employees implemented 2,000–3,000 suggestions during the first four years of gain-sharing, or approximately 1.7 suggestions per employee per year. Unfor-tunately, the gainsharing coordinators maintained efficient suggestion records for only the first four months under the plan. At the end of these first four months, the fifteen gainsharing teams voted on 399 sugges-tions, of which 244 were accepted and implemented, 33 withdrawn, and 122 needed further investigation. The gainsharing coordinators decided that the teams could best use their time to analyze, discuss, and imple-ment suggestions rather than keep accurate formal records. The go-get-ters running the team meetings, who did not want the extra burden of keeping records, agreed. According to the coordinators and production employees, the only formally written suggestions entailed ideas that ei-ther were very costly or affected another work cell.

Many of the initial suggestions reviewed by the gainsharing teams were "comfort" suggestions. In addition to immediate changes in ineffi-cient work processes, union members wanted better work seats and more lighting, tools, fans, and floor mats. A backlog in reviewing and ap-proving suggestions developed because nearly four hundred sugges-tions were submitted by union members during the first four months of gainsharing. Some fence-sitters and opponents refused to submit addi-tional suggestions until the first wave was reviewed and implemented. Those most reluctant to get involved in gainsharing activities were older union members. In their fifties and with more than thirty years' senior-ity, they were accustomed to and preferred old work relationships. In ad-dition, even if they did not improve their work methods, their jobs were protected by their seniority status in the union.

As is noted below in the discussion on the group-based bonus, em-ployees were unable to generate a bonus because of a very expensive warranty problem that occurred shortly after gainsharing was imple-mented. Go-getter production employees continued to provide many suggestions despite the lack of gainsharing payouts. Some fence-sitters began to withhold their suggestions, however, because they were work-ing more efficiently yet were not earning a gainsharing bonus. Adversar-ial union members told other union members that managers knew beforehand about the new warranty problem and implemented gain-sharing to pay for these excessive costs. Union leaders did not try to dif-fuse this false perception. The lack of gainsharing payouts eventually led to the defeat of pro-gainsharing union officials in 1989.

As was noted in Chapter 7, management turnover was quite high at the production facilities owned by the parent corporation. Managers were transferred frequently, to apply knowledge they had gained at their previous facility or to learn new skills as they moved up the managerial hierarchy. In 1989, corporate headquarters changed facility managers at Innovations-Brotherhood. Unlike the new facility manager at Innovations, the new Innovations-Brotherhood facility manager did not merge the corporate-based Excellence-in-Manufacturing program with gainsharing. Instead, he was preoccupied with responding to a recently elected set of anti-management/gainsharing union leaders. Whereas the new union officers interpreted their 1989 election as a sign to reduce team-building interactions with managers, the new facility manager pushed in the opposite direction, asking the gainsharing steering committee to develop policies that would increase interaction and trust between management and union members.

I attended the July 1992 steering committee meeting, consisting of four management and four nonmanagement employees. The meeting was chaired by both gainsharing coordinators. Its purpose was to vote on the June "Beyond the Call of Duty" nominations and announce June's gainsharing bonus results. This was the first meeting for two of the four union members assigned to the steering committee. In general, the production employees had substantial input into the discussion. Several times during the meeting, the two new union representatives mentioned how surprised they were about the openness of the discussions.

These new union representatives requested an explanation of the Beyond the Call of Duty nomination process. One of the new members who had previously won this award said he did not think he deserved it because he had simply been doing his job. The person who originally nominated him for the award was at the meeting and pointed out that his performance had been exemplary. Another union member questioned whether it was appropriate to give the award to a union member with bad work habits, even if the particular suggestion or action meriting the award was exemplary. His question raised several issues that were debated extensively. Two managers argued that receiving the award could change the union member's bad work habits. The steering committee concluded that the award should be based on a specific suggestion or action, not an employee's work habit history. The two submitted nominees were granted awards.

Before the July gainsharing bonus calculation was discussed, one of the new union representatives told those in attendance that his supervisor did not seem pleased that he was leaving his work cell to attend a gainsharing meeting. The management gainsharing coordinator promised to speak with the supervisor about the importance of attending this monthly meeting.

The controller then provided an explanation of the gainsharing bonus calculation for June. The facility had earned a profit of $389,000 on sales of $8 million, for an ROI (return on investment) of 4.9 percent. Warranty expenditures were $546,000 for the month. She announced that the production employees had outperformed the historical standard for three of the four new gainsharing bonus factors—inventory days, scrap, and work attendnace—resulting in a total gainsharing bonus of 2 percent ($27,000), which would be shared equally between the employees and Innovations-Brotherhood. The facility would keep $13,500 and the remaining $13,500 would be distributed among all facility employees, which meant approximately $30 for each of the 450 employees. A new union representative said that all of the cost savings should be distributed to the employees. The controller explained that management reinvested the facility's share of the bonus in the factory.

The last issue discussed at this hour-long meeting was the possibility of creating a fifth gainsharing bonus factor—health and wellness. The gainsharing coordinators had begun collecting and analyzing data that charted the number of accidents per employee, per work cell, per month for the previous year. They were awaiting data from the industry association for comparable facilities. They asked everyone to consider how each of the accidents could be measured according to the intensity of injury and how this data could serve as a benchmark for a new gainsharing bonus factor.

I also attended the July 1992 review board meeting held the following day, which was attended by twenty-two management and nonmanagement employees. The one-hour meeting was chaired by the union gainsharing coordinator. No employee suggestions were on the agenda because they had all been accepted or rejected by the cell review teams. The two primary issues discussed at the meeting were the gainsharing bonus for June and seven new categories that the corporation wanted the facility to benchmark. Production employees had many questions about both issues. Managers used these questions as an opportunity to explain how the facility did business.

The controller's presentation on the gainsharing bonus exemplifies the general interaction between management and nonmanagement employees at the meeting. During the meeting she used the same overhead slide outlining the gainsharing bonus calculation that she had shown during her presentation to the steering committee the previous day. Although the warranty costs were no longer part of the gainsharing bonus calculation, several production employees asked how management determined whether Innovations-Brotherhood or the customer was at fault for the clutch problem. The production employees provided several examples of returned clutches whose damage seemed to have been caused by the customer and wanted to know why the facility should incur the repair costs. The facility manager agreed that some of the damaged clutches were the customer's fault. But in the new, competitive market, Innovations-Brotherhood had to do everything it could to keep the customer satisfied, even if that meant accepting questionable warranty claims.

Team Structure

As recommended by the gainsharing consultant, the twenty-two quality circles established prior to gainsharing were collapsed into ten gainsharing teams (one per work cell) when gainsharing was implemented in July 1988. At the time of the field study, there were fifteen gainsharing teams. Each work cell elected a gainsharing team leader and a review board representative. The gainsharing teams could accept and implement suggestions that cost less than $500. Five cell review teams also were created to communicate ideas among work cells that performed the same tasks but operated during different shifts. The cell review teams consisted of the gainsharing team leader, the review board representative from each of the three shifts, and the cell manager. The cell review teams could accept and implement suggestions that cost between $500 and $3,000. Last, a review board was established consisting of the facility manager, controller, cell supervisors, union president, chief steward, one union review board representative from each gainsharing team, all gainsharing steering committee members, and the two gainsharing coordinators.

As expected, many of the quality circle leaders won the first set of elections for gainsharing team leaders. With the exception of elected team leaders and review board representatives, attendance at gainsharing team meetings was voluntary. Initially, most union members, except a few opponents, attended the gainsharing team meetings out of curiosity. When no bonuses were earned, adversarial union members began to attend the gainsharing meetings to find out what was going on. Although they did not disrupt the meetings, their presence was felt. They would sit in a corner, say nothing during the meeting, and disparage meeting events on the shop floor afterward. If a manager attending the meeting said something that demonstrated his ignorance about some aspect of the production process, the adversarial union members would spread jokes at the manager's expense.

As work cells and gainsharing evolved, it became obvious to upper management that supervisors had to be taught how to manage employee participation. Fence-sitter and oppositional supervisors were told to allow the gainsharing teams to implement even those suggestions that seemed trivial or inappropriate. Management's view was that if teams felt constrained in implementing small suggestions, they would never advance to the stage of developing and implementing major ones. In addition, it was important for work cell employees to believe that they could stop production to discuss work-related issues. Supervisors would have to trust, within reason, that discussions among union members were related to work rather than question them whenever they stepped away from their production tasks.

Some union members were shirking their work responsibilities, however. This had a negative impact on the other union members, who began to wonder why they should continue to work hard while others did not. Before gainsharing, a union member suspected of "slacking off" would be subjected to a time-study and an increase in hourly production targets. With gainsharing, there was no piece-rate incentive to modify. Also, it was much more difficult for supervisors to quantify employee productivity, especially when lower than usual hourly production totals could be the result of a team meeting or a new cell assignment. Some oppositional managers and supervisors quit because they could not tolerate the ambiguity.

The experience of Buddy, a reliable production employee who had been earning high piece-rate bonuses, is representative of the dynamics associated with these changes for union members. Buddy would malign management and encourage other union members to get involved in activities detrimental to efficient production, such as rigging the fire hoses so that they would spray unsuspecting people. But he also viewed the new work cells and gainsharing teams as a constructive opportunity to change the way he worked. He ran for the position of team leader and won because go-getters, fence-sitters, and opponents all trusted him. He made suggestions, encouraged others to make suggestions, implemented work process changes, and occasionally annoyed managers just to amuse himself.

When Buddy later served as a review board representative, he experienced "culture shock" at these meetings. First, he had little interest in the financial and production data with which the meetings began. Second, he was not sure that the meetings were legitimate because the shop-floor view of them was negative: The meetings were thought to consist of union members doing either management's job or rubber-stamping management decisions.

Buddy concluded that contrary to the popular opinion on the shop floor, union members and managers participating actively in gainsharing activities were very sincere. He dedicated himself to being a good gainsharing team leader and review board representative, and he found these activities very fulfilling. Then some of his adversarial union friends accused him of "sucking up" to management. Whenever he argued a point that gave management the benefit of the doubt, an opponent or a fence-sitter would sniff his clothes and say: "You smell like management." When he stopped work to attend meetings, oppositional managers and union members accused him of "goofing off" and trying to get out of production work. It did not help that no bonuses were being earned because of the warranty problem.

After six months of being a gainsharing team leader, Buddy declared, "I don't need this," resigned from his gainsharing duties, and went back to just doing his job. A few months later, he was bored and realized that gainsharing involvement had made his job fun. He ran for team leader again and was reelected. This time, he assigned a few opponents, including the union steward who was a member of his work cell, to several decision-making teams. According to Buddy, "I had to figure out if what was said was sincere or just bull and who was just griping for the sake of it." The new oppositional team members were surprised to see union members trying to solve work process problems, even without managers in attendance.

In 1990, the recession, along with the new competition and the warranty problem, negatively affected the gainsharing teams. Sales, which had been $7 million per month in 1988, declined steadily to a low of $4.4 million in July 1991. In 1990 management began a series of layoffs based on seniority, followed by a series of "bumpings" initiated by union members wanting more desirable shifts. As a result, there were tremendous changes in team dynamics, particularly in the teams led by younger union members, who were either laid off or assigned to a less desirable work cell or shift because they lacked seniority. When business picked up and jobs were added, another round of team turnovers occurred when previously bumped union members requested jobs on the more desirable shifts as they became available. Thus, work cell and gainsharing team assignments were constantly in flux.

In December 1990, the facility manager implemented major cost-cutting measures across facility operations, including an indefinite cancellation of gainsharing team meetings. By early spring the facility manager had second thoughts about this decision. Because communication with employees had been reduced, obvious and necessary changes were not being made by frustrated union members. The facility manager rescheduled the gainsharing team meetings beginning June 1991.

One suggestion common to several June gainsharing team meetings was the need to clean the facility. Maintenance problems had been delayed, and work areas were not organized appropriately because of the cost reductions that had been initiated. Management devised a "housekeeping" contest that awarded the cleanest work cell a pizza. Two hours prior to what was supposed to be a surprise audit, a forewarned supervisor encouraged one of his work cells to close down operations and clean in order to win the contest. Later that day, the work cell worked two hours overtime to make up for the lost production time. When that work cell won the housekeeping award, union members complained that the contest was contrary to both union and gainsharing philosophies, because the whole was sacrificed so that a few people could win a pizza. Management canceled the contest. Some managers were struck by how quickly gainsharing had become identified with union solidarity.

Union members debated the theoretical consistency of linking individual awards with the gainsharing program. For instance, in November 1991, management began the monthly Beyond the Call of Duty award whereby managers and union members nominated those who had provided extra assistance. Gainsharing steering committee members voted on which of four levels of awards, if any, should be given to a nominee. The highest-level award was a choice of two hundred lottery tickets, a portable color television, ten shares of company stock, a $500 savings bond, or a $200 charitable contribution. One of the first union winners declined the award because, as a self-proclaimed opponent, he considered it as a bribe from management that was "pro-individual" and "anti-brotherhood." The gainsharing teams debated the depth of these sentiments among the employees. They concluded that the awards were welcomed by a large majority of union members. This particular individual award system was still in effect at the time of the field study.

Group-Based Bonus

During four years of gainsharing, the average monthly bonus payout was 0.4 percent ($12). As shown in Table 8-1, the breakdown per year is 0 percent (July–December 1988), 0 percent (1989), 0.2 percent (1990), 0.3 percent (1991), and 0.97 percent (January–June 1992).

Before gainsharing was implemented, it was obvious to both management and union leaders that a piece-rate bonus system did not make sense as a reward for appropriate work-cell behaviors, such as rotating

Table 8–1. Innovations-Brotherhood: Monthly gainsharing bonus payouts (%)

	1988	1989	1990	1991	1992
January	—	0.0	0.0	0.80	0.65
February	—	0.0	0.0	0.35	0.90
March	—	0.0	0.0	0.20	1.65
April	—	0.0	0.65[b]	0.40	0.85
May	—	0.0	0.40	0.10	0.80
June	—	0.0	0.05	0.10	1.00
July	0.0	0.0	0.20	0.25	
August	0.0	0.0	0.10	0.15	
September	0.0	0.0	0.0	0.35	
October	0.0	0.0	0.05	0.65	
November	0.0	0.0	0.30	0.30	
December	0.0	0.0	0.65	0.30	
Average monthly bonus % per employee	0.0	0.0	0.2	0.3	0.97
Average monthly bonus $ per employee[a]	$0	$0	$6	$9	$29
Reserve pool %	0.0	0.0	n.a.	n.a.	n.a.
Year-end reserve pool $ per employee	$0	$0	n.a.	n.a.	n.a.

[a]Average production employee salary: $17 an hour, $2,958 a month, or $35,368 a year.

[b]Original bonus calculation changed to a four-factor calculation, and the reserve pool was eliminated.

n.a.: Not applicable because the year-end reserve pool was eliminated in April 1990.

jobs and attending meetings. The union president agreed privately to support management efforts to explore gainsharing as a pay alternative, but publicly he would neither support nor condemn the effort because of its negative financial effects on union members currently earning substantial piece-rate bonuses. The union vice president agreed to shoulder the praise or blame for the gainsharing bonus.

Two bonus-related issues were raised at the gainsharing steering committee meetings: management commitment to gainsharing, and the nature of the bonus calculation. First, union members believed that they were taking all the risks. They had heard stories about other facilities whose adversarial managers sabotaged the gainsharing system by not allowing nonmanagement employees the time needed to write suggestions or hold gainsharing meetings. To increase management's stake in the financial bonus, the facility manager substituted the gainsharing bonus for already existing managerial bonuses, which were linked to schooling and extra hours worked, and which he wanted to eliminate anyway.

The second issue pertained to the basis for calculating the group-based bonus. The gainsharing consultant recommended a simple calculation based on factors that nonmanagement employees affected directly. In response, management proposed several narrow financial measures, such as labor hours and amount of scrap produced. But the union countered with a broad and ambiguous financial measure—ROI. The facility manager argued against ROI because it contained too many items beyond the control of union members (such as sales volume and market fluctuations). Simply put, ROI was not a meaningful measure of daily improvements in the work process. Union leaders remained adamant, and the steering committee adopted ROI as the historical standard.

Why did union members on the gainsharing steering committee lobby so strongly for ROI? Although the company's stock is publicly traded, each facility's ROI was kept confidential. Union officers suspected that the facility's ROI was quite high (24 percent), but they were not sure. They wanted access to ROI numbers so that they could use the information to improve their collective bargaining strategy. Also, management's willingness to share ROI information with the union would be a sign of good faith in gainsharing. None of this was stated explicitly during the steering committee meetings. Instead, the union simply maintained that ROI would be the most appropriate measure, and management conceded. From management's perspective, if union members wanted to rely on an ambiguous factor, such as ROI, they were willing to give it a try; when the union realized that it was not an appropriate measure, some other measure could be adopted. Management had no idea that this was a collective bargaining ploy by the union until, with the union's permission, I told the new facility manager at the time of the field study. (He laughed.)

Immediately after gainsharing was implemented, the financial bonus calculation was severely negatively affected by a new product warranty problem. Warranty costs for the facility had typically been about $20,000 a month. In early 1988 there was a major design flaw in a new clutch, and by June, warranty costs had risen to $50,000 a month—a problem not anticipated by management. In July, just as gainsharing started, warranties increased to $150,000 a month and rose steadily until they stabilized at $400,000 a month by the end of the year. Over the next two years, the faulty product design became a $12 million warranty problem. Although some of the warranty problems were questionable, management accepted all returns because of the two new competitors that had entered the market.

These warranty costs made it impossible for union members to earn a financial bonus. Based on historical standards, the facility had to earn an ROI of more than 24 percent before union members earned a gainsharing bonus. ROI for September 1988 dipped to 20 percent, and it further declined to 14.3 percent in July 1989, one year after gainsharing had been implemented. According to management, if warranties had not been included in the ROI or if some other calculation had been used, a bonus would have been earned. But this was not the case.

Because no bonuses had been paid out, gainsharing was the key campaign issue for the 1989 union elections. The public positions on gainsharing held by the five incumbent union officers were as follows: president—neutral; vice president—strong supporter; chief steward—mild supporter; treasurer—strong supporter; and secretary—neutral. When two union members strongly opposed to gainsharing ran for president and vice president, respectively, the incumbent president responded by making several very public antigainsharing statements. In turn, the incumbent vice president created a progainsharing ticket, running with a friend for president and vice president. Two antigainsharing union members ran for the offices of chief steward and treasurer; the incumbent neutral secretary ran unopposed.

The incumbent won the presidential election with 60 percent of the vote, compared to 25 percent for the antigainsharing challenger and 15 percent for the progainsharing challenger. Antigainsharing candidates won the offices of vice president and chief steward. In a very close race, the progainsharing incumbent treasurer was reelected. Union members were surprised by the closeness of this particular vote because the incumbent had been an excellent treasurer for the past nine years and was much more qualified than the antigainsharing challenger. The newly elected union officers interpreted the results as a signal that union members wanted to retain their distance from management.

A facility-wide employee attitude survey taken one year after gainsharing implementation showed that contrary to management's expectations, trust between management and union members had actually declined. A survey administered to thirteen union leaders in October 1987, when gainsharing was initially being explored, asked whether they strongly agreed (scored a "5") or strongly disagreed (scored a "1") with the statement "Employees here trust management." The average score was 2.2. By June 1989, this score had declined to 1.8. The gainsharing steering committee discussed the employee attitude survey results and decided to remove warranty costs from the ROI calculation.

As mentioned earlier, a new facility manager arrived in 1989, and his primary agenda item was improving trust between management and the newly elected antimanagement/antigainsharing union officials. A task team of management and union officials visited other production facilities with progressive management-labor relationships and recommended four major changes, which were soon implemented. First, all management staff meetings were opened to union officers. Second, managers discarded their ties and gave up their reserved parking spaces. Third, a new company letterhead included both union and company insignias. Fourth, the gainsharing bonus calculation was revised a second time.

It was obvious to everyone on the steering committee that the ROI measure had to be abandoned in favor of measures related more directly to daily production. Four new factors were adopted for the bonus calculation: operating expense to sales—29 percent; inventory days—thirty days; scrap parts per million—55,000; and attendance—96.7 percent. A financial bonus would be earned if one of these measures improved. For instance, each employee would earn a $30 bonus in a month that achieved the following goals: a 27 percent operating-expense-to-sales ratio; twenty-seven inventory days; 50,000 parts per million of scrap; and 97.4 percent attendance. The year-end reserve pool, which had always been a deficit, was eliminated. Management also agreed to continue to report ROI at the monthly review board meetings.

Shortly after the new bonus calculation took effect, a few bonuses were earned. They were so small, however, that some union members joked that "the monthly bonus payout is convenient because you can put it into the coffee machine." The steering committee decided to change the payout system from a monthly to a semiannual distribution.

Sales increased in early 1992 and by March had reached the July 1988 level of $7 million per month. At the time of the 1992 field study, managers believed that the facility had entered a recovery stage. Yet because of complaints by adversarial union members about the lack of gainsharing bonuses, some managers argued for their elimination. At the same time, a majority of managers believed that this action would generate additional ill-feeling among other union members, most of whom wanted to keep the bonus.

To address the bonus problem, the gainsharing steering committee reviewed additional factors that could be part of the calculation. For instance, they explored ways to include aspects of division operations affected by union members. Gainsharing was not an issue during the 1992 union elections. At the time of the field study, an estimated 25 percent of the union members were strongly involved in gainsharing activities, and 10 percent were opponents. The remaining 65 percent were fence-sitters.

The Outcomes Propositions

There is a strong consensus among management and union members, even those who are still adversarial, that gainsharing is essential to Innovations-Brotherhood. Both management and union members benefited directly and indirectly from four years of gainsharing.

Benefits

Direct benefits to both management and union members included better production processes, new machinery, improved product quality, more in-house work, improved collective bargaining negotiations, and fewer grievances.

Better Production Processes. The 2,000 to 3,000 gainsharing suggestions offered by union members have greatly improved the production process, generated tremendous financial savings for Innovations-Brotherhood, and improved working conditions. For instance, one work cell had been filling boxes with scrap and disposing of them in a heat treatment dumper permanently located on the other side of the facility, at a cost of at least $60 a shift. The cell purchased a $4,700 movable dumper that saved Innovations-Brotherhood at least $50,000 in the first year alone and saved the union members a lot of physical stress. A new procedure for receiving steel developed by an office team saved the facility $12,000 a year.

New Machinery. Using their gainsharing team's monthly budget, union members have purchased many new machines and the best available tools to improve product quality and reduce production time.

Improved Product Quality. Many team discussions pertain to making a high-quality product on the first try. Shoddy work is likely to be detected earlier in the production process and eliminated, rather than passed on to the next group or to the customer.

More In-House Work. A union member suggested the purchase of a machine that would permit the facility to produce its own materials rather than purchase them from suppliers. The $35,500 machine saved Innovations-Brotherhood $396,000 in vendor costs and brought in additional jobs.

Improved Collective Bargaining. In 1992, union and management agreed to begin contract negotiations early, and they settled early. Communication has been better and more frequent. Because all management staff meetings are open to union officers, some potentially difficult collective bargaining issues are discussed prior to formal negotiations. In particular, this helped Innovations-Brotherhood in its response to a crisis in health-care costs—an issue that had already led to a union strike at another corporate facility. Union officers who attended management meetings on health-care costs viewed problem in the same way as management. A joint management-union team was formed to examine the issue. In addition, the union knew the facility's ROI numbers, which helped their side of the bargaining.

Fewer Grievances. Before 1988, the facility averaged thirty pending grievances a day. With the creation of work cells and implementation of gainsharing, only about twenty grievances have been filed, and none during the past two years. According to one supervisor, the union members "can only really file a grievance against themselves because they organize their own work, set their own schedules, and set their own work quotas." Rather than write up a grievance, union members submit the problem as a gainsharing suggestion and discuss it at the next gainsharing team meeting.

Direct benefits to management and indirect benefits to union members included greater worker identification with facility problems, an easier decision-making process for tough decisions, greater quantifiability of production factors, direct communication with union members, rather than through union officers, less need for management supervision, and recycling and energy savings.

Greater Worker Identification with Facility Problems. Management believes that union members are much more responsive to a host of organizational problems that they would previously have ignored. For instance, an office employee who knew that a competitor was underpricing them attended a different gainsharing team meeting to determine how the work cell could reduce costs to meet the competitor's price. Operators who, prior to gainsharing, would allow a machine to be installed wrongly and then complain about it to management are now fully responsible for installing all new machines.

Union members have developed a better understanding that the facility's profitability ensures their own job security. In response to a management promise not to lay off union members as a result of suggestions that improved the work process, one work cell reorganized itself such that two positions were unnecessary. The two union members, who agreed to this arrangement, were bumped to another shift without any complaints. As a sign of the barriers that have been broken, the facility manager challenges visitors to guess which people attending a meeting are managers and which are union members. At a meeting of eight people, I was wrong about three of them.

Before gainsharing, management feared what union members would say if they met customers. After gainsharing implementation, union members were permitted to speak directly to customers about their product. A team of union members visited a customer and determined that color coding Innovations-Brotherhood's parts would greatly reduce miscommunication. Union members visited suppliers as well, giving advice on how to improve their product.

Easier Decision-Making Process. With union officers attending management staff meetings, the union serves as a buffer for tough decisions. For instance, before gainsharing, management would notify the union just prior to a layoff. Now union officers analyze the financial data and are able to foresee when layoffs appear inevitable. Union officers urge members to work harder or smarter to prevent a layoff. If not preventable, the layoff is at least anticipated. Similarly, as noted earlier, union members are exploring alternative ways of funding health-care benefits.

Greater Quantifiability of Production Factors. Gainsharing suggestions and the bonus calculation have forced managers to better quantify facility operations. Anything that union members affect and that can be measured may be included in the bonus. For instance, managers are trying to determine how to quantify customer service and certain shipping factors.

Direct Communication with Union Members. Before gainsharing, managers often felt compelled to speak with union officers before suggesting that an employee change his or her work methods. In addition, union members would not perform someone else's job, and they would ask the union to clarify new directions from management. Now union members demand that managers communicate directly with them.

Less Need for Management Supervision. Gainsharing gives union members who serve as work-cell team leaders responsibility for some discipline issues. Because cell members organize themselves, they encourage each other to put in a fair day's work. Supervisors no longer have to monitor behavior constantly. When there is a major discipline problem, union members demand that the supervisor take appropriate action. There is also less need to supervise the implementation of production changes because the union members take responsibility for them.

Recycling and Energy Savings. Gainsharing has greatly increased recycling facility-wide. One employee suggested that a baler be purchased to recycle cardboard. Within nine months, one department recycled 27,745 sheets, thereby saving $11,000. A union member actively involved in environmental issues determined how to recycle computer paper throughout the facility and where to sell it.

Direct benefits to union members and indirect benefits to management included easier work tasks, greater voice in decision making, better managers, leadership opportunities, and improved health and safety.

Easier Work Tasks. The statement most often made by union members regarding the benefits of gainsharing is that "it makes my job easier." If they do not like the way work is processed, they can change it. If factory ventilation is inadequate, they can purchase a fan. If their work is physically stressful, they can purchase a pulley. Some managers cringe at having this often-stated benefit, interpreting the word "easier" to mean "slacking off."

Greater Voice in Decision Making. Gainsharing provides union members with another outlet for expressing opinions about facility operations. They can fulfill their work needs through the team budgets and no longer have to convince supervisors that what is obviously needed should be purchased or redesigned. This latitude is particularly important in terms of health and safety improvements.

Better Managers. According to union members, gainsharing exposes bad managers because they can no longer "hide." These managers must face union members at team meetings and respond to their concerns. Some of Innovations-Brotherhood's worst managers have quit.

Leadership Opportunities. Before gainsharing, the only real leadership positions available for union members were within the union. Now they can become team representatives or join various task teams. Gainsharing allows some union members, such as Buddy, to take responsibility for their work rather than rely on a manager.

Improved Health and Safety. Many gainsharing suggestions pertain to health and safety improvements. For instance, teams have purchased exhaust fans for better ventilation, rubber mats to cover wet floors, and work station adjustments to prevent back problems and other common health ailments.

Conclusion

Each of the four conflict-of-interest propositions is examined below to aid understanding of how gainsharing evolved at this publicly owned union manufacturing facility.

P1: Manipulating the Transitional Process

The union was the primary power player during the transitional period. The union president privately supported gainsharing but publicly maintained a neutral position because of union politics. The union vice president agreed to shoulder the praise and blame for gainsharing. Most detrimentally, the union insisted that the gainsharing bonus be based on the facility's ROI, even though they knew that this calculation would not generate bonuses, in order to obtain ROI figures they could use to improve the union's collective bargaining strategy.

Management's acceptance of the union's ROI request was ambiguous. On the one hand, the facility manager wanted to develop trust with union officials by letting them decide how the financial bonus should be calculated. On the other hand, he knowingly accepted a bonus calculation that was not appropriate for measuring productivity improvements resulting from gainsharing. In addition, the facility manager appeased union objections about management commitment to gainsharing by substituting the gainsharing bonus for existing managerial bonuses he wanted to eliminate anyway.

Importantly, the facility manager adopted six strategies that encouraged extensive employee involvement in decision-making. These included creating a thirty-member gainsharing exploratory task force that consisted of twenty-five union members; creating two gainsharing coordinator positions, one assigned by management and the other by the union; allowing all production employees to attend gainsharing meetings; transforming all work-cell units into gainsharing teams; creating cell review teams to encourage nonmanagement communication among shifts; and rejecting the union's request to accept a 63.5 percent majority vote in favor of gainsharing in order to get the union more active in plan development.

P2: Interest-Group Power Struggles

Based on information gathered during the semistructured interviews, managers and supervisors represented the continuum of go-getters, fence-sitters, and opponents when gainsharing was implemented. Management fence-sitters and opponents questioned nonmanagement employees who stopped production to discuss gainsharing-related issues. Many of these managers and supervisors left Innovations-Brotherhood when it became apparent that gainsharing would continue indefinitely. Go-getter managers on the steering committee took a leading role in eliminating the out-of-control warranty expenses from the ROI bonus calculation and developed a more equitable bonus calculation that eventually replaced ROI. Strongly encouraged by the second facility manager, they also worked with the union on designing a new company letterhead with both the union's and company's insignia, eliminated reserved management parking spaces, abandoned the wearing of ties, opened all management staff meetings to union officers, and agreed to report monthly ROI calculations even after ROI was no longer being used as the basis for the gainsharing bonus. Although obviously a go-getter in the eyes of nonmanagement employees, the second facility manager temporarily canceled gainsharing team meetings because of the industry recession.

Go-getters among the nonmanagement employees won the initial set of elections for gainsharing team leaders and reserve board representatives. They assigned both nonmanagement fence-sitters and opponents to gainsharing-related task teams in the hopes of increasing their involvement. In alliance with the fence-sitters, go-getters submitted many "comfort" suggestions to improve working conditions. Both fence-sitters and opponents deliberately withheld suggestions during the first two years of gainsharing, when no bonuses were being earned because of the warranty problem and the ROI bonus calculation. They also withheld suggestions when there was a backlog in implementing suggestions.

Nonmanagement opponents attended the voluntary gainsharing team meetings to obtain information and disparage management. Some opponents used gainsharing discussions as an excuse for "slacking off." They ridiculed former opponents who became fence-sitters and former fence-sitters who became go-getters. Opponents used the lack of gainsharing bonus payouts as an issue to win several union office positions during the 1989 elections.

The dynamic nature of the go-getter, fence-sitter, and opponent typologies is evident in the behavior of the union president. The union president personally favored gainsharing implementation but did not believe it was in his political self-interest to be a public advocate for gainsharing. He took a fence-sitter posture, encouraging go-getters to get involved and agreeing with opponents who were highly critical of gainsharing. Although the union president was primarily responsible for getting management to agree on the ill-suited ROI bonus calculation, he did not diffuse the false perception of union members that using ROI was part of a strategic management trick to subsidize the out-of-control warranty problem. When he was challenged by a gainsharing opponent during the 1989 union elections, the union president made several anti-gainsharing statements, aligning himself with his adversarial constituency.

All three groups of nonmanagement employees are still evident after four years of gainsharing. An estimated 25 percent of the union members are strongly involved in gainsharing activities, and 10 percent are opponents. The remaining 65 percent are fence-sitters. According to the fence-sitters, they have seen many production improvements but very small bonus payouts. They disagree with opponents, who argue that gainsharing is a management trick to get union members to act like managers. Nonetheless, they will not align themselves with the go-getters unless gainsharing bonus payouts match the level of productivity improvements.

P3: Hidden and Suppressed Problems Surface

A variety of hidden and suppressed problems surfaced as a result of the more than two thousand suggestions accepted. Most suggestions corrected production inefficiencies. Other problems that surfaced as a result of gainsharing implementation include health and safety issues, the lack of group dynamics training for management and nonmanagement employees, the need for new tools and machines, and significant waste in the production process.

P4: Fulfilled Monetary and Nonmonetary Interests

Managers are looking forward to many more years of gainsharing. Gainsharing has generated many suggestions that have improved production and product quality. It has led to the purchase of new machinery, a decrease in employee grievances, an increase in workers' identification with facility issues, and has made the decision-making process for tough decisions easier. Managers are forced to quantify production factors better. They deal directly with union members and spend less time supervising work cells. Innovations-Brotherhood employees have begun several recycling efforts and have reduced energy costs significantly.

Despite the very small bonus payouts, nonmanagement go-getters, fence-sitters, and opponents also want gainsharing to continue. As have to managers, they too have benefited from improvements in the production process, new machinery, and product quality. Also, they have benefited from increased in-house work, improved collective bargaining negotiations, less stressful work tasks, a greater voice in decision making, better managers, new leadership opportunities, and improved health and safety.

Summary

Innovations-Brotherhood had difficulties with some of the conflict-of-interest exchange relationships diagramed in Figure 2-2. The facility manager allowed greater employee involvement by transforming work cells into gainsharing teams and permitting everyone to attend gainsharing team meetings. As a result, Innovations-Brotherhood received more than two thousand production-related performance improvement suggestions, which in turn significantly improved production output and reduced production costs.

Unfortunately, the union deliberately restricted the group-based financial bonus by demanding that the bonus calculation be based on the facility's ROI rather than factors that were a more direct measure of production improvements. For almost two years, there were no bonus payouts, despite the many production improvements. Even after the steering committee changed the bonus calculation to a four-factor score, payouts have been extremely small. In 1991, the average monthly bonus payout was $9, or the equivalent of about half an hour's worth of wages for the highly paid production employees. As a result, fence-sitters and opponents are restricting the degree to which they participate in employee involvement mechanisms and production process improvements. Nonetheless, nonmanagement go-getters are still actively involved in gainsharing activities.

9 Packaging International:
A Unionized ESOP Facility,
Abandoned Gainsharing

Packaging International is an employee-owned union facility located in a northeastern urban community. It was established in 1940 as the result of a merger between two other companies. Packaging International changed ownership in 1946, 1979, and 1984. It is a leading manufacturer in the highly competitive end-packaging equipment industry. Structurally, the company consists of two facilities—a production facility and an assembly facility—separated by a street. When gainsharing was implemented in July 1985, Packaging International employed 246 people; 70 percent were hourly union employees organized under the International Association of Machinists, 15 percent were management staff and sales personnel, 8 percent were nonunion engineers, and 7 percent were managers. Union employees earned approximately $25,000 a year. Average yearly net sales for 1982–84 were $17,049,000, with an average yearly profit of $695,000. Packaging International's products are sold in the United States, Canada, Mexico, Latin America, and the Far East.

In 1979, the new owner demanded a 30 percent return-on-investment which was very difficult for management to achieve without making short-term decisions that had long-term negative outcomes, such as decertifying the union and selling parts of Packaging International. Led by upper management, the privately owned facility was bought out by its employees in December 1984 at a price of $7.4 million. Stock was made available to all facility employees based on their hierarchical position to account for the obvious financial risks associated with the buyout. Of 40,000 shares, the president and two vice presidents controlled 29,000. Packaging International is governed by a board of directors consisting of the president, four vice presidents, two employee representatives (always engineers, not union members), and a person external to the organization. Thus, management controls a large majority of stock and five of the eight board of director votes. Despite owning a significant amount of stock, one vice president was fired when he "stepped out of line"—failing to act in concert with the other vice presidents and two employee representatives in siding with the president on an issue.

The union has had a rocky relationship with management, the last strike having occurred in 1979. After attending a speech by a gainsharing consultant in early 1985, Packaging International's president decided that gainsharing could serve as a way to improve quality, reduce costs, link pay to performance, and reduce the obvious barriers among managers, union members, and engineers. The national union had an anti-gainsharing policy because gainsharing blurred the border between management and labor, and it could be used by management to decertify the union. The local union dealt with this issue by substituting the term *quality plus plan* for *gainsharing*. Union leaders opposed to gainsharing included the outspoken vice president; those supporting it included the union president. An eight-member management and nonmanagement steering committee agreed to pursue implementation of gainsharing. A modified gainsharing plan was approved by more than 75 percent of the employees, and it was implemented on July 17, 1985. Packaging International suspended its Scanlon-type plan in April 1991.

Power Games Propositions

The two power games propositions are analyzed below according to management and nonmanagement reactions to three central aspects of Scanlon-type plans: the suggestion system, the team structure, and the group-based bonus. Related issues are also examined to explain why gainsharing was suspended.

Suggestion System

During six years of gainsharing, production employees implemented 8,114 suggestions. As shown in Table 9-1, the breakdown per year is 144 (1985), 722 (1986), 954 (1987), 986 (1988), 2,998 (1989), 2,280 (1990), and 30

Table 9–1.   Packaging International: Suggestions and bonuses per year

Year	Number of Accepted Suggestions	Bonus as a % of Wages
1985	144	2.2%
1986	722	0.9%
1987	954	0.8%
1988	986	1.1%
1989	2,998	1.1%
1990	2,280	1.2%
January–March 1991	30	1.6%
Total suggestions	8,114	
Average bonus		1.2%

(January–March 1991), or approximately 6.8 suggestions per employee per year.

The key position of gainsharing coordinator was given to a manager who was trusted by union members. He joined Packaging International in 1976, at age forty-five, as an assembly floor manager and was promoted to manufacturing manager. He was promoted to vice president of manufacturing just prior to the employee buyout in 1984. He preferred life as a manufacturing manager to that of a vice president (and major shareholder) and "jumped" at the opportunity to be the gainsharing coordinator, which he believed to be a central hands-on position within the facility.

During the first month of gainsharing, 80 percent of the employees attended team meetings to analyze 21 suggestions, which were mostly about redesigning equipment pieces, changing production processes, and purchasing new machines or tools. By the end of December, 144 suggestions had been accepted—an average of 0.65 suggestions per employee for the first five months of gainsharing. According to Packaging International records, the first 42 suggestions saved Packaging International approximately $96,500.

Production changes implemented by gainsharing teams during the first few months included developing a system to keep a complete supply of hardware with the preassembly department, developing a fixture for milling four pieces at a time, using a form so that engineers could update their parts list, reducing incoming shipping costs by 25 percent by using a different supplier, relocating the lathes storage area, combining all same-day invoices in one envelope, and inserting advertising leaflets with price quotes.

The overabundance of suggestions on correcting design problems led to a backlog in engineering. Many of the engineers tended to see the suggestions as critical of their work. Some engineers purposely delayed responding to the problems. Their sentiment was: "How dare production workers tell me that what I designed isn't the best!" In addition, the engineers refused to submit suggestions because it was their professional duty to solve problems. This led union members to further question the engineers' commitment to the program. The nonunion engineers tended to be both antimanagement and anti-union, so they accused management of giving in to the union when management criticized them.

An awards committee staffed with two managers and two union members, and led by the gainsharing coordinator, was formed to increase the number of suggestions. The committee initiated recognition awards for best suggestion of the month, team of the month, and employee of the month. Winners were given T-shirts, hats, and coffee mugs, and had their pictures taken and hung in the lobby. Committee members passed out gainsharing buttons and stickers, drew five names at random, and gave an award if the people whose names had been chosen were wearing the button or had the sticker on their machines. In addition, the gainsharing coordinator initiated a bimonthly newsletter to increase communication among departments and highlight team suggestions. All of this was very inexpensive.

The new gainsharing promotions had the biggest impact on the fence-sitters, giving them an additional reason to submit a suggestion for public evaluation. Although they were disappointed in the lack of bonuses, fence-sitters benefited by the many production process improvements initiated by go-getters, so they participated. They never volunteered to be team leaders, however. The few who became team representatives were pressured into the position. These favorable attitudes changed as a result of a series of layoffs Packaging International experienced in 1987. The ramifications were felt among the fence-sitters, some of whom maintained: "I give suggestions, then I see fifteen people laid off. To hell with giving suggestions."

Gainsharing suggestions received a big boost in December 1988 with the initiation of a "Q+ buck" program. The author of an accepted suggestion was awarded a Q+ buck, regardless of the value of the accepted suggestion. Employees could collect the Q+ bucks and exchange them for a gift certificate of equal value at a local store. As shown in Table 9-1, accepted suggestions increased dramatically from 986 (5 per employee) in 1988 to 2,998 (15 per employee) in 1989. The largest increases in accepted suggestions per team member per year were 8.6 to 47.5, 8.6 to 43.7, and 5.7 to 37.9, respectively.

Team Structure

The initial gainsharing plan consisted of eighteen department teams, a review board, and a group-based bonus. The department teams, which consisted of five to eight elected representatives and their supervisor, met once a month to discuss suggestions. They had the authority to implement any suggestion that had unanimous approval, did not affect another department, and cost less than $200 to implement. The thirty-one-member review board consisted of eighteen department team representatives (one per team), the union president, the company president, four vice presidents, the gainsharing coordinator, the industrial relations manager, the materials manager, the production facility machine shop manager, the assembly facility manager, and two product engineers. Suggestions required approval by two-thirds of those in attendance to be accepted.

The initial group of gainsharing team leaders were mostly lead men (nonmanagement employees with some formal responsibility for group performance) with cross-sectional training who tended to be outspoken and very knowledgeable. Other employees wanted these highly qualified workers to run for the position and win. These employees were excited about solving production problems on their own and the opportunity to work with "sincere managers." Gainsharing allowed them a chance to address issues that management had previously set aside, was not really interested in, or that got lost in the managerial shuffle. The teams met over morning coffee with the company president in attendance. The only team that did not meet the first month was that of the electricians, a group led by the adversarial union vice president. With the knowledge that most of the teams were functioning well and that attending eighteen team meetings a month was very time-consuming, the company president delegated the duty of attending all team meetings to the gainsharing coordinator.

According to interviewees, the initial review board meetings were quite interesting for all the participants. Union employees asked challenging questions and learned a lot about facility performance. They questioned each other and managers about the actual costs and cost savings associated with suggestions. If they believed a team was exaggerating these figures, they said so. At the first review board meeting, union employees suggested the need for future training programs on problem-solving techniques for both union members and managers. Management treated the review board meetings as a forum to educate employees about facility problems, for example, by going over a major customer problem step by step to demonstrate everything that went wrong throughout the process and discussing how each mistake cost significant amounts of money.

After one year of gainsharing, the original eighteen teams were reorganized, resulting in twelve active teams. During the industry-wide recession, the night shift was terminated, which eliminated one team. The six-member field sales team and ten-member field service team were combined into one field team. The six-member methods team and the twenty-two-member drill and assembly team were combined into an office and shop group. In both cases, the two new larger teams were formed because one of the two teams was not performing well and had significant daily interactions with the other team. The maintenance team existed but was inactive. Maintenance employees defined their gainsharing role as implementing—not offering—team suggestions. The foreman team was also inactive because, like the engineers, they believed that it was their job duty to find problems and make changes, and that they didn't need the gainsharing system.

There was one obvious oppositional team. In one and a half years of gainsharing, during which 866 suggestions were accepted, the electrician team had never met, and none of the nine members ever submitted a suggestion. This was very problematic on two counts. First, it was a symbolic "thorn in the side" of the gainsharing program. Every month, information tracking gainsharing suggestions was provided in newsletters, at meetings, and on bulletin boards. The listed number of suggestions for the electricians was always zero—a continual reminder to everyone about the problem. Second, the adversarial union vice president was an electrician, and in 1987, he was elected union president.

The union president in 1983–87 had been very supportive of gainsharing. But he was criticized by union members for sacrificing too many benefits at the time of the 1984 employee buyout, and he decided not to run for reelection. In 1987, the newly elected union president, who had previously served as vice president, was well known for his adversarial views regarding both management and gainsharing. Near retirement age, he strongly believed in the old confrontational ways of union-management relationships. Although the electricians boycotted all gainsharing meetings, he grudgingly attended the review board meetings in his new role as union president.

Despite the lack of support from the new union president and the powerful electricians' department, an April 1987 employee feedback survey indicated that plan satisfaction was relatively high, scoring a 3.7 on a 1 (low) to 5 (high) scale. Nonetheless, as measured by one survey item, there were no signs of improved trust in management. The most often stated complaints written on the 1987 survey forms pertained to managerial commitment. Respondents noted that some managers were not attending gainsharing meetings and did not respect union members who were active gainsharing participants. The company president responded to the survey results by putting supervisors and foremen through additional participatory management training at a local college.

Beginning in 1987, seniority-based layoffs due to the recession took a toll on gainsharing, because many go-getters and team leaders tended to be younger employees. They had seen gainsharing as a good opportunity to do something other than physical labor. The result of the layoffs was an older and more bitter workforce.

The company president pressured managers to attend gainsharing meetings after the new bonus calculation was established in April 1988. Two managers complained that gainsharing gave union employees too much control over them. The company president told these managers not to "confuse participation with permissiveness" and that poor work performers had to be disciplined by management.

Group-Based Bonus

During six years of gainsharing, the average monthly bonus payout was 1.2 percent ($25). As shown in Table 9-1, the breakdown per year is 2.2 percent (1985), 0.9 percent (1986), 0.8 percent (1987), 1.1 percent (1988), 1.1 percent (1989), and 1.2 percent (1990). Table 9-2 provides a monthly breakdown of bonus payouts.

The union had mixed feelings about the gainsharing bonus, believing that it had the potential to sidetrack the collective bargaining process. According to the union president, members did not want to be "bribed" into participating on account of the bonus. Thus the union agreed to start gainsharing in July 1985, even though no agreement had been reached on how the bonus would be calculated. Five months later, the steering committee, led by the company president, reached a final decision regarding the bonus calculation. A bonus would be earned when total costs as a percentage of net sales were less than the average facility ratio for 1982–1984 (95.92 percent). The employee share of the bonus would increase as actual costs, as a percentage of net sales, decreased.

Table 9–2. Packaging International: Monthly gainsharing bonus payouts (%)

	1985	1986	1987	1988	1989	1990
January	—	0.0	0.0	0.0	2.0	2.0
February	—	0.0	0.0	0.0	1.1	1.5
March	—	0.0	0.0	1.1[a]	1.0	1.3
April	—	0.0	2.1	2.5	1.7	
May	—	0.0	0.0	2.3	1.8	
June	—	0.0	2.1	1.6	2.7	9.8[b]
July	0.0	1.0	3.9	0.6	0.6	
August	0.5[c]	0.0	0.0	0.1	0.0	
September	0.0	0.0	0.0	0.0	0.0	0.0
October	0.2	2.1	0.7	1.0	0.0	
November	10.1	7.2	1.0	1.7	0.8	
December	2.1	0.0	0.0	1.8	3.1	0.0
Average monthly bonus % per employee	2.2	0.9	0.8	1.1	1.2	1.2
Average monthly bonus $ per employee[d]	$46	$19	$17	$23	$25	25
Reserve pool %	0.0	0.0	0.0	n.a.	n.a.	n.a.
Year-end reserve pool $ per employee	$0	$0	$0	n.a.	n.a.	n.a.

[a]Facility eliminated the reserve pool in March 1988.

[b]The monthly bonus changed to quarterly bonus beginning April 1990.

[c]The bonus payouts listed for 1985 were determined by company officials assuming that the agreed-upon calculation for January 1986 had been in existence when gainsharing began in July 1985.

[d]Average production employee salary: $12 an hour, $2,088 a month, or $25,056 a year.

The gainsharing consultant argued against the president's total cost ratio bonus plan because it contained too many factors (such as advertising, equipment depreciation, and sales commissions) that were beyond the control of production employees and engineers. The union agreed to support, on a trial basis, whatever bonus management developed, as long as it did not interfere with the collective bargaining contract. The engineers decided to accept whatever the union and management agreed on because they believed that gainsharing was primarily a new financial incentive for the lower-paid "nonprofessional" union employees.

Another unusual aspect of the mutually agreed upon bonus calculation was carrying over a year-end negative reserve pool to the following year. This policy was pushed by the company president, who argued that if people "dig themselves into a hole" they should "dig themselves out of it" rather than simply start over every twelve months. The union knew that most facilities eliminated any year-end reserve pool deficits yet did not argue the point because union leaders maintained that management had the discretion to determine what would be a fair bonus.

The company president believed that it was essential to the success of gainsharing for a bonus to be paid out for Christmas 1985, even though the bonus calculation approved by the steering committee would not be implemented until January. The steering committee agreed on a $75 bonus per employee. Based on the gainsharing bonus calculation numbers provided by management (see Table 9-1), employees should have earned approximately $270 for their work efforts during the first five months of gainsharing.

January 1986, which was the first month under the new bonus calculation system, yielded no bonus. Disputes arose immediately. Opponents complained that union members had improved some of their work behavior and yet received no bonus. Team representatives and managers who tried to explain the intricacies of the bonus calculation were met with skepticism. From the perspective of the opponents, they had worked hard and a lot of product had gone out the door. This lent credence to their belief that there were "two sets of books," one private and one public, and that the public one was being manipulated by management. The first monthly bonus was not earned until July. The opponents maintained that it did not make sense for union members earning an average of $10 an hour to reduce overtime in order to earn a gainsharing bonus, because no bonuses were forthcoming. This sentiment was particularly strong in the assembly facility, where the electricians worked, and which historically received the most overtime.

Gainsharing bonuses continued to be seldom and small. There were five bonus payouts in 1987, ranging from $14 to $81 per employee. Thus the financial incentive to cut costs in order to earn a gainsharing bonus was more than offset by the financial incentive to work overtime. For instance, although some managers believed the $4,000 gainsharing bonus payout for November 1987 was too large for Packaging International to incur in the midst of a recession, it still was just $20 per employee—the equivalent of two hours' pay. Nonetheless, some go-getters continued with their best efforts to make gainsharing work. One employee submitted seventy-five suggestions between July 1985 (when the plan began) and May 1988.

The steering committee met in April 1988 to change the bonus calculation retroactive to March. The negative carry-over from month to month and year to year was discouraging fence-sitters from participating. Too often, employees performed well for several months in a row but did not earn a bonus because of one month of poor financial results several months prior. The steering committee decided to eliminate the reserve pool. The new bonus calculation consisted of comparing a rotating three-month average with the historical 95.92 percent cost-to-net sales figure. Ten percent of the positive difference between actual costs and allowable costs would then be distributed among the employees. For instance, under the old calculation, there would have been no bonus for March 1988 because the combination of October 1987 and January 1988 created a large deficit in the reserve pool. With the new calculation, small bonuses were earned during the first five consecutive months.

Packaging International's best financial year since 1983 was 1988, which was also its second-best year since the mid-1970s. Profits before interest and taxes were $394,000 (51 percent) above projections, and $680,000 (140 percent) better than in 1987. In addition, at the end of the year, Packaging International began the Q+ buck program, which dramatically increased the number of employee suggestions. These suggestions, however, did not result in a corresponding increase in monthly gainsharing bonuses. Although bonuses were earned every month from January to July 1989, they averaged only $32 a month. These events only made the opponents more adversarial. Employees were offering many suggestions, yet the bonus payouts were minimal. Therefore, they argued, management was "playing with the books."

The opponents and a few fence-sitters responded by manipulating the Q+ buck game. First, they questioned why employee ideas were only worth a dollar each to Packaging International. Second, coalitions were formed between two teams that shared common work processes, wherein both teams would offer contradictory suggestions and accept them. For instance, team A would accept a suggestion to move item X into team B's work area, and team B would accept a suggestion to move item Y into team A's area. The following month, they would reverse their suggestions.

This type of game playing soured the other fence-sitters and the go-getters. They informed the gainsharing coordinator that not all suggestions should be rewarded equally: some accepted suggestions should be rewarded several Q+ bucks; others should receive none. The gainsharing coordinator argued that even though all suggestions were not of equal value, it was necessary to reward even bogus suggestions, because some day that person would feel guilty and then be compelled to offer a legitimate suggestion. By the end of 1989, the total number of accepted suggestions had skyrocketed to 2,941.

Gainsharing Suspension

In August 1989, the company president transferred the gainsharing coordinator to a small, but essential, tumultuous department with problematic union employees. The company president chose the field service manager, the largest nonexecutive stockholder who had been with the company since 1966, to be the new gainsharing coordinator.

It soon became evident that the new gainsharing coordinator was the wrong person for the job: he did not have the respect of union employees and lacked the previous coordinator's interpersonal communication skills and finesse. His field service expertise also kept him away from the facility for lengthy periods. Because gainsharing coordination was added to his other responsibilities, he tended to neglect his gainsharing duties when emergencies arose, which happened often. It was obvious to nonmanagement employees that the new coordinator had too many responsibilities. Even the go-getters began to question the company president's commitment to gainsharing.

An electrician was able to get the new gainsharing coordinator's attention by flagrantly manipulating the Q+ buck program. The electrician, who up to this point had boycotted all gainsharing meetings, sought "revenge" on an engineer he did not like by taking a blueprint and highlighting 280 legitimate, though minor and irrelevant, errors. He showed the corrected drawing to his foreman and demanded 280 Q+ bucks. When the foreman told him to "get lost," the electrician threatened to spend the entire day writing up 280 separate suggestions. The new gainsharing coordinator was asked to intervene. He dispensed a few inflammatory words at the electrician and went on to other pressing business.

As a result of these manipulations, the new coordinator decided that it was necessary to evaluate the quality of all accepted suggestions. He refused to give a Q+ buck for minor routing changes, or "human comfort" suggestions (for example, reducing the noise level by changing tires on in-facility trucks from steel to rubber), and "grievance" types of suggestions. The former gainsharing coordinator argued that it was essential to reward all types of suggestions because it encouraged people to submit better ones, and because it was good for team members to formally "air their gripes" at gainsharing meetings he attended. Responding to employee complaints allowed people to go on to other issues. The new gainsharing coordinator disagreed with this approach and drastically reduced the Q+ buck program in late 1990.

The new gainsharing coordinator's decisions swayed many fence-sitters to the side of the opponents. The opponents told others: "See, now the company wants something for nothing again. It's bad enough that the bonuses are pitiful, now our suggestions aren't even worth a buck anymore."

Beginning with the 1987 election of the adversarial electrician to the union presidency, the union constantly threatened to boycott gainsharing team meetings whenever the company president irritated them. As the relationship between the union and company president soured on many labor issues, the union increasingly used gainsharing as a weapon to either get the attention of or get even with the company president.

Based on the fourteen semistructured interviews, nobody could remember exactly when the first union boycott of a gainsharing meeting took place or exactly what caused it. The general sense was that the boycotts just naturally evolved beyond the electricians and any one of many squabbles between the company president and the union could have caused it. The electricians had been boycotting gainsharing since its inception, so when an electrician was elected union president, it became part of standard operating policy to boycott gainsharing team meetings to get even for injustices, real or perceived. The team meeting boycotts were neither officially ordered by the union nor part of long-range union planning. Instead, the electricians simply encouraged others to join their boycott when contentious issues were not resolved in the union's favor.

The first time a significant number of union members boycotted a review board meeting was October 1990. It was in response to a flippant, derogatory remark made by the company president, but there was disagreement as to the events that led up to the derogatory remark. According to some interviewees, at the previous review board meeting the company president sarcastically said that profits would have been much higher if not for all the overtime. The union president questioned whether the company president was accusing union workers of deliberately "slacking off" so that they could earn overtime pay. Harsh words were exchanged, and the next review board meeting was boycotted by some union members, including the union president.

Other interviewees recalled a different set of circumstances that led to the review board boycott. According to them, the company president accused the electricians of intentionally causing a major machine problem. The electricians maintained that the company president "didn't know what the ——— he was talking about," and as a sign of protest, the union president (an electrician) and a few other oppositional union members encouraged others to boycott the next review board meeting.

In either case, up to this point the union president had always attended review board meetings but never a department team meeting, because of his role as president. He said he would not attend another review board meeting until the company president apologized publicly. The company president refused to apologize. The lines were drawn. Other union employees began to boycott both their gainsharing meetings and the review board meetings in support of the union president.

From the perspective of the company president, the nature of the gainsharing meeting boycott had changed in that it was no longer just a few unruly electricians. Now fence-sitters and even some go-getters were boycotting. In addition, the union was personally taking its anger out on the gainsharing program, even though the program had nothing to do with the problem. According to union members, the union knew that despite his choice of a new coordinator, the company president was committed to gainsharing. So the union took its anger out on gainsharing to get the president's attention.

Soon review board meetings became a matter of embarrassment for the company president. Managers, some of whom did not want to be there, attended the regularly scheduled review board meeting, but the union employees did not, and the company president became increasingly frustrated. The meetings evolved into what was jokingly called the company president's "State of the Union" address. He opened the meeting with a monthly performance appraisal and then complained about the union.

The result of new restrictions on Q+ buck suggestions and the union boycott was a drastic reduction in gainsharing suggestions, from approximately 245 per month between January and November 1990, to 23 in December 1990, and 14 in January 1991. Some go-getters continued to hold team meetings and attend the review board meeting because they believed that it was wrong for the union to take out its hostilities on gainsharing. Nonetheless, they did not try to stop the growing boycott and would not speak out against the union, which protected their interests in many other areas of work life.

Then, according to the minutes of the January 25, 1991, review board meeting, "[the company president] said that he will no longer be an advisor for [gainsharing] and that he will be redirecting his efforts to other areas." In addition, the minutes stated, gainsharing "will no longer be a high priority on his list."

This announcement shocked everybody, including the opponents. The company president had been very proud of his participatory management experiment. The facility had reduced costs substantially as a result of the more than eight thousand implemented suggestions. Communications had improved greatly. Managers were now better trained in group dynamics. Union members were more focused on product quality and cutting costs. In addition to health and safety improvements, gainsharing suggestions also improved the quality of tools and machinery. There were still barriers separating management, the union, and the engineers, but they had been reduced during five and a half years of gainsharing. Obviously, the union and the company president were in the midst of an intense disagreement, but this was nothing new. Opponents argued that the company president withdrew his support because the bonus was finally going to be a substantial one.

When interviewed for this field study, the company president had a difficult time discussing what led him to withdraw his support for gainsharing. He described his experience in terms of "going through a divorce." In 1985 he and the union had joined hands around the concept of gainsharing. At the time, he believed that gainsharing would last forever. It was a "win-win situation" for everybody, he said. There was bickering over the years but they were similar to the "occasional quarrels that all married couples have." Then, the union "slapped" him in the face by encouraging others who were not electricians to boycott gainsharing. Worse yet, the fence-sitters and some go-getters obeyed. That was "the last straw" for him. His emotions were drained; it was "time to call the marriage off." As he put it, "I wanted to treat the workers like adults and it didn't work well. Union relations were just too hostile so we are now back to a more traditional relationship. I don't like it, but that's all we can do."

The go-getters assumed that the company president would change his mind. He was an emotional person, so his current negative emotions toward gainsharing could reverse over time. In addition, he did not cancel the next review board meeting but merely said that he would be redirecting his energies. Still, the union did not call off the boycott. With no teams meeting, and with the company president unwilling to attend the February review board meeting, the meeting was very subdued and anticlimactic. The March review board meeting was the last. During the first three months of 1991, 30 suggestions had been accepted—a per-employee yearly rate of 0.6. In comparison, the 1990 yearly average was 11.40 accepted suggestions per employee. The April meeting seemed unnecessary and was suspended until further notice.

During the field study, managers blamed the union for the suspension, the union blamed management, and the engineers blamed both groups, placing slightly greater blame on management for giving up. A few people insisted that gainsharing was suspended, not abandoned, but everyone else, including the company president, insisted that the democratic aspects of gainsharing were dead. According to the company president, gainsharing had "stopped the bleeding," and it was time to try something new. He believed that a new work-cell team system was a viable way to get employees to act on the production-improvement suggestions they had been withholding since gainsharing was suspended.

After the Scanlon-type plan was abandoned, two residual gainsharing features remained: the group-based financial bonus, calculated on a quarterly basis, and the steering committee meetings to discuss the financial bonus. In June 1991, the employees earned a quarterly bonus of $75 per person based on the gainsharing cost of sales to net sales bonus calculation. The bonus was changed again in December 1991 based on meeting a targeted level of shipment value.

Conclusion

As with the facilities in five previous case studies, gainsharing at this facility had a host of outcomes that benefited management and nonmanagement employees directly and indirectly during the six years of the plan. The 8,114 suggestions implemented by the union members greatly improved the production process and communications, generated significant financial savings for Packaging International, led to the purchase of new tools and machinery, improved product quality, reduced costs, reduced grievances, improved health and safety, created less stressful work tasks, and reduced production employee resistance to changes in the production process. Engineers started to review their designs with production employees about three years after gainsharing was implemented. Packaging International was one of twelve suppliers from among a population of 19,000 to win the Miller Brewing Award. Production employees monitored vendor cost estimates, a habit developed as a result of the gainsharing bonus. These benefits are clearly attributable to gainsharing implementation, despite the types of power games played by various interest groups.

This case study was undertaken to examine interest group reactions at a facility that had failed in its attempt to permanently institutionalize gainsharing. The reasons for the failure are analyzed below in terms of five interest groups: management, engineers, union go-getters, union fence-sitters, and union opponents.

Management

At this particular facility, the management team was dominated by the company president. The president would be appropriately classified as a "petty tyrant" (Ashforth 1994). He lorded his power over others. Most managers feared his unpredictable wrath. The one vice president who opposed the president publicly was fired at a board of directors meeting. As such, there were no gainsharing opponents among the managers. The president wanted gainsharing to succeed, and the managers supported his desires. The only manager classified by others as a go-getter was the first gainsharing coordinator. All other managers were classified as fence-sitters, who acted like go-getters whenever the president pressured them to be more active.

The president's most unhealthy manipulative gainsharing behaviors were related to the gainsharing bonus. Contrary to the gainsharing consultant's advice, the president developed an initial bonus calculation that benefited management's interests (three managers, including the president, controlled 75 percent of the company's stock) to the exclusion of the nonmanagement employees in two ways. First, the calculation was based on total costs rather than only cost factors that the production workers affected directly. For instance, the financial benefits of production improvements could be eliminated by an expensive marketing campaign. Second, reserve pool deficits were carried over rather than eliminated at year-end.

The president's conflicting emotions about the gainsharing bonus were also exemplified by his behavior regarding the unexpected Christmas 1985 gainsharing bonus and the manner in which the calculation was changed in 1988. Although the first bonus was officially scheduled for January 1986, the president wanted to inspire nonmanagement employees with a $75 gainsharing bonus at Christmas. This generous offering was actually a financial sham, however. According to facility records, employees had earned a $270 bonus. In 1988, when it was obvious that the calculation had to be changed, the president eliminated one obvious problem—the year-end reserve pool deficit—but not the other obvious problem—using total costs as the basis for the bonus.

The president also did not use good judgement in choosing the second gainsharing coordinator. His primary criterion was loyalty to Packaging International in terms of stock ownership and seniority, rather than the ability to manage people. In a cost-saving move, gainsharing duties were added to the field manager's existing job responsibilities rather than replacing some of them.

Last, the company president did the equivalent of declaring martial law when the opponent-led union boycott of gainsharing team meetings spread to fence-sitters and go-getters. In summarizing the political science literature on transforming dictatorships to democracies, O'Donnell and Schmitter (1986) have invoked the metaphor of a multilevel chess game to describe interest-group behavior. They note that "during the transition it is always possible for some contestants to kick over the board, or where authoritarian players still monopolize control over the pieces of organized violence, to remove their opponents by force" (67). Thus, the company president, suddenly realizing that the gainsharing chess board was attached to a union grievance chess board, declared an end to gainsharing.

Engineers

Eight percent of the facility's employees were engineers. They worked on the second floor of the assembly facility, segregated from both management and the union employees. They believed that writing suggestions and earning a financial bonus were contrary to their professional duty to reduce costs and implement improvement-related suggestions. From their perspective, gainsharing was an incentive aimed at motivating union employees. For the most part, the engineers were fence-sitters throughout Packaging International's six years of gainsharing. They did not participate in the early gainsharing calculation meetings nor did they care that gainsharing was abandoned.

On two occasions, an opponent coalition was formed within their ranks. The first time was when the initial wave of suggestions arrived regarding engineering designs. Several engineers were very defensive about hourly production employees criticizing their work. Their anxieties were alleviated somewhat because these suggestions were coming from go-getters they respected. The second time was when the union opponent threatened to submit 280 blueprint suggestions to correct 280 legitimate but irrelevant blueprint errors. The engineers were pleased when informed that the second gainsharing coordinator reprimanded the union opponent who threatened to submit the suggestions. Because production employees offered many helpful blueprint suggestions through gainsharing, the engineers began consulting production employees prior to completing their blueprints.

Union Go-Getters

Union go-getters were attracted to gainsharing because it provided them with a voice in workplace decisions and formal authority to make changes in the production process. The position of gainsharing representative was most appealing to the lead men—union production employees with cross-sectional training and some formal authority. Go-getters wanted employee participation and the gainsharing bonus, but they were willing to sacrifice the bonus for employee involvement. They did not complain about the obvious manipulations of the bonus calculation by the president because this was not a high-priority agenda item for them. When no bonuses were forthcoming, they defended managerial discretion for determining the calculation factors. These employees were more sensitive to receiving recognition awards and immediate dollar payouts for their suggestions during the Q+ buck program than the monthly financial bonuses.

Unlike the fence-sitters and the opponents, the go-getters interpreted the industry-wide recession as a motive to become even more active in gainsharing. Reducing costs could save jobs. The layoffs resulting from the recession had a significant negative impact on the ranks of go-getters. Many of the go-getters were younger employees, so the seniority-based layoff system resulted in the dismissal of many go-getters.

Go-getters defended the right of union members to be adversarial toward management and gainsharing. They unsuccessfully attempted to win over the opponents by showing how a gainsharing suggestion could make work less strenuous. They became annoyed with opponents who manipulated the Q+ buck game, but they argued in favor of the game's egalitarian rules because it encouraged fence-sitters to submit suggestions.

Nonetheless, go-getters were loyal union members. When given a choice between union allegiance or gainsharing at the time of the union boycott, the go-getters chose union allegiance. The union represented them in collective bargaining, grievance claims, and efforts to improve working conditions. They defended the right of union opponents to boycott meetings and grudgingly joined that boycott when it spread beyond the electricians. They were shocked when the president responded by suspending gainsharing but rationalized that the president's erratic action showed why the union was so necessary.

Union Fence-Sitters

Union fence-sitters trusted other members of the union to shape the rules of gainsharing in a way that benefited their interests. In this particular case, the fence-sitters were let down by both the go-getters and union leaders. The go-getters quickly acquiesced to management manipulation of the bonus because they were more interested in the participative component of gainsharing. Union leaders refused to participate in developing the bonus calculation because they did not want it to appear as if they were being "bribed" to participate. Thus, when no bonus was earned during the first official bonus month despite obvious production improvements, fence-sitters agreed with union opponents that management must be manipulating the books. The fence-sitters did respond well to both the recognition awards and Q+ buck program.

The Q+ buck program highlights the conflicting feelings of the fence-sitters. Receiving a dollar for a suggestion motivated many of them to offer suggestions they had been thinking about but never offered formally. Many of them became annoyed with union opponents who were blatantly manipulating the rules of the game, while other fence-sitters joined the manipulative games. When the second gainsharing coordinator changed the rules, however, many fence-sitters sided with the opponents. They believed that the new rules were too strict. The human comfort and grievance suggestions that previously improved their working conditions had been eliminated from Q+ buck consideration. An important opportunity to sway the fence-sitters to the side of the go-getters had been mismanaged. Fence-sitters easily chose to rally behind the union boycott rather than gainsharing.

Union Opponents

Union opponents refused to participate in deciding the rules for the gainsharing factor they cared about most—the financial bonus. Many of them fulfilled their desire to participate in decision-making processes by becoming active union members. This aspect of gainsharing did not appeal to them. The monthly financial bonus did appeal to them. If, however, they provided input on how the bonus calculation should be structured, then others might perceive them to be in favor of gainsharing. It was more important to them to appear "antigainsharing," so they refused to help devise an equitable calculation. When no bonuses were earned the first few months, the opponents argued that it was foolish for union members to try to reduce overtime. They asked the fence-sitters why someone should work hard to reduce overtime when, at the end of the month, there was no bonus.

The strongest opponent work group consisted of electricians. During the first year and a half, the electricians refused to hold a team meeting or offer a suggestion. When Packaging International provided recognition awards, which inspired the go-getters and fence-sitters, opponents accused other union members of selling out to management. Why should Packaging International provide an equitable gainsharing bonus, they asked, if employees were willing to settle for a cheap coffee mug with the company's name on it? When the recession-caused layoffs occurred, opponents argued that the layoffs were the result of all the efficiency-related suggestions the go-getters and the fence-sitters had implemented.

Thus, with the passage of time, gainsharing became a weapon used by union opponents against management. This was particularly evident during the Q+ dollar program. When the program began, adversarial union members criticized management for admitting that the suggestions of union employees were only worth a buck. These statements were made to encourage fence-sitters to withdraw from gainsharing participation. When this strategy failed, the oppositional union member who manipulated the new financial incentive system by threatening to submit 280 suggestions highlighting minor blueprint errors was regarded as a hero by the opponents. When the new gainsharing coordinator changed the rules to void such manipulative suggestions, oppositional union members told fence-sitters that their suggestions were now not even worth a buck. This was a no-win situation for gainsharing proponents, and a no-lose situation for gainsharing opponents. The ultimate union weapon was boycotting gainsharing meetings to gain the attention of the president on issues unrelated to gainsharing.

Summary

Packaging International had difficulties with all four conflict-of-interest exchange relationships diagrammed in Figure 2-2. The company president allowed greater employee involvement by assigning all employees to gainsharing teams. As a result, Packaging International received more than eight thousand production-related performance improvement suggestions, which, in turn, improved production output and reduced production costs significantly. On the other hand, the company president restricted the group-based financial bonus by choosing a very broad-based calculation and carrying over negative year-end reserve pool totals. Nonmanagement go-getters permitted this manipulation. Union officials refused to participate in developing the ground rules for gainsharing.

During six years of gainsharing, nonmanagement employees restricted their participation for a variety of reasons. Many engineers believed that gainsharing involvement was contrary to their professional status. Union electricians refused to participate because gainsharing blurred the distinction between the responsibilities of management and labor. Events associated with the second gainsharing coordinator led many nonmanagement fence-sitters to form an alliance with opponents. Whereas the first gainsharing coordinator encouraged employee participation by permitting the discussion of employee grievances at gainsharing team meetings and the submission of "creature comfort" suggestions, the second gainsharing eliminated both successful gainsharing amendments. In addition, the facility manager added gainsharing duties to the second gainsharing coordinator's already existing responsibilities, instead of substituting the new duties for some of the existing ones. The overworked coordinator lacked the communication skills of the first coordinator and used his fieldwork responsibilities away from Packaging International as an excuse for not appropriately managing gainsharing emergencies. At around this time, Packaging International's seniority-based layoff system caused tremendous changes in team dynamics, particularly when younger gainsharing team leaders were moved to a different work cell or laid off. All these activities, along with infrequent and small gainsharing bonuses, restricted employee participation, production process information, and employee wages.

Finally, oppositional union electricians never became involved in gainsharing activities. Management's ill-advised strategy of leaving them alone only solidified the oppositional power base. Opponents increased their power when an adversarial electrician was elected union president. Nongainsharing confrontations between the new adversarial union president and the company president, to the company president's surprise, strengthened the boycott of gainsharing activities. The facility manager abandoned gainsharing when nonmanagement go-getters reluctantly participated in the boycott.

PART IV

Summaries and Ethical Directions

10 Power Games, Outcomes, and Lessons Learned of Scanlon-Type Gainsharing Plans

In-depth case studies were conducted at the six manufacturing facilities for a particular reason. In addition to being nonunion and privately owned, Cylinder Lifts had small average monthly gainsharing bonuses (1.2 percent/$18). Foam Seats and Forestland had relatively modest average monthly gainsharing bonuses (5.2 percent/$63 and 6.8 percent/$85). Innovations had large average monthly bonuses (19.3 percent/$370). Innovations-Brotherhood had very small average monthly gainsharing bonuses (0.4 percent/$12). Packaging International, which had small average monthly gainsharing bonuses (1.2 percent/$25), was chosen because it abandoned gainsharing after six years.

Scanlon-Type Gainsharing Plan Paradoxes

The data in Table 10-1 strongly suggest that managers, consultants, and researchers should avoid simplistic one factor explanations for gainsharing successes and failures. If these facilities had been included in a large sample, determining which of the six facilities should be considered successes or failures would depend on how success was measured. If success was measured in terms of the average number of suggestions per employee per year, Innovations (4.9) and Cylinder Lifts (3.7) were quite successful, whereas Foam Seats (1.3) and Forestland (0.6) appear to be failures. In terms of average monthly gainsharing bonuses, however, Innovations (19.3 percent) was by far the most successful; Forestland (6.8 percent) and Foam Seats (5.2 percent) were moderately successful; and

Table 10–1.   Nonunion survey factors: Statistical means

Factor	Cylinder Lifts	Foam Seats	Forest Land	Innovations
Management support	3.3	3.1	3.8	3.3
Supervisor support	3.4	3.1	4.0	3.3
Team representative support	3.2	3.1	3.5	3.3
Employee support	3.1	3.1	3.6	3.5
Suggestion processing	3.2	3.2	3.6	3.2
Team meetings	3.5	3.1	3.5	3.1
Review board meetings	3.7	3.2	3.6	3.3
Bonus calculation	1.8	2.6	3.1	3.4
Facility-wide effort	3.2	3.3	3.9	3.7
Trust	2.4	2.7	3.1	3.0
Employee identity	3.3	3.0	3.4	3.3
Employee influence	2.4	3.0	3.3	3.3
Justice	2.9	3.0	3.1	3.1
Management style[a]	2.7	2.6	2.9	2.6
Average no. of suggestions per employee per year	3.7	1.3	0.6	4.9
Average monthly bonus %	1.2%	5.2%	6.8%	19.3%
Average monthly bonus $	$18	$63	$85	$370

[a]All factors measured with a 1–5 Likert scale (1=Strongly disagree, 3=Neutral, 5=Strongly agree), except management style, which was measured with a 1–4 Likert scale.

Cylinder Lifts (1.2 percent) was a failure. Why did Cylinder Lifts have the lowest gainsharing payouts yet a relatively high number of suggestions per employee? Why did Cylinder Lifts and Innovations have a similarly high number of suggestions per employee yet opposite extreme outcomes in terms of average monthly bonus payouts? Why did Foam Seats and Forestland have a very low number of suggestions per employee yet modest gainsharing payouts? Importantly, management and nonmanagement employees at all four facilities were looking forward to many more years of gainsharing.

The survey data gathered at the time of the field study add further complexity to the issue of gainsharing success and failure. (See Chapter 3 for a discussion of the gainsharing evaluation and attitude survey administered at the four nonunion facilities at the time of the field study.) Table 10-1 shows that the size of the gainsharing bonus is not very predictive of gainsharing support, efficiency of gainsharing activities, work climate, or management styles at the four nonunion facilities. Compare the results of Cylinder Lifts, which had the lowest gainsharing bonuses, with Innovations, which had the highest gainsharing bonuses. As should be expected, Innovations, as compared with Cylinder Lifts, had significantly higher scores for facility-wide gainsharing effort, fairness of the bonus calculation, employee support for gainsharing, trust, and employee influence. But why are the scores for management support, supervisor support, team representative support, suggestion processing, employee identity, and justice approximately the same for the two facilities? In addition, why does Cylinder Lifts, compared to Innovations, have higher scores for team meetings and review board meetings?

The data in Table 10-1 contain many other paradoxes. Why does Forestland, which has the lowest number of suggestions per employee, have the highest scores for management support, supervisor support, suggestion processing, and facility-wide gainsharing effort? Why does Innovations, which has the highest gainsharing bonuses, have such modest scores for management support, supervisor support, team representative support, suggestion processing, team meetings, trust, and justice? Finally, why, after four years of gainsharing, is the management style at all four nonunion facilities slightly below "consultative"—still a major step away from the goal of participatory management style?

It is because of these many complex questions that a theory of gainsharing grounded in the political science literature was developed and in-depth case studies were conducted at six facilities with Scanlon-type plans.

The literature review in Chapter 1 concluded with this question: Given that so much has been written about how to appropriately implement and manage Scanlon-type gainsharing plans, why don't managers just design them right, implement them appropriately, and support them so they will succeed? Chapter 2 provided several answers based on the political behaviors of workplace interest groups. For the most part, managers restrain employee involvement in decision making and employee wages, whereas nonmanagement employees restrain information about the production process and production output. Each interest group wants what the other interest group restrains.

Scanlon-type plans offer a democratic solution to this historical conflict of interests. As shown in Figure 2-2, by implementing a plan, managers allow nonmanagement employees greater access to decision making. As a result, nonmanagement employees provide information about problems with the production process and improve their production output. Last, nonmanagement employees earn a gainsharing bonus that reflects their production improvements.

Neither managers nor nonmanagement employees are monolithic interest groups. Based on insights from the political science literature on what happens when authoritarian right- or left-wing governments adopt democratic principles, management and nonmanagement interest groups can be further differentiated according to their reactions to gainsharing, namely, *go-getters*, *fence-sitters*, and *opponents*. The two power games and two outcomes propositions were derived to guide an understanding of the dynamics associated with each interest group during a facility's gainsharing experience. The field study revealed several common trends at the six facilities regarding the power games and outcomes propositions.

Power Games and Outcomes

P1: Manipulating the Transitional Process

The first proposition predicted that management and nonmanagement employees will likely manipulate the transitional process based on their own interests. Throughout this book, the Scanlon-type plan recommended by the consultant serves as an ideal version that all six facilities are measured against. The consultant has had more than twenty years of experience implementing the plans and has coauthored many books and articles on the subject. Given the unique context of each facility, the consultant presented a form of gainsharing that entailed a significant amount of employee involvement in both decision making and the financial gains from improved performance. The steering committees at each facility could either adopt or modify his recommendation. If they chose to modify it, the steering committee could further enhance or restrict the participatory mechanisms.

In terms of employee involvement in decision making, the gainsharing consultant made specific recommendations to all six facilities regarding the structure and process of the suggestion system, gainsharing teams, and review board. Two steering committees (at Forestland and Packaging International) accepted the gainsharing consultant's specific recommendations. Three steering committees (at Cylinder Lifts, Foam Seats, and Innovations) modified the recommendations and pursued strategies that would limit employee participation. One steering committee (at Innovations-Brotherhood) modified these recommendations and pursued a strategy that enhanced employee involvement. In addition, the facilities pursued strategies to enhance or restrict employee involvement that were unrelated to specific recommendations by the gainsharing consultant.

The consultant also made specific recommendations to all six facilities regarding the structure of and payout process for the group-based finan-

cial bonus. All six steering committees modified these recommendations. Managers at four facilities (Cylinder Lifts, Foam Seats, Forestland,
and Packaging International) pursued strategies that made it more difficult for employees to earn a gainsharing bonus. At International-Brotherhood, the union pursued a strategy that made the gainsharing bonus
more difficult to earn. The management at only one facility (Innovations)
made the gainsharing bonus easier for employees to earn. Strategies to
enhance or restrict the gainsharing bonus that were unrelated to specific
recommendations by the gainsharing consultant were implemented as
well.

Specific power games that management and nonmanagement employees pursued during the transitional process at the six facilities are
listed below in terms of four central aspects of Scanlon-type plans: the
group-based financial bonus, department teams, the review board, and
the suggestion system / gainsharing coordination. As noted in Chapter 2,
although a negative connotation is typically placed on the concept of
power, it is a neutral term. Power games may therefore be either constructive or detrimental.

Constructive Group-Based Financial Bonus Power Games
1. Managers choose a 75/25 bonus ratio—75 percent for employees
and 25 percent for the facility—rather than a 50/50 ratio (Innovations).

Detrimental Group-Based Financial Bonus Power Games
1. Managers choose a bonus calculation that is linked only indirectly
to improved performance, thus giving them flexibility to manipulate accounting numbers to minimize the bonus earned (Cylinder Lifts, Foam
Seats, Packaging International).
2. Managers choose a historical standard based on a year of high productivity and profitability, rather than on a three-year standard that
would allow for peaks and valleys (Cylinder Lifts).
3. Managers choose a weighted calculation for the historical base period, with the most recent year—which is the most productive year—
counting for one-half of the standard (Forestland).
4. Managers choose a 33/67 bonus ratio—33 percent for employees
and 67 percent for the facility—rather than a 50/50 ratio (Cylinder Lifts).
5. Managers choose to roll over negative reserve pool amounts to the
following fiscal year rather than eliminate them (Packaging International).
6. Managers cap the amount of employee bonuses that can be earned
during a year (Forestland).

7. Managers choose only compliant nonmanagement employees to be members of the steering committee (Cylinder Lifts, Foam Seats).

8. Union leaders support a bonus calculation that is linked only indirectly to improved performance because it contains an important financial factor that they can use in collective bargaining efforts (Innovations-Brotherhood).

9. Nonmanagement employees choose to roll over negative reserve pool amounts to the following fiscal year rather than eliminate them (Forestland).

10. Nonmanagement employees refuse to contribute to bonus calculation discussions so that they can blame management for manipulating the calculation if bonuses are not earned (all facilities).

11. Engineers refuse to contribute to calculation discussions because it is "beneath" them (Packaging International).

Constructive Department Team Power Games

1. Managers assign everyone to a gainsharing team (Forestland, Innovations-Brotherhood).

2. Managers transform work cells into gainsharing teams (Innovations-Brotherhood).

3. Managers create intershift teams in addition to shift teams to work out problems among work shifts (Innovations-Brotherhood).

4. Managers encourage nonmanagement employees to discuss employee grievances at team meetings (Forestland, Innovations, Innovations-Brotherhood, Packaging International).

Detrimental Department Team Power Games

1. To minimize costs, managers create one team for the entire facility, with one member per department on the team, rather than a team for every department (Cylinder Lifts).

2. Managers create one team for the entire department across shifts rather than one team per shift (Foam Seats).

3. Managers create one team for the entire department rather than one team per work cell (Innovations).

4. Managers assign a management employee, rather than a nonmanagement employee, to manage the department team meetings (Foam Seats).

5. Managers discourage nonmanagement employees from attending department team meetings by scheduling them to work when their team meetings are being held (Cylinder Lifts, Foam Seats, Packaging International).

6. Managers schedule team meetings after working hours (Foam Seats).

7. Nonmanagement employees elect an unqualified team representative (that is, one who may have difficulty reading or writing) (Cylinder Lifts).

8. Nonmanagement employees chastise team representatives for acting like managers (all facilities).

9. Nonmanagement employees interrupt team meetings (all facilities).

Constructive Review Board Power Games

1. Managers develop a review board with more nonmanagement employees than management employees (Cylinder Lifts, Innovations, Innovations-Brotherhood).

2. Managers encourage nonmanagement employees to solve suggestion disputes (Cylinder Lifts).

Detrimental Review Board Power Games

1. Managers develop a review board with more management than nonmanagement employees so that they can be certain to win any votes on contentious issues (Cylinder Lifts, Innovations).

2. Managers dominate the agenda and discussions (Foam Seats).

3. Nonmanagement employees raise contentious nongainsharing-related issues (Packaging International).

Constructive Suggestion System/Gainsharing Coordinator Power Games

1. Managers provide awards for employee suggestions (all facilities).

2. Managers permit nonmanagement employees to determine the gainsharing coordinator (Foam Seats, Innovations-Brotherhood).

3. Managers assign nonmanagement employees to task teams to discuss problems with the gainsharing system (all facilities).

Detrimental Suggestion System/Gainsharing Coordinator Power Games

1. Managers do not allocate sufficient time or money to implement suggestions (Cylinder Lifts, Foam Seats, Packaging International).

2. Managers choose a gainsharing coordinator without obtaining input from nonmanagement employees (Cylinder Lifts, Foam Seats, Forestland, Innovations, Packaging International).

3. Management adds the new gainsharing coordination responsibilities to an employee's full-time work duties (Cylinder Lifts, Foam Seats, Innovations).

4. Team representatives reject suggestions or delay accepting sugges-

tions for political reasons—for example, they dislike the employee or the department team making the suggestion (all facilities).

5. A key organizational interest group that is responsible for implementing many suggestions (e.g., engineers or maintenance employees) intentionally delays implementation (Foam Seats, Packaging International).

P2: Interest Group Power Struggles

The second proposition predicted that power struggles will likely arise among and between go-getters, fence-sitters, and opponents in both management and nonmanagement interest groups. Each of the six interest groups exhibited unique behavior regarding employee suggestions, gainsharing teams, and the group-based financial bonus. (See Tables 10-2 and 10-3 for a summary of interest group attitudes and behaviors as they relate to various gainsharing activities.)

Management Go-Getters. Management go-getters included the facility manager or owner at each facility. They chose to implement gainsharing because they believed that it would generate many favorable outcomes. All six facilities had other managers who were go-getters. At two facilities (Forestland and Innovations), all of the managers were categorized as go-getters. The other four facilities had managers who were also fence-sitters or opponents.

Management go-getters considered the submission of suggestions by nonmanagement employees to be a tremendous opportunity to learn about production process issues. To encourage more suggestions, management go-getters guaranteed that efficiency-related gainsharing suggestions would not result in employee layoffs. If a suggestion eliminated a particular job task, that employee would be shifted to another job task. Management go-getters also developed a wide variety of incentives to encourage employee suggestions, such as the 100/100/100 contest at Innovations and the Q+ buck game at Packaging International. Other incentives included facility jackets, coffee mugs, gift certificates, parking spaces, and employee of the month awards.

One management go-getter decided to adopt weekly, rather than monthly, gainsharing team meetings. Some management go-getters assigned all, rather than some, nonmanagement employees to gainsharing teams. They also created task teams to explore gainsharing-related issues. The facility manager at Forestland had to stop attending team meetings so that nonmanagement employees on the teams would take responsibility for their own decisions.

Table 10–2. Management attitudes and behaviors toward gainsharing activities

Interest Group	Suggestion System	Teams	Financial Bonus
Go-Getters	• The suggestion system provided an opportunity to learn about production process problems • Managers guaranteed employees that they would not be laid off as a result of a suggestion or production improvements • Employees were given rewards for submitting suggestions	• The facility created task teams for gainsharing-related issues • Weekly team meetings were instituted • All employees were assigned to teams • Nonmanagement employees were encouraged to take responsibility for team decisions	• The bonus calculation was manipulated to favor the facility • Managers were embarrassed when facility profits increased but no gainsharing bonus was paid out • The bonus calculation was revised to be more equitable
Fence-Sitters	• Suggestions seemed to be criticisms of managers' work • The facility manager might use the suggestions to evaluate employees' performance negatively • Nonmanagement employees should not make changes without management permission	• Team meetings may have been an unnecessary waste of time • Production employees attending meetings may have been slacking off	• Production improvements may have been achieved without the financial bonus
Opponents	• Suggestion submissions were discouraged • Suggestions were thought to be criticisms of managers' work • The facility manager would use suggestions to evaluate performance negatively • Nonmanagement employees should not make changes without management permission • Production employees discussing suggestions are just slacking off	• Team meetings were an unnecessary waste of time • Production employees attending meetings were scolded for slacking off	• Production improvements could have been achieved without the financial bonus

Table 10-3. Nonmanagement attitudes and behaviors toward gainsharing activities

Interest Group	Suggestion System	Teams	Financial Bonus
Go-Getters	• Responded quickly to suggestions • Continued to offer suggestions even though bonuses were small • Submitted suggestions on behalf of fence-sitters and opponents • Tried to make fence-sitters and opponents feel guilty when bonuses were earned • Wanted individual recognition for their suggestions • Formed coalitions for key suggestions	• Ran for initial team leadership positions • Took full responsibility for team activities • Attended other team meetings • Competed with other teams for productivity improvements • Put opponents and fence-sitters on task teams	• Permitted bonus manipulation by managers because they were primarily interested in employee involvement in decision making
Fence-Sitters	• Trusted nonmanagement go-getters until proven otherwise • Offered "safe" suggestions • Monitored their suggestion's evolution closely • Withheld suggestions when bonuses were low • Felt guilty for withholding suggestions when bonuses were earned • Assumed managers knew about production problems • Did not like to make changes without management's permission	• Preferred that go-getters took team leadership positions • Did not want to be forced to attend meetings	• Motivated strongly by bonus payouts • Withheld suggestions until bonus payouts were forthcoming

Table 10-3.   (*Continued*)

Interest Group	Suggestion System	Teams	Financial Bonus
Opponents	• Submitted very critical suggestions • Monitored their suggestion's evolution closely • Assumed managers only wanted cheap suggestions • Critical of go-getters for rejecting suggestions	• Refused to vote • Treated vote as a joke • Embarrassed and denigrated management and nonmanagement go-getters at meetings • Did not want to be forced to attend meetings	• Motivated strongly by bonus payouts • Assumed managers were manipulating the bonus • Assumed savings were being used to subsidize other costs rather than for the bonus • Analyzed bonus in terms of potential overtime losses • Monitored shipments in relation to bonus payouts • Believed bonus should be based on equal monetary payouts, not equal percentage of salary

Management go-getters were embarrassed if facility profits increased, but no gainsharing bonus was earned. When this occurred over several consecutive months or years, these managers were compelled to revise the bonus calculation so that it would better reflect the many performance improvements implemented by nonmanagement employees. Nonetheless, many management go-getters were willing to accept or participate in bonus calculation manipulations that favored the facility over nonmanagement employees.

Management Fence-Sitters. Four of the six facilities (Cylinder Lifts, Foam Seats, Innovations-Brotherhood, and Packaging International) had management fence-sitters. This was the largest management interest group at these facilities. Gainsharing was the facility manager's experiment, and management fence-sitters responded favorably when asked. For the most part, they considered gainsharing to be extra work, meetings, and paperwork.

Management fence-sitters were critical of nonmanagement employees who stopped the production process to discuss production gainsharing issues or to attend team meetings. They believed that employees might be using gainsharing as an excuse to put less effort into their work. Management fence-sitters tended to regard nonmanagement employee suggestions as criticisms of their performance. High-quality suggestions made them feel as though they were performing their job duties inadequately. They feared that the facility manager might conclude that they were not performing their jobs well. In addition, they were not comfortable with nonmanagement employees making changes in something that management designed.

Management fence-sitters also avoided attending gainsharing meetings because they believed that the meetings were a waste of time.

Moreover, they wondered whether the bonus payouts were necessary to obtain the benefits of gainsharing. These sentiments were particularly strong among Forestland and Innovations' managers located at corporate headquarters.

Management Opponents. Four of the six facilities (Cylinder Lifts, Foam Seats, Innovations-Brotherhood, and Packaging International) had management opponents. They constituted a small proportion of the managers at these facilities. For the most part, they considered gainsharing to be the latest management fad that, like other previous fads, would be abandoned by the facility manager when it inevitably failed. Gainsharing meant unnecessary extra work, meetings, and paperwork. Management opponents either became fence-sitters or quit.

Management opponents shared many of the sentiments listed above for management fence-sitters but to a more extreme degree. They discouraged nonmanagement employees from submitting gainsharing suggestions. They scolded nonmanagement employees who stopped the production process to discuss production gainsharing issues and made disparaging remarks to employees who submitted suggestions. Like the fence-sitters, management opponents interpreted employee suggestions as critical of their performance abilities. High-quality suggestions made them feel as though they were inadequately performing their job duties. They feared that the facility manager would conclude that they were not performing their jobs well. In addition, management opponents sometimes scolded nonmanagement employees who made changes in the production process without first obtaining permission or took time from production work to attend team meetings.

Many management opponents refused to attend gainsharing meetings because they believed the meetings were a waste of time. If they did attend, they would not share ideas on how to improve suggestions being discussed. Management opponents also believed that production improvements were obtainable without the gainsharing bonus.

Nonmanagement Go-Getters. All six facilities had nonmanagement go-getters. Importantly, nonmanagement go-getters were not coopted by management as a result of gainsharing. They were willing to put pressure on nonmanagement fence-sitters and opponents to participate in gainsharing activities, but they were not willing to discipline oppositional co-workers. When faced with an ultimatum to support either management or the union, nonmanagement go-getters at International-Brotherhood supported the union. From the perspective of nonmanagement go-getters, there were clear distinctions between managers and themselves, no matter how much responsibility they were willing to assume. Managers had higher wages, attractive offices, better cars, greater autonomy, and the authority to hire and fire. At the time of the field studies, nonmanagement go-getters were the most influential nonmanagement group at two of the six facilities (Forestland and Innovations).

Nonmanagement go-getters offered many suggestions for improving their work areas, making better quality products, and improving overall facility performance. They also wanted to do as much as possible to avoid potential layoffs. They continued to offer suggestions even if financial bonuses were small and management was manipulating the bonus calculation, because they were primarily interested in the employee involvement mechanism of gainsharing. They also wanted to receive individual recognition for their suggestions and fought against trends to put a team name on a suggestion that one employee was primarily responsible for developing.

Nonmanagement go-getters formed coalitions with other teams for key suggestions that were expensive or had high management opposition (such as health and safety improvements or the purchase of new machines). They submitted suggestions on behalf of fence-sitters and opponents to get them more involved, help generate a bonus, or encourage prosocial sentiments. Nonmanagement go-getters felt obligated to respond as quickly as possible to these suggestions. They also tried to make fence-sitters and opponents feel guilty for not contributing suggestions when bonuses were earned.

Nonmanagement go-getters wanted to be elected to positions of responsibility. They took responsibility for team activities and attended other gainsharing team meetings to see how they operated and what issues they dealt with. They also competed among themselves to determine which team or department could generate the most productivity improvements. They assigned fence-sitters and opponents to task teams with the hope of increasing their commitment to gainsharing.

Nonmanagement go-getters permitted managers to manipulate the bonus calculation because they were primarily interested in employee participation, not the bonus. Nonmanagement go-getters at Cylinder Lifts argued that the manipulation was fair because the owner was risking his capital. At Forestland, they insisted that it was unfair for the facility to have to absorb year-end reserve pool deficits.

Nonmanagement Fence-Sitters. Fence-sitters were the largest group of nonmanagement employees when gainsharing was implemented at all six facilities. Both nonmanagement go-getters and nonmanagement opponents attempted to form alliances with them. Nonmanagement fence-sitters trusted that the go-getters represented their best interests in gainsharing activities until proven otherwise. At the time of the field studies, nonmanagement fence-sitters were the dominant interest group at two of the six facilities (Cylinder Lifts and International-Brotherhood), both of which had many beneficial production changes but very small financial bonuses.

Nonmanagement fence-sitters struggled with the idea that managers really wanted their suggestions. They assumed that managers were aware of production problems. If a problem was obvious to a fence-sitter they assumed that it was also obvious to management. Unlike go-getters, nonmanagement fence-sitters were very hesitant to make any production process changes without management approval. They tended to offer suggestions that made their jobs less stressful (such as moving supplies closer to the work area) and would not arouse any criticism or controversy. They also offered many health and safety suggestions.

Fence-sitters observed closely how long it took their suggestions to be placed on the team agenda and then discussed and implemented. The quicker the suggestions were processed, the quicker they offered another suggestion. They felt guilty when a substantial gainsharing bonus was generated while they were still withholding helpful suggestions. They also justified withholding production improvement suggestions because of low bonus payouts.

Nonmanagement fence-sitters wanted go-getters to take team leadership responsibilities. They defined their contribution to gainsharing in terms of working efficiently on the production floor and submitting an occasional suggestion. They rebelled against being forced to attend team meetings.

These fence-sitters also carefully monitored the frequency and size of each bonus. They were much more motivated by the financial rewards from gainsharing than by employee involvement mechanisms. From their perspective, management had promised that under gainsharing, bonuses would be earned based on production process improvements. In these employees' view, if bonuses were forthcoming, then gainsharing was legitimate, and they would offer suggestions. If bonuses were not forthcoming, however, then fence-sitters assumed that management was being manipulative, and they lost faith in the gainsharing system. Non-management fence-sitters responded well to other financial incentives for submitting suggestions, such as the Q+ buck program at Packaging International. They also responded well to other suggestion rewards, such as winning a coffee mug or T-shirt.

Nonmanagement Opponents. All six facilities had nonmanagement opponents at the beginning of gainsharing implementation and several years later. At the time of the field studies, opponents were the most influential nonmanagement group at two of the six facilities (Foam Seats and Packaging International). Nonmanagement opponents did not trust management. From their perspective, gainsharing implementation was the latest attempt by management to exploit nonmanagement employees by "getting something" (production performance improvements) for "nothing" (no bonus, or a very small one). They fueled negative perceptions of gainsharing activities and were cynical about production improvements that benefited them.

Nonmanagement opponents took advantage of problems with the suggestion process to persuade nonmanagement fence-sitters to withhold their involvement. If suggestion processing was slow, opponents told fence-sitters that the system was not legitimate. If a suggestion was rejected, they told fence-sitters that the go-getters running the teams really did not want their suggestions. If an expensive suggestion was rejected, they told fence-sitters that management only wanted inexpensive suggestions. The occasional suggestion offered by nonmanagement opponents was either highly critical of previous managerial decisions or related to health and safety.

Many nonmanagement opponents refrained from voting in team representative elections because they believed they would be "selling out" by doing so. At Cylinder Lifts, a coalition of nonmanagement opponents elected a very shy production employee who could neither read nor write to be a gainsharing team representative. Their motivation was to force the facility manager to issue a recall election, which he did not do. They rebelled against being forced to attend gainsharing meetings by embarrassing or denigrating managers. They accused nonmanagement go-getters of selling out to management.

Nonmanagement opponents were convinced that managers manipulated the calculation until proven otherwise. From their perspective, managers used the financial improvements generated by gainsharing suggestions and production process changes to subsidize other facility costs rather than distribute the savings as a bonus. They also opposed the manner in which the gainsharing bonus was distributed. According to federal law, gainsharing bonuses must be distributed as an equal percentage of employee wages (e.g., 5 percent for everyone) rather than an equal monetary amount ($100 for everyone). Opponents argued that the bonus system was unfair because managers, who had higher wages than production employees, earned larger monetary bonuses.

When bonuses were not forthcoming, the opponents formed alliances with shipping employees to document the financial value of shipments. Opponents maintained that gainsharing bonuses should be forthcoming if the financial value of shipments were higher than the historical standard or if profits increased. If there was no bonus, then managers were manipulating the bonus calculation. When bonuses were paid, nonmanagement opponents believed they earned them, despite their lack of suggestions or team participation, because they had worked hard on the production floor. Last, many opponents weighed the amount of the gainsharing bonus against the amount of overtime income lost due to productivity improvements. If the gainsharing bonuses were consistently larger, such as at Innovations, then their opposition decreased.

Each of the six facilities had opponents who evolved into fence-sitters or go-getters either because of the size of the financial bonus or some significant change in the production process that improved the opponent's daily work tasks. Nonetheless, even at Innovations, which had average monthly gainsharing bonus payouts of 19.3 percent, there were nonmanagement opponents who expected management to cancel the bonus payouts.

P3 and P4: Gainsharing Outcomes

The third proposition predicted that hidden and suppressed social and economic problems will surface shortly after gainsharing implementation. The fourth proposition predicted that management and nonmanagement employees will likely continue to support gainsharing as long as it fulfills some of their monetary or nonmonetary interests. The findings related to these two propositions are grouped together because the monetary and nonmonetary interests include appropriate reactions to the hidden and suppressed social and economic problems that sur-

Table 10–4.   Gainsharing outcomes common to all six facilities

Direct Benefits to Management and Nonmanagement Employees	Direct Benefits to Management; Indirect Benefits to Nonmanagement Employees	Direct Benefits to Nonmanagement Employees; Indirect Benefits to Management
1. Better production process 2. New tools and machinery 3. Increased training and development 4. Improved product quality 5. Improved communications 6. Group dynamics training 7. Better managers	1. Significant cost savings 2. Recycling and energy savings 3. Less employee resistance to production changes 4. Greater worker identity with facility problems 5. Easier process for tough decisions 6. Greater quantifiability of production factors 7. Less need for supervision 8. Improved customer relations 9. Improved supplier relations	1. Improved health and safety 2. Less stressful work tasks 3. Greater voice in decision making 4. Reduced employee grievances 5. Leadership opportunities

faced shortly after gainsharing implementation. (See Tables 10-4 and 10-5 for a summary of the outcomes as they directly or indirectly benefited management and nonmanagement employees.)

Table 10-4 summarizes trends in outcomes that occurred at all six facilities after gainsharing implementation. These outcomes occurred regardless of the specific types of power games that ensued at each facility. Based on the case studies, it is obvious that the less detrimental the power games, the better the outcomes. For instance, gainsharing implementation improved product quality at all six facilities. Even when management restricted both employee involvement in the decision-making process and the calculation of financial bonuses, product quality improved. At the same time, product quality improvements were more likely to continually occur for extended periods when management enhanced both employee involvement in decision making and the determination of financial bonuses.

Direct Benefits to Management and Nonmanagement Employees. All six facilities improved their *production process* as a result of gainsharing. The number of suggestions implemented per facility were 1,478 over four years at Cylinder Lifts, 776 suggestions over four years at Foam Seats, at least 121 suggestions over four years at Forestland, 4,238 suggestions

Table 10–5.   Gainsharing outcomes specific to only one or a few facilities

Direct Benefits to Management and Nonmanagement Employees	Direct Benefits to Management; Indirect Benefits to Nonmanagement Employees	Direct Benefits to Nonmanagement Employees; Indirect Benefits to Management
1. New promotion avenues 2. More in-house work 3. Improved collective bargaining negotiations	1. Direct communication with union members rather than through union officers	1. Basic education course 2. New performance evaluation system 3. More job rotation 4. Alternatives to mandatory layoffs 5. Clothing allowance 6. Employee uniforms 7. Credit union 8. Change in paydays 9. Recreational activities 10. Higher wages

over six years at Innovations, 2,000–3,000 suggestions over four years at Innovations-Brotherhood, and 8,114 suggestions over six years at Packaging International.

Some of the suggestions recommended the purchase of *new tools and machinery*. Poduction employees wanted the best tools on the market for performing their job tasks. As a result, all six facilities had to increase *training and development* for those using the new machines. The training and development extended to other job tasks as well. For instance, because so many suggestions at Packaging International were related to problems with machines designed by engineers, managers trained production employees to read engineering blueprints.

The nonmanagement employee suggestions, new machines, and increased training and development ultimately contributed to improved *product quality*. Cylinder Lifts was certified as a qualified supplier; Foam Seats won its customer's gold medal achievement award and mark of excellence award; Innovations was designated a certified parts supplier; Packaging International won the Miller Brewing award; and Forestland was able to win a supplier certification award on a yearly basis. As discussed earlier, factors other than gainsharing contributed to these many awards. Nonetheless, managers at all six facilities assigned a great deal of credit to gainsharing. Because of the gainsharing bonus and team activities, employees were highly motivated to prevent defective products from being sent to customers.

The suggestion system, gainsharing task teams, and review boards all led to *improved communications* at each facility. A tremendous amount of production-related information was being shared between departments and between management and nonmanagement employees. Most facilities found it necessary to display more bulletin boards on the production floor to handle the extra communications. All of the facilities also found it necessary to initiate *group dynamics training* for both management and nonmanagement employees participating on gainsharing teams. Managers were trained in how to receive critical comments from production employees. Both management and nonmanagement employees were also trained in how to run effective team meetings. Both the facility manager and production employees at all six facilities maintained that after several years of gainsharing, the facility had *better managers*. Managers were better informed about production issues and were much more likely to speak directly with nonmanagement employees about solving production problems.

There were three direct benefits to management and nonmanagement employees that occurred at only one or two of the six facilities. Cylinder Lifts used the gainsharing team system to create *new promotion avenues* for nonmanagement employees. At Foam Seats, the nonmanagement gainsharing coordinator was hoping that successful performance would translate into a management position. At Innovations-Brotherhood, gainsharing suggestions led to *more in-house work* for the facility. In addition, managers attributed the *improvements in collective bargaining negotiations* to the increased communication between management and union employees that gainsharing fostered. Importantly, union leaders at Innovations-Brotherhood attributed the collective bargaining improvements to both better communication and having obtained the ROI number for the facility.

Direct Benefits to Management, Indirect Benefits to Nonmanagement Employees. All six facilities realized *significant cost savings* as a result of gainsharing. This included net savings of $300,000 at Cylinder Lifts, $471,100 at Forestland, and $540,313 at Foam Seats. Innovations, which had the largest gainsharing bonus payouts, had net payroll savings of $311,589 during the three years prior to the field study. One particular significant cost saving experienced by all six facilities was *recycling and energy savings*. This was one area that production employees immediately addressed after gainsharing implementation. They knew that they were wasting energy and product materials, but prior to gainsharing, they lacked strong motivation to do anything about it.

All six facilities experienced *less employee resistance to production changes* because many of the changes were being initiated by co-workers. In addition, gainsharing interactions and information sharing, particularly the sharing of financial data, led to *greater worker identification with facility problems*. With this greater awareness by the production employees, managers believed that gainsharing created a work culture with an *easier process for tough decisions*. For instance, because managers at Innovations-Brotherhood shared health cost data with production employees and the union, and these costs were discussed at gainsharing team meetings, management and the union were working cooperatively on a plan to reduce health costs. Prior to gainsharing, management would have simply tried to impose health cost reductions on the union.

All six facilities had *greater quantifiability of production factors* because production employees wanted to earn gainsharing bonuses. These employees believed that if something could be measured, then historical standards could be developed to serve as the basis for another gainsharing bonus factor. There was also *less need for supervision*, because the gainsharing bonus focused the efforts of nonmanagement employees on their production tasks. For instance, Innovations-Brotherhood was able to eliminate an entire level of supervisors after several years of gainsharing.

Managers at all six facilities noted that *customer relations* had improved as a result of gainsharing. As noted above in the discussion on product quality, all of the facilities won awards from their customers. Managers at several facilities also claimed that gainsharing increased employees' respect for the customer. For example, at Forestland, production employees became more service oriented because customer sales and returns affected the gainsharing bonus. Innovations extended its gainsharing training workshops to customer personnel.

Managers at all six facilities noted that *supplier relations* had improved as a result of gainsharing. Some gainsharing suggestions forced management to develop better relations with suppliers. For example, production employees at Foam Seats provided product quality improvement suggestions to suppliers and requested that management end relations with suppliers of low-quality products. At Innovations, production employees submitted several product improvement suggestions directly to suppliers. Managers at Cylinder Lifts initiated a program of inviting suppliers to visit the facility in order to familiarize themselves with facility operations.

Finally, one direct benefit to management experienced at Innovations-Brotherhood is most likely applicable to many union facilities. As a result of gainsharing, managers were able to *communicate directly with union members* rather than through union officers. Prior to gainsharing implementation, managers spoke to union officers before suggesting that employees change their work methods. After gainsharing, union members demanded that managers communicate directly with them.

Direct Benefits to Nonmanagement, Indirect Benefits to Management Employees. All six facilities reported significant *health and safety improvements.* Production employees used the gainsharing suggestion system, gainsharing team meetings, and team budgets to implement health and safety changes. For example, a hoist was purchased at Cylinder Lifts for a worker who had two hernias. After a maintenance worker was severely injured, a platform and guard rail were purchased at Foam Seats to prevent future mishaps. At Forestland, the facility paid for a complete medical physical for its employees. So many health and safety suggestions were submitted at Innovations that a safety committee was formed.

Probably the benefit mentioned most often by production employees was that gainsharing made *work tasks less stressful.* Over and over, production employees reported that the suggestion system made their jobs easier to perform because they could reorganize their work environments as they saw fit. For example, they did not have to go through several layers of management to move necessary supplies closer to where the job task was being performed. Instead, they simply submitted a gainsharing suggestion to have the materials moved.

The suggestion system and gainsharing team format provided production employees with a *greater voice in decision making.* This is a primary purpose of gainsharing, and it was achieved at all six facilities. The greater voice in decision making and discretionary team budgets led to a *reduction in employee grievances.* Grievances were submitted as gainsharing suggestions and discussed at team meetings. Under gainsharing, production employees had the budgetary authority to make the necessary changes. According to several interviewees, managers were much more responsive to claims that a particular policy or procedure was unfair as a result of gainsharing interactions.

Production employees at all six facilities also saw gainsharing in terms of *leadership opportunities.* Some production workers wanted greater responsibilities without entering the ranks of management. Gainsharing gave them a chance to lead team meetings and organize their work group.

Many of the direct benefits to nonmanagement employees and indirect benefits to management were achieved by only some of the six facilities. These benefits resulted from problems that were specific to a facility. For instance, managers at Cylinder Lifts and Forestland realized that some employees did not participate in gainsharing activities because they did not know how to read or write. As a result, both facilities started *basic education courses* to help employees receive high school equivalency diplomas. A production employee at Cylinder Lifts submitted a suggestion that all employees should evaluate their own performance, and this suggestion resulted in a *new performance evaluation system*. Production employees at Foam Seats, Forestland, and Innovations continually submitted suggestions requesting *job rotation*. Management and nonmanagement employees at Foam Seats and Forestland attributed new *layoff policies* to gainsharing interactions. *Clothing allowances, employee uniforms,* and *credit union membership* were the direct results of gainsharing suggestions submitted by production employees at Foam Seats. A *change in paydays* and *recreational activities* were the direct result of gainsharing suggestions submitted at Forestland. The only production employees to receive substantially *higher wages* as a result of the gainsharing bonus were those at Innovations.

Community Benefits?

As described above, owners, managers, nonmanagement employees, customers, and suppliers have all benefited from the implementation of Scanlon-type plans at the six facilities. What about the local community? Does it also benefit in some way?

Importantly, none of the interviewees at any of the facilities mentioned that gainsharing improved relationships with the local community. In a review of the suggestion logs, only one community-related suggestion was found: an employee at Foam Seats suggested that an unused garbage receptacle be returned to the town. Although gainsharing team representatives are citizens as well as employees, citizen concerns were not introduced through gainsharing mechanisms. This is a limitation of only using gainsharing, a middle-range form of democracy, as the model for organizational democracy. Because production employees do not voice community concerns, it is essential for companies to create stakeholder panels with external stakeholders who represent community groups, as part of the decision-making process (Collins and Barkdull 1995).

Although there were no direct links between gainsharing implementation and improvements in community policies and outcomes, gainsharing generated several significant beneficial policies and outcomes that were in the public interest. Production employee suggestions pertaining to recycling materials, energy efficiency, and scrap reduction contribute to solving local and national environmental problems. Another public interest benefit was the establishment of a General Equivalency Diploma (GED) program at Cylinder Lifts and Forestland. The classes that managers at these facilities offer to their production employees contribute to solving the problem of illiteracy. These findings suggest that gainsharing plans should be more actively encouraged as a matter of public policy in terms of providing tax incentives for gainsharing implementation.

Research Limitations

There are several caveats to the validity of the research that limit the findings of this study. I entered these facilities after they had had at least four years of gainsharing experience and asked interviewees to reflect on past events. Sometimes interviewees struggled with recalling and interpreting various events. This problem was most evident with Packaging International employees, who had difficulty recalling and interpreting the specific events that led to the final showdown between the president of the company and the union. Research is needed that documents gainsharing events as they evolve rather than after they occur.

Although there are many benefits to conducting field study research, some of these benefits generate limitations. Managers rarely pursue only one intervention strategy and then wait for the results before pursuing other strategies—an assumption often made in laboratory experiments. Instead, managers often pursue multiple strategies when attacking a problem such as product quality. Whenever possible, I relied on evidence from gainsharing suggestion logs and verified this information with key informants. But product quality improvements could have resulted from variables interviewees either overlooked or inappropriately discounted. In addition, some facilities had inadequate record-keeping systems. For instance, those interviewed at Innovations insisted that product returns declined substantially after gainsharing implementation, but no documentation was available to verify this empirical claim. Similarly, managers at Cylinder Lifts claimed that some suppliers increased their customer base based on recommendations from their employees, but there was no reasonable way to determine how many.

Another research limitation was the lack of a control group. The outcomes, or lack of them, could be a function of nongainsharing issues, such as the business environment or competitive issues. Finally, all of the facilities experienced managerial turnover. The power games and gainsharing outcomes described in this book may be more a function of personality characteristics rather than gainsharing attributes. All of these limitations suggest corresponding areas for future research.

Some Future Research Questions

In addition to research that would overcome the limitations stated above, many other areas demand future research. The six case studies were undertaken to explore why gainsharing researchers have been reporting ambiguous results on production outcomes and changes in work climate. It is now possible to create a composite profile of experiences from the six case studies. Each attribute of the composite profile represents an area for future research. Some of these attributes were proposed in Chapter 2. They are restated here with supporting evidence from the case studies. Research using larger databases should be explored to determine their degree of generalizability.

Managers typically implement Scanlon-type plans to increase productivity, not because they want to institute democratic values. Managers create steering committees, which, for the most part, rubber stamp how they want to implement gainsharing. Nonmanagement employees permit managers to determine the initial set of gainsharing rules because planning management systems has been the traditional role of management. Because of costs, managers are likely to reject a gainsharing consultant's recommendations for the optimal mix of employee involvement in decisions and the financial group-based bonus. Managers believe that the potential outcomes of gainsharing can be achieved with less than optimal forms of employee involvement. They want to obtain these expected outcomes as inexpensively as possible. When this is not possible, they revert to the original recommendations.

Most managers will follow the lead and wishes of the facility manager. If gainsharing lasts more than one year and the facility manager continues to demonstrate significant support for it, oppositional managers will either quit or take a fence-sitter position. If the facility manager becomes skeptical about gainsharing, then go-getter managers will reduce their support of gainsharing activities. The further a manager is from the daily performance of nonmanagement employees, the more likely the manager will believe that continually high bonuses are the result of a faulty bonus calculation or poor management, rather than nonmanagement effort.

Nonmanagement employees fall into three categories that, if graphed according to number of members, would be bell-shaped. A few nonmanagement employees will be go-getters; most will be fence-sitters; and a few will be oppositional. A facility will have all three types of nonmanagement employees regardless of the degree of gainsharing success or level of gainsharing bonus. After several years of gainsharing, however, the percentage of nonmanagement employees in each group will reflect the monthly group-based bonus payouts. If the many productivity improvements stemming from go-getter suggestions and the improved work methods of all nonmanagement employees generate high bonus payouts, then some fence-sitters will become go-getters, and most opponents will become fence-sitters or go-getters. This change in behaviors and attitudes will occur because fence-sitters and opponents have developed faith in the fairness of the new system of management or because they feel guilty for withholding suggestions while earning a bonus. Nonetheless, there will always be some nonmanagement opponents. If the work methods and productivity improvements generate only modest gainsharing bonus payouts, then there will be few changes in group membership, with some go-getters becoming fence-sitters or opponents. If the work methods and productivity improvements do not generate any financial bonuses, then some fence-sitters will become opponents, and most go-getters will become fence-sitters or opponents. Nonetheless, there will always be some nonmanagement go-getters.

Employee age has mixed predictive ability regarding gainsharing participation. Some young and old employees see gainsharing as an opportunity to take responsibility at work but lack the education necessary to become active participants in decision making. Some young employees see gainsharing as an opportunity to avoid an early layoff, whereas some old employees see gainsharing as an opportunity to avoid a layoff prior to retirement. For some old employees, gainsharing is an opportunity to express their accumulated knowledge about production. Some old employees will be oppositional because of their historical experiences with adversarial managers. Some young employees identify with oppositional older employees because they are rebellious toward authority. Many young and old nonmanagement employees will be fence-sitters.

If high financial bonuses are being earned, nonmanagement employees give managers more benefit of the doubt. These improved attitudes and behaviors do not translate into higher scores for trust in management on employee feedback surveys, however. Instead, nonmanagement employees are likely to increase their trust expectation levels over time, causing middle-of-the-road responses to survey items. The more trust management has earned, the greater the expected level of trust. Nonmanagement employees do not express high levels of trust in management because there is always some action, activity, or event that managers undertake that nonmanagement employees will question. Oppositional nonmanagement employees use these situations to remind nonmanagement go-getters and fence-sitters that managers should never be trusted fully. On the other hand, gainsharing can lead to a significant decline in the level of trust in management, particularly if the financial bonuses do not adequately reflect improvements in the production process.

Importantly, trust in management and the level of the financial bonuses are not the primary predictors of whether nonmanagement employees believe gainsharing should be maintained. Instead, nonmanagement employees ultimately judge gainsharing according to other self-interests and group interests. If nonmanagement employees have been able to improve health and safety conditions, address grievances, and make their stressful work tasks easier, then gainsharing will be considered worthwhile.

Last, it is important that researchers be very cautious when making generalizations about survey research on gainsharing. Foam Seats and Innovations both received 3.1 scores for team meetings. Interviews revealed, however, that the dynamics of the teams were very different at these two facilities. At Foam Seats, production employees had lost interest in team participation because of the low bonus payouts. At Innovations, the teams were experiencing many transitional problems caused by the implementation of a new team system.

Managing the Power Games

Politics is a fact of life. As Aristotle noted more than two thousand years ago, human beings are political animals. We live in relationship with others; no one is an island. The world in which we live has always been and will always be hierarchical. The existence of hierarchy fosters political games because only a few can make it to the top. In the early 1500s, Machiavelli was attacked for classifying the morality of political games on the basis of outcomes rather than on the process itself. Whatever successfully contributed to amassing power was right. From a Machiavellian perspective, Bill Clinton, Donald Trump, and Si Newhouse are good political players. But for the moralist, individuals who have successfully advanced to the top of their professions are not necessarily good political players, because some of the methods they may have used to make it to the top are morally suspect—they have exploited others and lied to the public at various points in their ascent.

As discussed in Chapter 2, gainsharing implementation typically reduces power differentials between management and labor—management becomes more accountable to labor and vice versa. The political battles begin with the process of determining the initial set of rules for the structure of the group-based bonus calculation, department teams, the review board, and the suggestion system. Political science research on the transformation of dictatorships into democracies suggests that former authoritarian rulers will manipulate the transitional process to safeguard their already entrenched self-interest. This certainly happened at each facility. These types of political games are temptations that require immediate restraint, and both management and nonmanagement employees should challenge them immediately. Gainsharing can be extremely beneficial to both management and nonmanagement employees if these political games are managed appropriately.

There are many things facilities can do to avoid pitfalls that could lead to the failure of a Scanlon-type plan because of political problems. The recommendations below are categorized according to overall issues and specific management issues related to the suggestion system/gainsharing coordinator, gainsharing teams, and the group-based financial bonus.

Overall Issues

1. The responsibility for gainsharing success should rest with a team of managers, not just the CEO or the facility manager. Management fence-sitters and opponents must have the freedom to be critical about the gainsharing plan, and their criticisms must be addressed.

2. It is necessary to create a social network of management and nonmanagement gainsharing supporters at the beginning of gainsharing implementation that could be appealed to in difficult times.

3. Engineers and other professionals must be included in the discussion of how they can best serve gainsharing. It is important to increase the amount of social interaction between professional and nonprofessional employees. For instance, distributing engineers among production teams can help eradicate some prejudices held by both groups.

4. Managers should recognize that gainsharing does not fulfill all employee needs. Some managers believe that gainsharing can prevent

unionization or decertify a union. As demonstrated at Packaging International, gainsharing does not break nonmanagement employee bonds with the union. Gainsharing fulfills the need of some employees to become active participants in the facility's decision-making process, but even these employees recognize that the union provides them with a wide range of other benefits.

5. To increase nonmanagement employee commitment to gainsharing, nonmanagement employees should vote on implementing and renewing gainsharing.

6. Gainsharing go-getters must challenge detrimental political games, particularly in facilities where there is a history of adversarial management-nonmanagement relations. If these games are not addressed, the ill will that they foster will accumulate until a major issue arises that makes very public everything people thought they were getting away with.

7. Any discussions that result in changing the rules of gainsharing should include nonmanagement employees. It is important to meet with key go-getters, fence-sitters, and opponents to determine the best way to implement necessary changes in the gainsharing system.

8. Management and nonmanagement employees must develop strategies to integrate opponents into the gainsharing system. Leaving them alone increases their opposition.

9. Managers should expect the gainsharing system to have opponents, even after many years. The presence of opponents does not mean gainsharing is failing. It is important to keep their presence in perspective; their negative outlook should be balanced with the positive changes that go-getters and fence-sitters generate.

10. Managers should think of gainsharing as part of a facility's evolutionary process; it is not the final goal. There are many other ways to give additional responsibilities to nonmanagement go-getters and fence-sitters. As in all evolving democracies, paradise will always be several steps away in gainsharing organizations.

Suggestion System/Gainsharing Coordinator Issues

1. Management and nonmanagement employees should have a voice in choosing the gainsharing coordinator. The gainsharing coordinator needs the trust of both groups.

2. The gainsharing coordinator must be relieved of a comparable amount of duties. Gainsharing duties should not be added to the employee's already full-time duties.

3. Managers should be clearly informed that the more suggestions production employees submit, the better they will be evaluated by the facility manager. The facility manager should never suggest that a large number of suggestions are a symptom of poor management performance.

4. Management fence-sitters and opponents should be reminded why it is essential for nonmanagement employees to stop the production process to discuss solutions to production problems.

5. Management opponents should be punished for scolding production employees who discuss production problems.

6. A wide range of incentives for gainsharing participation should be offered because different groups of employees are sensitive to different incentives. Participation opportunities, monetary rewards, and recognition rewards are all essential motivators.

7. Human comfort and grievance-type suggestions should be permitted. These are salient issues for nonmanagement employees, particularly for fence-sitters. Allowing nonmanagement employees to raise these suggestions through gainsharing enables employees to focus more—not less—on gainsharing issues.

8. Managers need to consistently encourage nonmanagement fence-sitters to offer and implement suggestions. Fence-sitters should be thanked for highlighting problems that management was unaware of.

9. Managers should publicly reinforce nonmanagement employees who are willing to risk stopping production to discuss and analyze productivity improvement suggestions.

10. Suggestions offered by nonmanagement fence-sitters must be processed as quickly as possible. Fence-sitters closely monitor the progress of their suggestions before submitting more.

11. Nonmanagement go-getters should be encouraged to work with fence-sitters and opponents to formulate and submit suggestions.

12. When financial bonuses are earned, a special effort should be made to encourage nonmanagement fence-sitters to submit new suggestions. Fence-sitters tend to feel guilty when bonuses are earned while they are withholding suggestions.

13. Individual recognition awards should be given for suggestions. Managers should not expect or demand that all suggestions be developed by a team, rather than by individuals.

14. Nonmanagement go-getters should be encouraged to form coalitions with other gainsharing teams to help pass complex or costly suggestions.

15. It should be expected that some nonmanagement opponents will submit very critical suggestions just to irritate managers.

16. Expensive suggestions should be implemented early in the gain-sharing process to prevent nonmanagement employees from thinking that only "cheap ideas" are desired.

Gainsharing Team Issues

1. Managers should develop special work contracts that protect the jobs of nonmanagement go-getters with low seniority, even in unionized facilities. Protection from layoffs should be a function of both seniority and certain performance attributes, such as gainsharing leadership.

2. Gainsharing teams should be formed at the lowest possible hierarchical level within the organization. If a facility is organized according to work teams, then work teams should be transformed into gainsharing teams. Ideally, all employees should be on gainsharing teams that meet weekly for relatively short periods.

3. Gainsharing teams should be limited to employees who work on the same shift. They share common work experiences. Small intershift teams should be developed to smooth out problems among shifts.

4. Gainsharing team meetings should occur on facility time. Meetings that are scheduled after regular working hours may unintentionally exclude employees who use daycare services.

5. Whenever possible, task teams and review board meetings should have more nonmanagement than management employees. This fosters a sense of decision responsibility among nonmanagement employees.

6. Management and nonmanagement employees on gainsharing teams and the review board should be trained in group dynamics and how to run effective team meetings.

7. Management fence-sitters and opponents should be reminded that team meetings are essential for nonmanagement employees.

8. Management opponents who scold nonmanagement employees for attending team meetings should be reprimanded.

9. Nonmanagement employees should be encouraged to take responsibility for team decisions. If nonmanagement employees expect managers attending their meetings to make the ultimate decision, then managers should not attend the meetings.

10. Nonmanagement go-getters should be encouraged to attend other gainsharing team meetings to learn why they are successful or unsuccessful.

11. Nonmanagement fence-sitters should not be expected to run for the position of team representative. Nonetheless, nonmanagement go-getters should encourage fence-sitters to chair gainsharing meetings so that they will have a greater commitment to gainsharing.

12. Nonmanagement fence-sitters should be required to attend gain-sharing team meetings. It is a positive step in support of gainsharing when nonmanagement fence-sitters observe and eventually interact with the go-getters running the team meetings.

13. Nonmanagement opponents should attend some team meetings. This should be decided on a case-by-case basis. Opponents who deliber-ately disrupt team meetings should be permitted to attend only an occa-sional meeting. Nonetheless, they should not be ignored by managers. Ignoring nonmanagement opponents strengthens their convictions. They need to be challenged to participate in a constructive manner.

Group-Based Financial Bonus Issues

1. Opponents, fence-sitters, and go-getters must play an active role in determining the gainsharing bonus calculation. Everyone must be will-ing to take ownership of the calculation.

2. Managers need to be reminded that the bonus is not a gift to unde-serving employees. The employees earn a bonus because many of the changes they made would not have been offered to management if the gainsharing system was not in place. The need for some of the changes will appear to be very obvious after the fact. Managers should remember that before gainsharing, these obvious changes were not being made.

3. The bonus calculation must be clearly linked to performance im-provements that employees affect directly. If production employees im-prove their performance and more and better-quality products are shipped every month, a bonus should be forthcoming. Otherwise, em-ployees will view the bonus distribution as very subjective.

4. The historical standard should include rotating several years of per-formance. If only the most recent best year counts as the historical stan-dard, surpassing this standard will be frustrating and demoralizing for production employees.

5. Reserve-pool deficits should be eliminated at the end of every year, even if production employees argue otherwise. Every year should be seen as a fresh start.

6. Nonmanagement fence-sitters and opponents are particularly sensi-tive to bonus payouts. When bonuses are earned and paid, fence-sitters

and opponents should be personally thanked for their contributions to improved performance.

7. Nonmanagement fence-sitters and opponents should be reminded why it is in their financial self-interest to receive a gainsharing bonus by working more efficiently rather than receive overtime wages by working less efficiently.

11 The Ethical Superiority of
Participatory Management

In Chapter 1, it was noted that involving employees in decisions that affect them directly has been praised in the management literature for more than a century. Many of the best-selling management books published during the past two decades emphasize the need for organizations to decentralize and empower their employees. During the heady revolutionary days of the 1960s, Slater and Bennis (1990) declared the inevitability of democracy at the workplace. Twenty-five years later, in a retrospection of that article, the authors claimed that they were right (Slater and Bennis 1990).

Unfortunately, the data do not support their claim. Using high-end estimates, Scanlon-type gainsharing plans may be found in some form at 26 percent of the Fortune 1000 firms (Lawler, Mohrman, and Ledford 1992), at 9 percent of firms with more than 500 employees (Dulworth and Usilaner 1987; Freund and Epstein 1984), and at 4 percent of firms that employ human resource professionals (Markham, Scott, and Little 1992).

One explanation for this slow evolution is that participatory management mechanisms often do not live up to the claims made for them. For instance, Wagner (1994) found no statistically significant support for concluding that consultative participation forms of management had a positive relationship to either performance outcomes or work satisfaction. He concluded that employee participation in decision making may not be worthwhile to pursue.

The six case studies described in this book were undertaken to obtain a better understanding of the mixed empirical results reported in participatory management research. In Chapter 10, I concluded that the mixed results are caused by inappropriate managerial responses to the power games associated with participatory management. All employees are participants in these power games. But managers can do many things to avoid the political pitfalls that could lead to the failure of a Scanlon-type plan. If these power games are managed appropriately, the plans can work.

Are the results worth the effort? The evidence reported in this book strongly suggests an affirmative response. All six facilities achieved significant improvements in productivity and work methods. Nonetheless, the president of Packaging International abandoned gainsharing after six years. At Innovations and Forestland, managers at corporate headquarters were questioning whether gainsharing benefits could be achieved without paying such large financial bonuses to employees.

Managers might be more likely to explore why participatory management is not working and to make appropriate corrections if participatory management had an ethical foundation in addition to an economic one. Organization theorists and managers are in need of a moral compass. Scanlon-type plans may not be the best form of employee involvement, but they aim in the right direction. Participatory management is inevitable because of its moral standing. Top-down authoritarian forms of management do not figure in conceptions of humane societies.

This final chapter argues in favor of the inevitability of participatory management on the basis of its coherence to the social-philosophical assumptions about human nature that, in the United States underlie the forms of political arrangements (democracy) and economic arrangements (mixed economy). The United States has been an international force in persuading other nations to adopt a democratic political system and a mixed economy. It is time for the nation to look inward at its prominent organizational systems.

As shown in Table 11-1, a range of political arrangements parallels a range of economic arrangements. These parallels are based on shared social philosophies about the relationship between sovereign and subjects in the political and economic realms. Historically, the authoritarian model has been dismissed from both political and economic discussions in the United States. Currently, the framework for these is defined by communitarians and libertarians.

Some of the fundamental social-philosophical assumptions about human nature and social organization made by political and economic theorists, and embodied in some of our most significant political and economic institutions, are diametrically opposed to some of the assumptions

Table 11-1. Ethical foundations of political, economic, and organization theories

	Authoritarianism	Communitarianism	Libertarianism
Political Theory			
Example	Dictatorship	Representative democracy	Direct democracy
Role of sovereign	Government commands in all matters	Government establishes goals and monitors for harms and deviances	Government monitors for harms
Role of subjects	Citizens obey commands for peace	Interest groups pursue self- group, and national interests	Citizens pursue self-interest
Economic Theory			
Example	Planned economy	Mixed economy	Market economy
Role of sovereign	Government commands in all matters	Government establishes goals and monitors for harms and deviances	Government monitors for harms
Role of subjects	Managers obey commands for GNP	Managers pursue self-, group, and national interests	Managers pursue self-interest
Organization Theory			
Example	Traditional management	Participatory management	Self-management
Role of Sovereign	Managers command in all matters	Managers establish goals and monitor for harms and deviances	Managers monitor for harms
Role of Subjects	Employees obey commands for wages	Employees pursue self-, group, and company interests	Employees pursue self-interests

about human nature and social organization made by organization theorists and embodied in a large number of organizational structures. Several admirable efforts have been made that link organization theory with political theory, particularly among scholars writing on workplace democracy and employee rights (Bowles and Gintis 1993; Dahl 1985; Ewing 1977; Pateman 1970; Scott and Hart 1971). This chapter develops a much broader social-philosophical framework into which these other works can fit:

1. Communitarian and libertarian forms of social arrangements have been well established in both political and economic theory to be ethically superior to authoritarian forms of social arrangements.
2. In political and economic theory, communitarianism represents the status quo, and libertarianism offers ethically legitimate challenges to the status quo.
3. Organization theory is still dominated by an authoritarian model, with communitarianism offered as a pragmatic (rather than ethical) challenge to the status quo.
4. From an ethical perspective, the authoritarian model should have been dismissed long ago, and the current debate in organization theory should consist of libertarian challenges to communitarian forms of organizational structures and policies.

Managers and scholars seeking to create more humane and fair organizations should ground their critiques and counterproposals within the same social-philosophical framework that dominates the nation's political and economic debates. To advance this line of inquiry, one must first consider three contentious assumptions underlying that framework.

Key Theoretical Assumptions

The first key assumption is that organizational systems are analogous to political and economic systems. Reasoning by analogy is a very useful process for understanding a concept by drawing comparisons with other concepts that are similar but not identical to it in several key attributes. The debatable issue is whether the concepts being compared are similar in important ways (leading to a good analogy) or in trivial ways (leading to a false analogy), and whether the significant differences are compelling enough to dismiss the analogy. For instance, there are significant differences in purpose between political systems (maintaining peace and justice) and economic systems (increasing GNP). Nonetheless, political concepts are often used to analyze and develop policy recommendations for economic systems, and economic concepts are often used to analyze and develop policy recommendations for political systems, because the two systems share some significant similarities.

In a now-classic article, March (1962) maintained that "the organization is properly viewed as a political system and that viewing the firm as such a system both clarifies conventional economic theory of the firm and (in conjunction with recent developments in theoretical languages) suggests some ways of dealing with classical problems in the theory of political systems generally" (663). He highlighted three main organizational concerns that are central to political theory: conflict resolution, preference ordering, and allocation of scarce resources. These concepts are interrelated, since many conflicts involve preference ordering and resource allocations. Such conflicts occur with both internal (employees) and external (community leaders, public interest groups) stakeholders. March was primarily concerned with the former. According to March, it is wrong to assume that "conflict is resolved by the employment contract, or—more generally—by the factor prices and that the result is a joint preference ordering of some sort or other" (669).

Political concepts have entered organization theory literature in the areas of political coalitions at the workplace (Astley and Zajac 1991), power (Pfeffer 1992), machiavellianism (Buskirk 1974; Collins 1992; Jay 1967), and workplace justice (Sheppard, Lewicki, and Minton, 1992). Zahra (1985) reports that 82 percent of managers surveyed agreed or agreed strongly with the statement "effective executives must be successful company politicians." According to Ashforth and Lee (1990), political behavior can be very dysfunctional. The business sections of bookstores are filled with intriguing stories of political problems that have lead to the downfall of business leaders, managers, and organizations.

A key similarity among political, economic, and organizational systems is the way in which control is exercised. As shown in Table 11-1, this control is exercised in the context of a sovereign/subject relationship. How should people be governed and conflicts resolved? People can either be trusted and extended significant liberties or not be trusted and made subject to the extensive power of a sovereign. If people can be trusted to behave appropriately when granted political and economic liberty, why should they not be trusted to behave appropriately when granted liberty within organizations? Why should organizations be exempt from the normal rules of morality?

Importantly, each of the social-philosophical assumptions, when applied to different systems, results in different techniques. For instance,

Table 11-1 does not imply that because political authoritarians may imprison dissidents, organizational authoritarians also imprison dissidents. Instead, both political and organizational authoritarians command in all matters, though the techniques for carrying out their commands differ with the contextual features of their unique operating systems. All too often, managers, organization theorists, and other business scholars readily dismiss organizational communitarianism on the grounds that representative democracy is very messy (Jensen 1993). Table 11-1 does not, however, suggest that the specific techniques of representative democracy be imposed on organizations. Instead, it suggests that participatory management and representative democracy share many social-philosophical assumptions.

The second key assumption is that the social-philosophical assumptions of political systems, economic systems, and organizational systems should be similar. The desire for value congruence and the creation of a "well-ordered society" is the foundation of moral philosophy. The justifications for value congruences, on both the individual and societal levels of analysis, include the unity of self, the essentiality of cooperation, and the creation of stability. John Rawls is just one of a great number of philosophers who have argued this point. In his modern classic *A Theory of Justice*, Rawls follows in the philosophical tradition of Aristotle, Kant, and Mill by arguing that the individual goal is "the unity of the self," whereby people free of contradictions and hypocrisies pursue a rational plan that fits within a personal and societal definition of "the good" (1971: 561). Value consistency among social systems is the trademark of a well-ordered society, and value contradictions are the seeds of individual and social unrest. Value congruence is often essential for cooperation, because there must be some agreement on basic rules and shared values for cooperation to occur. Value congruence thus leads to more stable relationships and a more stable society.

Importantly, not all value congruence is acceptable. Philosophers assume there is a set of values, or a range of acceptable values, that is indeed better than other values. More than two thousand years ago, Aristotle argued that life has an ultimate purpose—happiness—which is achieved through a combination of intellectual virtue, moral virtue, health, and wealth. Specifically what should be included in moral virtue has been a subject of significant philosophical debate. Aristotle's list of virtues has been criticized, defended, and amended.

For example, business ethicist Robert Solomon (1993) maintains that the basic virtues of business include justice, honesty, fairness, trust, toughness, friendliness, honor, loyalty, shame, competition, caring, and compassion. Freeman and Gilbert (1988) provide a slightly different list of socially acceptable values under the heading of "common morality," which includes promise keeping, nonmalevolence, mutual aid, respect for persons, and respect for property. The values of freedom, fairness, and security are at the heart of Donaldson's list (1989: 81) of fundamental international rights that multinationals must respect.

Just as important, not all values in these value sets are equal. Solomon (1993), following in the steps of Aristotle, is in very crowded company when claiming that justice is the ultimate virtue, both in corporate life and life in general. Hence both competition and compassion are to be obtained in reference to justice. As Rawls (1971) argues, "A society is well-ordered when it is not only designed to advance the good of its members but when it is also effectively regulated by a public conception of justice" (4–5). Justice is not simply an attribute of government; it is central to the operation of all systems of organization. Within both for-profit and non-profit organizations, justice considerations weigh heavily in making, applying, and interpreting policies and rules (Sheppard, Lewicki, and Minton 1992). As business ethicists have long argued, business activities should be evaluated according to these widely held values.

The third key assumption is that ethical arguments are superior to economic ones. This is such a well-accepted assumption in philosophy that one is hard pressed to find an article in the past fifteen years of *Journal of Business Ethics* or the past five years of *Business Ethics Quarterly* that comes close to arguing the reverse—that economic arguments are superior to ethical ones. But one is hard pressed to find scholarly articles in economics and business journals in which economic evidence is discounted on moral grounds. Business ethicists have attributed the latter phenomenon to a phase in the evolution of ideas that is probably ending. According to Shepard et al. (1995) pre-industrial society operated under a paradigm of moral unity whereby "business activity was linked to society's values of morality" (577). With the rise of industrialism, business activity was "freed from moral constraints by the alleged 'invisible hand' of efficient markets (the amoral theory of business)," but "[now] some variant of the moral unity paradigm may be recurring in post-industrial society." The moral unity paradigm has been dominant for most of the history of civilization and is central to the field of business ethics; moreover, as was argued with the preceding assumptions, it is making some headway in the field of organization theory.

Economic techniques and data are ultimately justified according to some moral assessment and principles (Hausman and McPherson 1993). In addition, just as not all value sets are equal, not all arguments based on ethics are equal. It has long been established that deontological and utilitarian ethical theories take precedence over egoism, social group relativism, and cultural relativism (Brady and Dunn 1995). Lower-level ethical theories are often justified according to higher-level ethical theories. This ranking of ethical theories is made explicit in Kohlberg's (1981) stages of moral development. One need only go back to the original writings of Adam Smith, the father of capitalism, to understand the appropriate relationship between economic and ethical arguments. The economic arguments in *The Wealth of Nations* are justified by the ethical arguments found in both *The Wealth of Nations* and *The Theory of Moral Sentiments* (Collins 1988; Werhane 1991). Smith justifies the individual pursuit of economic self-interest on the grounds that it will increase a nation's standard of living and thus afford the greatest good for the greatest number of people (utilitarian reasoning). In addition, Smith assumes explicitly that individuals restrain their self-interested tendencies because of sympathy, respect for others, and avoidance of harm (deontological reasons). Thus, economics is an essential source of information used in decision making, but economic decisions are evaluated according to deontological and utilitarian moral principles.

From a historical perspective, the social-philosophical assumptions of much of organization theory and practice remain two to three hundred years behind the social-philosophical assumptions that generated the new governance process implemented as the United States. Organization theory has much to gain from historical analysis (Kieser 1994). The following summary of historical developments in political and economic theory may be compared with the current status of organization theory.

Political Debates in the United States

Opposition to authoritarian political philosophy has a long history in the United States. Many of the initial waves of European immigrants who traveled across the Atlantic Ocean to settle in the New World were fleeing political and religious oppression. During the late sixteenth century, Queen Elizabeth sought to unify the subjects of England under the Anglican Church. By act of parliament, all clergy of England were made to accept particular religious creeds, such as the Book of Common Prayer, the Thirty-Nine Articles, and the Queen's religious sovereignty. Those who did not accept these creeds were persecuted; publications were censored, assemblies disbanded, congregations fined, preachers imprisoned, and property confiscated (Brachlow 1988; Cragg 1957; Durant and Durant 1961). Failure to adhere to a particular religious doctrine, whether Anglicanism in England, Catholicism in France, or Lutheranism in Germany, Denmark, and Sweden, could result in torture and exile. Religious dissenters could not hold political or military office, or enter most universities.

In addition to those seeking political and religious freedom, immigrants to the New World included peasants, fortune hunters, and criminals. Many of the early political debates within and between groups of settlers concerned the degree of allegiance the group should maintain to its European sovereign. Who ought to govern life in the colonies—Spain, the Netherlands, France, England, or the colonists themselves? For better or worse, military victories by the British against their European rivals centralized British sovereignship until the Revolutionary War.

Many but not all colonists preferred self-rule. In the Declaration of Independence, Thomas Jefferson referred to King George of England as a despot and tyrant who refused to allow the colonists to establish their own legislative and judicial bodies. Without the consent of colonial leaders, the king imposed an army and police force, collected taxes, determined trade policies, and according to the Declaration, "plundered our seas, ravaged our Coasts, burnt our towns, and destroyed the lives of our people." In declaring their freedom from generations of rule by monarchs and nobles, colonial political leaders were faced with the same problem from which many of them or their ancestors had fled: how to maintain peace among a population of 2.5 million, whose members were of a variety of religions intolerant of other religions, most notably Anglicanism, Puritanism, and Presbyterianism (Perry 1944).

Both libertarians and communitarians credit John Locke's ([1690] 1960) *Two Treatises of Government* for establishing the legitimacy of government based on the consent of the governed and providing the ethical basis for defending the structures, processes, and policies of democratic governments (Lodge 1976; Rothbard 1978). Locke argued that desirable ends can be achieved and undesirable ends avoided when there is only one sovereign group *and* that sovereign's law-making ability is based on the consent of the governed. According to Locke, God created a humanity that is free and rational. If no system of central control existed, people (other than a few degenerates) would restrain their behavior according to their reason, which dictates that they should not harm others. Therefore, peace could be maintained in civil society if the sovereign allowed its subjects extensive liberties. Subjects could be trusted to pursue their own self-interest in a manner that would improve the general welfare. The sovereign, who should be accountable to the law, could continue to make and maintain laws on the condition that those laws be in the public interest and have the consent of the subjects. A lack of consent by subjects would undermine the legitimacy of the sovereign to govern. The overriding principle of government should be the protection of individual liberty.

Thus, the U.S. Constitution established minimal government. Persons fulfilling the role of sovereign were accountable to the consent of the governed, and tremendous restrictions were placed on government's power over individuals. The Bill of Rights was amended to the Constitution to further limit governmental powers. Individuals were granted the right to freedom of religion, speech, press, arms, and due process.

Since independence, political debates have flourished among communitarians (Bellah et al., 1985, 1991; Dahl 1982; Dworkin 1977; Rawls 1971; Sandel 1982; Walzer 1983) and between communitarians and libertarians (Machan 1974, 1990; Nozick 1974; Rothbard 1978). Proponents of political authoritarianism are relegated to the fringes of political discourse (Mendel 1979).

Issues in the Bill of Rights are useful in defining and distinguishing between libertarians and communitarians. Libertarians interpret individual rights as being absolute (Newman 1984; Rothbard 1978). They rebel against monitoring powers assigned to the government, with the exception of judicial oversight for physical harm. For liberty to flourish, they hold that a nonintrusive judicial system is needed to ensure individual rights by protecting citizens against physical harm imposed on them by others. Libertarians emphasize negative rights—the right not to have one's liberty or property infringed upon by government—and oppose positive rights, such as a right or entitlement to health care or education. They believe laws pertaining to moral or private issues should be repealed, thus enhancing individual liberty.

From a libertarian perspective, the taxing and monitoring powers of government should be curtailed greatly. In accordance with the goals of the American Civil Liberties Union, libertarians such as Tibor Machan (1988) maintain that "much that is evil will have to remain protected from suppression—just as the defender of free speech and worship realizes that yellow journalism found in many tabloids and the televangelism practice of some corrupt preachers is due protection" (5). Important libertarian public policy recommendations include government sale of large landholdings to private citizens and significant reduction in military expenditures based on allowing the citizens of foreign countries to solve their own problems. Libertarians oppose government funding of the arts and laws that limit individual choices about sex or abortion.

Libertarians view interest-group-based politics as corrupting the democratic process and oppressing individual differences (Newman 1984; Rothbard 1978). The libertarian ideal is utopian—no government. The concept of a community will is the antithesis of libertarianism. The preferred model would be a direct democracy that has a very limited function, similar to colonial New England town meetings where occasionally citizens met to resolve some dispute or communal need. Though not immune from interest group politics, such meetings provide a fairly level playing ground for individual participants. A more modern image of this libertarian political ideal is a Ross Perot electronic town hall meeting that presents key issues to all the citizens and each enters his or her preference into a computer, thus eliminating the need for elected representatives. Government does serve a minimal purpose for libertarians, the key word being *minimal*.

Proponents of communitarianism, like libertarians, accept the importance of individual liberty and reject authoritarianism. Communitarians differ from libertarians in that they treat liberty as a relative right, not an absolute right, and hence are much more willing to restrain the right of free speech when it conflicts with some other principle, such as the good of the community (Dworkin 1977). They reject libertarianism on the grounds that it results in social isolation (Bellah et al., 1991; Durkheim 1933; Fromm 1941) or moral relativism (Kirk 1960, 1988). Individuals are believed to find meaning in their lives by identifying with a social or moral collective.

Throughout this discussion, the term *communitarian* is applied to a political philosophy, not just the specific growing political movement led by Amitai Etzioni (1993). Etzioni's Communitarian movement consists of liberals and conservatives, Democrats and Republicans, who want to emphasize what they have in common—opposition to "radical individualists, such as libertarians and the American Civil Liberties Union" who overemphasize rights (11)—rather than political policies that divide them. Etzioni wants what both liberals and conservatives desire—"a judicious mix of self-interest, self-expression, and commitment to the commons—of rights and responsibilities" (26). Communitarians accept the primacy of liberty over authoritarianism and the primacy of specific community outcomes (moral rectitude and/or social justice) over individual liberty.

In the broader use of the term, communitarians disagree strongly among themselves about what constitutes legitimate intervention on behalf of community welfare. *Conservative* communitarians justify government intervention on the grounds of *moral rectitude*; that is, a representative democracy should develop legislation that encourages moral activities and discourages supposedly immoral or sinful activities (Kirk

1960). For example, Kirk (1960) argues that Jeffersonian democracy was too tolerant in allowing sinful individuals to pursue their immoral vices and thus erred on the side of moral relativism. It overemphasized the equality of human beings, which can never be achieved, and underemphasized respect for authority and moral order. In this sense, direct democracy lacks a moral compass. John Adams, like his English counterpart Edmund Burke, stood for a representative form of democracy that would restrain liberty on the basis of religious beliefs and pragmatic considerations. In his view, human beings are fallible; because some will pursue immoral interests out of emotional weakness and ignorance, moral authorities are needed to direct the nation's activities.

According to conservative communitarians, the moral situation of the country worsened during the Industrial Revolution. Wealth passed from small business owners and farmers who were in constant personal contact with their employees, to impersonal, financially driven industrialists ignorant of older traditions. Industrialization and the extensive application of the division of labor broke down personal relationships such that "the wealthy man ceased to be magistrate and patron; he ceased to be neighbor to the poor man; he became a mass-man, very often, with no purpose in life but aggrandizement" (Kirk 1988). Liberals humanely yet mistakenly demanded that government respond to their needs. Eventually people began to expect government to solve social problems that could be solved only through individual effort and moral education. Taxes increased, government expanded into a welfare state, and social problems worsened. Thus, modern conservative communitarians, though agreeing with some libertarian policies that would reduce the size of government bureaucracy and get government out of the private lives of its citizens, demand that government ban abortions, ban homosexual activities, imprison casual drug users, put warning labels on music, and have public school teachers lead students in prayer, all for the sake of the moral community.

Liberal communitarians justify government intervention on the grounds of *social justice* and believe that government should develop legislation that aids the disadvantaged (Rawls 1971). They see democratic societies as lacking a level playing field—human beings with particular characteristics have undeserved social advantages over others (being born male rather than female, wealthy rather than poor, white rather than black)—and believe that this is not fair or just. According to liberal communitarians, the problems of industrialization were compounded by the calvinistic and social darwinist moral perspectives of business leaders. Carnegie (1900/1962) and others preached that material wealth was a function of hard work and God's blessing, and that poverty was a function of laziness and exclusion from God's blessings. They maintained that government should remain minimal, because natural laws are at work whereby the strongest deservedly rise to the top and the weakest deservedly stay on the bottom of the social ladder, thus preserving appropriate inequalities in political power and wealth for the good of the community.

The growing social gap between rich and poor fueled the liberal political programs of Theodore and Franklin Roosevelt. They argued that social justice demanded that government play a more active role in determining and fulfilling community and human needs. Franklin Roosevelt maintained that government should begin social planning and restricting the liberties of the wealthy for the benefit of the economically worst off. His solution was the development of a welfare state—rather than socialism, communism, or some other authoritarian model. Importantly, liberty was still the first priority but not the only priority of government. This tradition was carried through to Lyndon Johnson's Great Society project. Thus, liberal communitarians, though agreeing with some libertarian policies that would restrain government from interfering with an individual's private morality, demand that government provide funds for child care services, national health care, prenatal care, infant nutrition, education, and public housing, all for the sake of the social justice.

In summary, political debates in the United States revolve around the tension within communitarianism (liberal versus conservative) and between communitarianism and libertarianism. Both liberal and conservative communitarians accept the primacy of liberty over authoritarianism and argue that the sovereign is justified in restraining liberty to avoid certain undesirable community outcomes. Liberal communitarians seek to make amends for social injustices attributable to accident of birth. They maintain that the sovereign should trust individuals on moral issues but intervene to correct what they perceive to be well-embedded social problems, such as poverty or discrimination. Conservative communitarians seek to make amends for moral injustices attributed to a perverse use of free will. They maintain that the sovereign should trust individuals to solve social problems voluntarily but intervene to correct for what they perceive to be immoral activities, such as abortion or homosexuality. Libertarians maintain that even if the activity or community welfare outcome is immoral or unjust, every person's liberty should be tolerated unless people are being harmed physically. Proponents of authoritarianism are not welcomed to debates in the public arena and are ridiculed for supporting an ethically undesirable political philosophy.

Economic Debates in the United States

The evolution of economic debates in the United States shares a common ethical foundation with the evolution of political debates, so only brief summaries are given here. The opposition to authoritarian economic philosophy—a planned economy—has a long history in the United States. Many from the initial wave of European immigrants were escaping from economic oppression as well as political oppression. Today, most economic debates are among proponents of communitarianism (Galbraith 1958, 1967, 1973; Kirk 1960; Nader, Green, and Seligman 1976; Reich 1983; Reich and Donahue 1985; Stone 1976) and between communitarians and libertarians (Friedman 1962; Gilder 1981; Hayek 1944; Machan 1990; Mises 1949; Rand 1967). Proponents of economic authoritarianism are spurned, particularly since the collapse of the pre-1989 Russian economy, and remain on the fringes of political debate (Mendel 1979).

Adam Smith's ([1776] 1976) theoretical conception of capitalism was a reaction against the authoritarian abuses of mercantilism. Smith maintained that the mercantilist policies of government-sanctioned monopolies, import quotas, guilds, and many other economic restrictions generated poverty, not wealth. He argued that the general welfare could be better advanced by allowing all citizens, not just a handful of merchants with government connections, to pursue their economic self-interest. According to Smith ([1759] 1976), the presence of moral sentiments—as well as the development of one's conscience, belief in God, and fear of the law—restrains most individuals from pursuing self-interest in a way that may harm others. Hence, government intervention should be limited to providing a system of justice, a military, and some essential public goods (such as roads), all of which are unlikely to be generated by the individual pursuit of economic self-interest (Collins 1988; Collins and Barkdull 1995). Decisions about what to produce, the quantity and quality of production, the means of distribution, price, and levels of employment should be made on the managerial level, not by government officials. Although constrained by sociological factors—such as class status or geography—laborers should be given the liberty to choose places of employment.

Libertarians place the blame for the United States' economic problems on unnecessary government intervention in the economy and the oligopolistic practices of large business organizations (Rothbard 1978). At the time of the Industrial Revolution, the leaders of industry consolidated their economic power and controlled politicians to such an extent that legislation was enacted to protect them from competitors. Government intervention increased during the Great Depression, and in the libertarians' view, the application of Keynesian economic theory only worsened the situation. Further, New Deal legislation led to the development of a welfare state, resulting in a mixed economy rather than a market economy.

According to proponents of libertarian economic theory, government is currently too intrusive in the economic sector and should abolish the welfare state (Friedman 1962; Murray 1984; Rothbard 1978). They propose that government intervention in the economy be limited to establishing laws that foster economic competition and that all laws restricting economic activity be eliminated. Also, they hold that the government has mistakenly categorized as public goods a large number of goods and services that should be privatized, including national defense, police and fire protection, transportation, water and sewer services, garbage collection, the judicial system, prisons, and mail service. Libertarians contend that rather than government imposing services on citizens, services should be provided by private enterprises and be purchased by citizens.

Conservative communitarians agree with libertarians that government should rescind most regulation of economic activity, disband regulatory bureaucracies, foster competition, and privatize many goods and services now provided by government. However, they note that the commerce clause of the U.S. Constitution delegates to government the power to regulate some economic activities and transactions for the benefit of community welfare. From their perspective, government is justified in restraining economic activity that is either based on or fosters immorality.

Liberal communitarians argue that government intervention is justified when the public good is not promoted by the individual pursuit of self-interest (such as mail service to all households, regardless of economic status) or when powerful economic actors do not have a sense of justice to restrain their liberty (as in some wage disputes between management and labor). They hold that social justice demands some industrial policy planning on the national level (Galbraith 1967; Lodge 1976). According to liberal communitarians, government regulation should be enacted when the market system does not appropriately monitor itself for inefficiencies, producer rents, externalities, inadequacy of information, unequal bargaining power, moral hazards, and resource scarcity (Breyer 1982).

Congruence between Political and Economic
Social Philosophies

Theoretical links have been established among the various political
and economic social philosophies. As shown in Figure 11-1, dictatorships and planned economies are linked by an authoritarian social philosophy; direct democracy and a market economy are linked by a libertarian social philosophy; and representative democracy and a mixed
economy are linked by a communitarian social philosophy.

According to Mises (1949), Friedman (1962), and Novak (1982), there
is congruence between the libertarian social philosophies of democracy
and a market economy. Both systems establish extensive limits on the
sovereign's coercive powers and establish individual liberty as a priority. More importantly, democracy and a market economy are interpene-
trating systems that feed off one another. Friedman's central argument in
Capitalism and Freedom is that "there is an intimate connection between
economics and politics, that only certain combinations of political and
economic arrangements are possible, and that in particular, a society
which is socialist cannot also be democratic, in the sense of guaranteeing
individual freedom" (7–8). Neoclassical economists maintain that an
erosion of economic liberty by government is likely to be followed by an
erosion of political liberty. An important central debate pertaining to the
current transformation of authoritarian governments to democratic capitalism (the former Soviet Union, China) is whether political freedom
should precede economic freedom, or vice versa (Diamond and Plattner
1993).

According to Marx, Lenin, and Mao, there is congruence between the
authoritarian social philosophies of dictatorship and a planned economy
(Mendel 1979). Both systems establish extensive limits on individual liberty and encourage the sovereign's use of coercive powers. For instance,
Lenin ([1902] 1963) compared the role of a political leader with that of an
orchestra conductor who knows "who is playing which violin and
where, where and what instrument [each person] has learned and is
learning to play, who is playing wrongly, where and why . . . and who
should be transferred, who and where, in order to correct the disso-
nance" (20). Lenin maintained that political and economic success could
come about only through an absolute unity of will among all people, implemented through the single will of their political leaders.

The United States is neither a direct democracy nor a pure market
economy. Instead, it is a representative democracy with a mixed economy, both of which depend on a large federal bureaucracy. In 1990, the

federal government collected $1.155 trillion in revenue and spent $1.393 trillion. Federal office space is equivalent to all of the office space in the nation's ten largest cities multiplied by a factor of four. Hence, liberty matters greatly, but not to the exclusion of political and economic goals established by the sovereign on the basis of a communitarian social philosophy. The sovereign is held accountable to the subjects. According to Lodge (1984), the United States is evolving toward political and economic communitarianism despite the efforts of libertarians to stop that process.

In summary, communitarian political and economic arrangements are considered ethically superior to competing authoritarian arrangements because they fit widely held views of human nature and have generated many socially desirable outcomes. In reference to human nature, communitarian social arrangements allow people to freely pursue their self-interest, care about the welfare of others, and rely on "reason" to restrain their self-interested tendencies so as not to harm others. On the basis of its social-philosophical assumptions, the U.S. government protects the liberty of citizens to pursue their political and economic interests and intervenes when individuals misuse their freedom as a result of individual fallibility or selfishness or when certain public goods are not generated. Although many social problems remain to be addressed, representative democracy and the mixed economy have greatly improved community welfare in the United States. Importantly, communitarians borrow many ideas from libertarians. Liberal communitarians join forces with libertarians in opposing government policies advocated by conservatives concerned with moral rectitude. Conservative communitarians join forces with libertarians in opposing government policies advocated by liberals concerned with social justice.

Organization Theory and Political/Economic Social Philosophies

Authoritarian managerial power at the workplace has a long history that includes the institution of slavery in Greece, Rome, and the United States. As is evident in the writings of social darwinists (Carnegie [1900] 1962), tyrannical power is a deserved reward for success in climbing the organizational ladder. Typically, organization theorists attribute the structures and processes of traditionally managed companies to the theoretical work of Taylor ([1911] 1947), Fayol ([1949] 1967), and Weber ([1947] 1959), all of whom were concerned to various degrees with the bureaucratic nature of organizational activities, assignment of planning activities solely to management personnel, and precise determination of the nature of work tasks to be performed by nonmanagement employees. In general, these organization theorists maintained that managers should determine policies and impose them on organizational members. Organizations should have a hierarchical chain of command and the communication process should flow from the upper levels of management to the lowest levels of the organization. Nonmanagement employees should not contribute to managerial decisions unless they are so commanded by managers.

Organization theorists who chronicle "organizational reality," particularly Weber ([1947] 1959), can aid the understanding of managerial authoritarianism. Weber provided several managerial justifications for bureaucracy that are also a very strong defense of the authoritarian model for organizations. He contended that managers need to (1) coordinate the services of many workers on a continual basis, (2) rationally exploit similar types of work through unified command, (3) provide continuous common supervision to achieve a technically rational organization of work, (4) establish expert training, (5) discipline workers, (6) derive decisions based on high levels of technical efficiency, (7) maximize technical rationality, (8) maintain technical and commercial secrets, (9) speculate on business policy, and (10) establish bargaining superiority. Weber concluded that "experience tends universally to show that the purely bureaucratic type of administrative organization—that is, the monocratic variety of bureaucracy—is, from a purely technical point of view, capable of attaining the highest degree of efficiency and is in this sense formally the most rational known means of carrying out imperative control over human beings" (337).

By far the most ardent defender of the similarities in social-philosophical assumptions among authoritarian political, economic, and organization theories was Lenin. He strongly argued that the sovereign should dictate in matters of politics and the economy, and also that Soviet business organizations should implement Taylorism, the key component of the authoritarian organization model. Lenin maintained that the educational and cultural level of the masses had to be raised significantly, along with worker discipline, skill, effectiveness, and the intensity of labor, to increase productivity to a level beyond that in capitalist nations. Therefore, Soviet managers would have to adopt the best achievement of capitalism—authoritarian-based scientific management. Lenin (1917/ 1975) argued that organizational success depended on managers being able to "organize in Russia the study and teaching of the Taylor system and systematically try it out and adopt it to our own ends" (447). He demanded that people unquestioningly subordinate themselves "to a single will of the leaders of labor" (455).

How prevalent is organizational authoritarianism in the 1990s? Apparently, no studies have measured the degree of authoritarianism in organizations nationwide. Nonetheless, the following five indicators suggest that authoritarianism remains prevalent: research on the prevalence of participatory management processes, the lack of civil liberties at the workplace, the experiences of corporate culture scholars, anecdotes in both the scholarly and general business literature, and the nature of management education programs.

First, research documenting the prevalence of participatory management practices and policies of companies reveals that companies are still very resistant to them. Lawler, Mohrman, and Ledford (1992) surveyed Fortune 1000 firms and categorized them according to the percentage of employees covered by a variety of participatory management practices. Using 40 percent of the employees covered as a cutoff (still less than half of all employees), they found that only 3 percent of the firms had substantially used gainsharing, 11 percent used quality circles, and 3 percent of those with unions had union-management quality of work life committees. Even a relatively easy-to-administer communitarian practice such as obtaining survey feedback was being used substantially by only 31 percent of the respondents. For his book of case studies on resolving employee grievances, Ewing (1989), a Harvard Business School professor with many contacts, wrote to "several hundred" companies and could find only thirty to fifty with a due process grievance procedure for nonunion employees; the other companies had at most an open-door policy.

Second, the lack of civil liberties within organizations fosters authoritarianism. As argued by Ewing (1977: 3), Americans are denied the "freedom of press, speech, and assembly, due process of law, privacy, freedom of conscience, and other important rights" when they are at work. This lack of civil liberties is apparent in nonprofit as well as for-profit organizations. The literature on whistle-blowing provides numerous cases documenting employees' unsuccessful attempts to exercise civil liberties at the workplace (Miceli and Near 1992).

Third, the depth of an authoritarian culture within traditionally managed business organizations is particularly evident in the works of corporate culture theorists. Whether referred to as a bureaucratic culture (Kilmann 1984), a control paradigm (Lawler 1986), a traditional paradigm (Veltrop and Harrington 1988), a rational model (Peters and Water-

man 1982), or the Old Guard (O'Toole 1985), the cultures that organizational consultants find in the companies they are attempting to transform
are very similar in one respect—they are authoritarian. After decades of
modifications in organization theory, work within business organizations remains highly organized, compartmentalized, and controlled through
managerial command.

Fourth, a vast number of anecdotes in both the scholarly and general
business literature suggest the prevalence of authoritarianism. The business ethics literature is filled with examples of the "just do it" mentality
in organizations. For example, an in-depth survey of thirty graduates of
Harvard's MBA program found that eleven had faced strong organizational pressures from above to act in an unethical manner (Bardaracco
and Webb 1995). Recent books such as *The Force* (Dorsey 1994) and *Liar's
Poker* (Lewis 1989), among many others, have documented the authoritarian tendencies of managers in America's largest and most influential
organizations. Even such "socially responsible" firms as Ben and Jerry's
(Lager 1994) and the Body Shop (Entine 1994) have struggled with their
very public efforts to abide by the communitarian ethos.

A similar deduction is evident in the growing literature on the need to
reform boards of directors. If CEOs expect blind allegiance from the
powerful business personalities who sit on corporate boards (Park 1995;
Pound 1995), what is the likelihood that they sincerely encourage employee participation further down the organizational hierarchy? Most
agency theory-based solutions to the problem of controlling managers
through corporate governance mechanisms favor more narrowly aligning managerial interests with shareholder interests, thus increasing the
likelihood of organizational authoritarianism, and reject the communitarian solution of placing stakeholders other than business people on
boards (Hart 1995; Jensen 1993).

Fifth, the nature of management education programs also encourages
authoritarian tendencies. Although the Organization Behavior group at
the Harvard Business School has long had a preference for employee
participation (Ewing 1990), MBA graduates from Harvard and other
leading business schools advocate controlling employees on the basis of
financial considerations (the need to reduce overhead, inventory, assets,
labor costs) rather than communitarian social-philosophical considerations (Collins 1996; Robinson 1994).

Importantly, the social philosophical framework developed thus far
does not depend on whether one believes that authoritarianism or communitarianism is the dominant organizational paradigm in theory or in
practice. Instead, the argument put forth here is that the communitarian

paradigm is ethically superior, and that the central focus of organization theory should be the debates among competing or complementary communitarian forms of management and between communitarian and libertarian forms of management. The field has not yet reached that stage of social-philosophical evolution, however.

If it is true that people are self-interested, concerned about the welfare of others, and rational yet imperfect, what type of organizational structures, processes, and policies should managers create to govern them while they perform work tasks? As suggested in Table 11-1, the system should be based on the same social-philosophical assumptions about sovereigns and subjects that underlie representative democracy and the mixed economy. The sovereign, in this case management, should establish goals and monitor for harm and deviance. Subjects (in this case, nonmanagement employees) should be able to fulfill their individual and work group interests while accomplishing company goals established by managers, with their input.

A wide variety of participatory management structures, processes, and policies that are based on a communitarian social philosophy appear in the literature on management and business ethics (Donaldson 1982; Freund and Epstein 1984; Huse and Cummings 1975/1985; Kelso and Hetter 1967; Lawler 1986; Stone 1976). These participatory management features differ according to the size, scope, and form of employee involvement. They increase employee involvement in the company's decision-making process while enabling managers to intervene when employee decisions fail to achieve organizational goals.

Libertarian models of organizational arrangements are underdeveloped. One of the few systematic efforts in this area was by Freeman and Gilbert (1988). In the tradition of John Locke, they proposed that when granted freedom and liberty, individuals typically guide their behavior by the precepts of common morality. Most individuals tend to keep promises, respect the rights of others, and refrain from harming those nearby. Individuals are good citizens not only in a democratic political system but also in a corporate environment.

In a libertarian organization, agreements between management and nonmanagement employees would be grounded in the values of freedom and liberty, with an appropriate fit between the personal projects of individuals and the goals of the organization. Freeman and Gilbert suggest that companies adopt a personal projects enterprise strategy whereby individuals have the liberty to pursue personal projects that coincide with organizational goals. A foundational ethic for such an organization culture is personal autonomy. The result would not be anarchy, because there would be congruence between an individual's personal projects and organizational goals. Thus, Freeman and Gilbert reverse the logic of authoritarianism by arguing that a business organization should serve as a means to individual ends instead of people serving as means to organizational ends. In this sense, companies exist as a set of contractual arrangements (Keeley 1988, 1995), and managers should act as brokers of other people's personal projects. Policies and procedures within organizations should be guided by the principles of personal autonomy, conventional rights, respect for persons, and voluntary agreements. A more radical libertarian alternative would be to give each member of an organization an equal voice in management decisions, thus abolishing organizational hierarchy (Lindenfeld and Rothschild-Witt 1982).

The number of organization scholars noting the onset of a new managerial revolution and encouraging the implementation of participatory management systems has been growing steadily for more than three decades (Lawler, Mohrman, and Ledford 1992; McGregor 1960; Preston and Post 1974). Despite the proclamations by some academics that workplace democracy has arrived because "the pyramid-shaped organization chart has gone the way of the Edsel" (Slater and Bennis, 1990: 174) or that the participatory management "revolution itself is clearly underway" (Preston and Post 1974: 484), the many indicators listed above suggest that organizations are adopting participatory management techniques only superficially, if at all. Why do managers continue to choose—and some organization theorists support—organizational patterns that are based on authoritarianism and reject alternative organizational patterns? Three very important objections to organizational communitarianism are that managers should be categorized as subjects with extensive liberty rather than as sovereigns whose liberties should be restricted, communitarianism is an experimental ethical luxury; and few employees advocate participation. All three objections demonstrate the depth to which authoritarian assumptions still underlie thinking about how companies should be governed. Each requires further elaboration and counterarguments.

The first objection is often assumed and rarely stated. As noted previously, most organization theorists do not explicitly state their social-philosophical assumptions (Scott and Hart 1971). One of the rare exceptions can be found in the writings of Locke and his colleagues. Locke and Schweiger (1979) categorized theorists making communitarian-based recommendations as left-wing authoritarians and defended their own authoritarian recommendations on libertarian grounds. According to them, managers (as political subjects) are granted the liberty by government to manage however they desire; if managers prefer to be authoritarians, so be it. Unfortunately, Locke and Schweiger fail to distinguish that although managers are subjects on the political level of analysis, they are sovereigns on the organizational level of analysis. Hence, those who have benefited greatly from political and economic liberty impose authoritarianism within the organizations they manage. While performing their jobs as organizational sovereigns, managers should follow the same rules that are applied to political sovereigns, not political subjects. It is essential to constrain the liberty of sovereigns because of the power they wield in their respective systems.

Advocates of the second objection maintain that communitarianism is an experimental ethical luxury that organizations cannot afford in the competitive global environment. Two of America's most significant global competitors, however—Germany and Japan—have many companies that operate according to communitarian principles. Union representation on boards of directors is legislated in Germany. Japanese companies are the source of many of the communitarian innovations with which American managers are experimenting. In addition, political dictators and proponents of planned economies could apply the same logic to support authoritarian political and economic models. Short-term performance pressures are often used as justification by dictators for maintaining martial law policies on a permanent basis. Similarly, managers are quick to use short-term performance to justify declaring martial law conditions within their organizations on a permanent basis.

Many of the criticisms leveled against the adoption of participatory management parallel Aristotle's (1984) and Lenin's (1904/1975) criticisms of democracy (Ross and Collins 1987). The concern is that involving nonmanagement employees in a company's decision-making process may lead to organizational mediocrity, rule by the uneducated and unskilled, bureaucracy, instability, and lack of accountability. Scholars need to counter this rejection of communitarianism with the many examples of communitarian success and emphasize the often overlooked negative effects of "petty tyrants" (Ashforth 1994). Several literature reviews and surveys have concluded that communitarian companies can operate very efficiently and effectively (Cotton et al., 1988; Glaser 1976; Lawler, Mohrman, and Ledford 1992; Miller and Monge 1986; Wagner and Gooding 1987), and most management textbooks contain examples of successful efforts. In particular, research conducted by Tannenbaum and colleagues on employee participation consistently shows that control in organizations is not a zero-sum game; the greater the decentralization of control, the greater the total control within the organization

(Bartolke et al., 1982; Tannenbaum 1986; Tannenbaum and Cooke 1979). If managed appropriately, communitarianism can work.

Third, organization theorists who defend the traditional authoritarian model often point out that organizational members are content with that model (Locke and Schweiger 1979; Locke, Schweiger, and Latham 1986). After all, nonmanagement employees are not agitating for radical change in how organizations are governed. Employees may not want to participate in organizational decision making. For instance, 65 percent of Japanese employees participate in their company's suggestion program, but only 13 percent of employees do so in the United States (Kilburn 1988).

This type of counterargument against organizational communitarianism simply demonstrates the acceptance of authoritarianism as an organizational form of governance within U.S. organizations. Analogous arguments are not acceptable in the nation's political and economic debates. For instance, should democracy be abandoned because less than 50 percent of eligible citizens vote? Rather than reaching such an extremist conclusion, political scientists and politicians struggle to find ways of encouraging more citizens to vote because they believe democracy is ethically superior to other forms of governance. Hofstede (1994) provides a more constructive response by arguing that the lack of employee support for communitarian mechanisms may be a reflection of their concern about immediate physical needs, such as job security, safe working conditions, and adequate wages, rather than a rejection of higher-level psychological needs, such as freedom and liberty at the workplace.

A key obstacle in the adoption of communitarian policies and procedures is a lack of management leadership on the issue. America's political and economic revolutions were advocated by a power elite of wealthy property owners. They took leading roles in breaking away from unjust authoritarian English impositions on their political and economic lives. A significant number of wealthy property owners realized that it was in their interest to take certain risks in demanding their political and economic freedoms. Currently, the power elite property owners are not, for the most part, on the participatory management bandwagon. The occasional treatises written by CEOs in praise of participatory management (DePree 1989) fall far short of rallying fellow CEOs to support the right of all employees to participate in organization decisions. The rhetoric has been in the media since the 1960s, but the commitment is lacking. Until a substantial number of the power elite who currently govern American companies become committed to the ethical superiority of participatory management, its inevitability will be postponed.

There are connections among the metasystems presented in Table 11-1. An overemphasis on the authoritarian model for organizations has an effect on activities in the economic and political spheres. Because subjects do not receive appropriate recourse from organizational sovereigns, they appeal to the political sovereign for help. Hence, problems between sovereign and subjects within the organization are debated on the economic and/or political level of analysis where the organizational sovereigns are subject to government. The failure of organizational sovereigns to respond to the needs and interests of organizational subjects has resulted in extensive government regulation in such areas as union formation, prenotification of employees about plant closings, minimum wages, occupational health and safety, and discrimination.

It is important to qualify this argument on two counts. First, no dire predictions are being made about the collapse of political and economic liberty due to the prevalence of organizational authoritarianism. Rather, the comparative differences in social-philosophical patterns give rise to claims of hypocrisy and organizational inefficiency. For example, although most managers claim that honesty, sense of humor, loyalty to fellow workers, and independence are very important features of an efficiently operated organization, those features are not always found in the companies where the managers work (Maccoby 1976). These communitarian goals require the reformation of organizations.

Second, the critique of organizational authoritarianism can be applied to all organizations, not just business organizations, although certain types such as the military may claim exemption. Political democracies suspend certain liberties on the basis of community welfare justifications, and the same logic should be true for organizations. The important point is that the standard should be democratic organizations with a few authoritarian exceptions, rather than authoritarian organizations with a few participatory management exceptions.

Conclusion

Debates in political and economic theory are typically framed by the tension within communitarianism and between communitarianism and libertarianism. Organization theory, however, is well grounded in authoritarianism. Authoritarian governance processes for business organizations are typically justified on the grounds that they are essential for achieving very specific organizational tasks and because business organizations operate in hostile internal and external environments. The social-philosophical assumptions for governing that are rejected by political and economic theorists—namely, that sovereigns should dictate to subjects—are readily accepted by many organization theorists. Because wages are provided in exchange for services rendered, and employees have the liberty to enter or exit those transactions, defenders argue that authoritarianism is a transactional advancement in work relations, compared with the slavery systems of Egyptian, Greek, and Roman civilizations and the feudal system of the Middle Ages. The preservation of the authoritarian model demonstrates that much present thinking about how companies should be organized and directed is largely attributable to the continuity of authoritarianism throughout much of human history. However, changing conceptions of th meaning of human life has brought into question the ability of such ancient authoritarian systems to serve human needs adequately.

From an organizational perspective, if companies were organized on the basis of communitarian or libertarian policies and such structures can be demonstrated to be as successful as authoritarian companies, these alternative models of organizational relations, which are compatible with widely held assumptions about human nature and governance processes, should be adopted because of ethical considerations. Like current political and economic debates, organization theory debates should consist of disagreements among communitarians over managers intervening in the life of employees, and between communitarians and libertarians on the self-management of all organizational activities.

The communitarian and libertarian models are preferable because they are based on a belief in the essential goodness of most human beings and aim at encouraging personal liberty, as long as the pursuit of liberty is beneficial to the larger community. This concept is at the ethical foundation of the dominant political and economic theories of the United States. It should also be the ethical foundation of organization theory. Obviously, more theoretical and practical work needs to be done in this area of organization analysis. One path to resolving the conflict is through participatory management, a form of management control that is more consistent with the nation's dominant political and economic paradigms than with the prevailing authoritarian form. Businesses will not become good democratic team players, respecting the interests of parties outside the organization, until they first respect the interests of those within the organization.

Common recommendations offered by both organization and business ethics theorists for addressing business ethics problems include sensitizing managers to ethical issues, training managers in ethical reasoning, and adopting codes of ethics. Each of these solutions is necessary but not sufficient. They touch on but do not dig deeply enough into the real ethical problem underlying business activities. The problem is at the level of organizational relationships and it should be resolved at that level. Solutions to the current ethical paralysis between organizations and their stakeholders should include the democratization of organizations. Several important theoretical and empirical research questions remain: What are the most efficient and effective modes of participation? What modes are better in which situations? What are the obstacles to change, and how can they be overcome? These types of questions ought to be the framework for debate. In addition, new forms of organizational systems should be developed from the communitarian and libertarian political philosophies described here.

With authoritarianism the status quo for many organizations and communitarian alternatives viewed as radical change, organization theory remains several centuries behind political theory and economic theory. In the United States, the shift from the authoritarian political and economic model entailed a military uprising led by a vanguard of enlightened subjects. What will it take to finally make the shift from authoritarianism to communitarianism in organizational governance? Unions and other employee associations should take leadership roles. There is no uprising by subjects demanding participatory management, but not all political paradigm shifts require a military revolt. Most recently, the shift from authoritarian to communitarian political theory in Russia was led by an enlightened sovereign. Currently, society is relying on enlightened managers, such as Max DePree (1989), the chairman and CEO of Herman Miller, and organizational consultants, such as Tom Peters, to lead the way. Business school professors try to shape the attitudes of the future CEOs in their courses, hoping their efforts will lead to particular organizational design preferences (Lewin and Stephens 1994). Managers with authoritarian attitudes will emphasize the dark side of the new organizational forms being proposed (Victor and Stephens 1994). It is therefore essential that organization theorists also play a central role in the transformation. They can do so not by producing politically biased research but by reflecting consistently on how their theories and research are related to the framework developed in Table 11-1. Unless organization theorists develop policy recommendations based on the strongly held communitarian social philosophical assumptions, necessary changes will continue to be slow, piecemeal, and faddish.

References

Ackoff, R. L. 1994. *The Democratic Organization*. New York: Oxford University Press.

Aktouf, O. 1992. "Management and Theories of Organizations in the 1990s: Toward a Critical Radical Humanism?" *Academy of Management Review* 17: 407–431.

Aristotle. 1984. *The Politics*. New York: Penguin Books.

Ashforth, B. E. 1994. "Petty Tyranny in Organizations." *Human Relations* 47: 755–778.

Ashforth, B. E., and R. T. Lee. 1990. "Defensive Behavior in Organizations: A Preliminary Model." *Human Relations* 43:621–648.

Astley, W. G., and E. J. Zajac. 1991. "Intraorganizational Power and Organizational Design: Reconciling Rational and Coalitional Models of Organization." *Organization Science* 2:399–411.

Azzarello, J. A. 1992/93. "Long-Time Environmental Leadership Pays Off in Many Ways at Herman Miller." *Total Quality Environmental Management* 2 (Winter): 187–191.

Baloyra, E. A. ed. 1987. *Comparing New Democracies: Transition and Consolidation in the Mediterranean and the Southern Cone*. Boulder, Colo.: Westview Press.

Bardaracco, J. L., and A. P. Webb. 1995. "Business Ethics: A View From the Trenches." *California Management Review* 37 (2):8–28.

Bartolke, K., W. Eschweiler, D. Flechsenberger, and A. S. Tannenbaum. 1982. "Workers' Participation and the Distribution of Control as Perceived by Members of Ten German Companies." *Administrative Science Quarterly* 27: 380–397.

Belcher, J. G. 1994. "Gainsharing and Variable Pay: The State of the Art." *Compensation and Benefits Review* 26 (May–June): 50–60.

Bellah, R. N., R. Madsen, W. M. Sullivan, A. Swidler, and S. M. Tipton. 1985. *Habits of the Heart*. Berkeley: University of California Press.

———. 1991. *The Good Society*. New York: Vintage Books.

Bergmann, A. E. 1975. "Industrial Democracy in Germany: The Battle for Power." *Journal of General Management* 2 (Summer): 20–29.

Bernstein, P. 1982. "Necessary Elements for Effective Worker Participation in Decision-Making." In *Workplace Democracy and Social Change*, edited by F. Lindenfeld and J. Rothschild-Whitt, 51–81. Boston: Porter Sargent Publishers.

Borzutzky, S. T. 1987. "The Pinochet Regime: Crisis and Consolidation." In *Authoritarians and Democrats: Regime Transition in Latin America*, edited by J. M. Malloy and M. A. Seligson, 67–89. Pittsburgh: University of Pittsburgh Press.

Bowles, S., and H. Gintis. 1993. "A Political and Economic Case for the Democratic Enterprise." *Economics and Philosophy* 9:75–100.

Brachlow, S. 1988. *The Communion of Saints*. New York: Oxford University Press.

Brady, F. N., and C. P. Dunn. 1995. "Business Meta-Ethics." *Business Ethics Quarterly* 5:385–398.

Braverman, H. 1974. *Labor and Monopoly Capital: The Degradation of Work in the Twentieth Century*. New York: Monthly Review Press.

Breyer, S. G. 1982. *Regulation and Its Reform*. Cambridge: Harvard University Press.

Brownell, P. 1981. "Participation in Budgeting, Locus of Control, and Organizational Effectiveness." *Accounting Review* 56:844–858.

Bullock, R. J., and E. E. Lawler. 1984. "Gainsharing: A Few Questions, and Fewer Answers." *Human Resource Management* 23 (Spring): 23–40.

Bullock, R. J., and M. E. Tubbs. 1990. "A Case Meta-Analysis of Gainsharing Plans as Organization Development Interventions." *Journal of Applied Behavioral Science* 26:383–404.

Buskirk, R. H. 1974. *Modern Management and Machiavelli*. New York: Mentor Books.

Carnegie, A. [1900] 1962. *The Gospel of Wealth*. Cambridge: The Belknap Press of Harvard University Press.

Clegg, S. 1979. *The Theory of Power and Organization*. Boston: Routledge and Kegan Paul.

———, ed. 1990. *Organization Theory and Class Analysis: New Approaches and New Issues*. New York: Walter de Gruyter.

Collins, D. 1988. "Adam Smith's Social Contract." *Business and Professional Ethics Journal* 7:119–146.

———. 1992. "An Ethical Analysis of Organizational Power at Salomon Brothers." *Business Ethics Quarterly* 2:367–377.

———. 1996. "The Voluntary Brainwashing of Humanities Students in Stanford's MBA Program: Student Complaints and Some Recommendations." *Business Ethics Quarterly* 6:391–411.

Collins, D., and J. Barkdull. 1995. "Capitalism, Environmentalism, and Mediating Structures: From Adam Smith to Stakeholder Panels." *Environmental Ethics* 17:227–244.

Conaghan, C. M. 1987. "Party Politics and Democratization in Ecuador." In *Authoritarians and Democrats: Regime Transition in Latin America*, edited by J. M.

Malloy and M. A. Seligson, 145–163. Pittsburgh: University of Pittsburgh Press.

Copley, F. B. 1923. *Frederick W. Taylor: Father of Scientific Management*. New York: Harper & Brothers.

Cotton, J. L., D. A. Vollrath, K. L. Froggatt, M. L. Lengnick-Hall, and K. R. Jennings. 1988. "Employee Participation: Diverse Forms and Different Outcomes." *Academy of Management Review* 13:8–22.

Cragg, G. R. 1957. *Puritanism in the Period of the Great Persecution, 1660–1688*. New York: Cambridge University Press.

Cyert, R. M., and J. G. March. 1963. *A Behavioral Theory of the Firm*. Englewood Cliffs, N.J.: Prentice-Hall.

Dachler, H. P., and B. Wilpert. 1978. "Conceptual Dimensions and Boundaries of Participation in Organizations: A Critical Evaluation." *Administrative Science Quarterly* 23:1–39.

Dahl, R. 1982. *Dilemmas of Pluralist Democracy*. New Haven: Yale University Press.

———. 1985. *A Preface to Economic Democracy*. Berkeley: University of California Press.

———. 1989. *Democracy and Its Critics*. New Haven: Yale University Press.

Davenport, R. W. 1958. "Enterprise for Everyman." In *The Scanlon Plan*, edited by F. G. Lesieur, 17–33. New York: John Wiley & Sons.

DePree, M. 1989. *Leadership Is an Art*. New York: Doubleday.

Diamond, L., J. J. Linz, and S. M. Lipset, eds. 1989. *Democracy in Developing Countries*. Vol. 4: *Latin America*. Boulder, Colorado: Lynne Rienner.

Diamond, L., and M. F. Plattner. 1993. *Capitalism, Socialism, and Democracy Revisited*. Baltimore: Johns Hopkins University Press.

Di Palma, G. 1990. *To Craft Democracies*. Berkeley: University of California Press.

Doherty, E. M., W. R. Nord, and J. L. McAdams. 1989. "Gainsharing and Organization Development: A Productive Synergy." *Journal of Applied Behavioral Science* 25:209–229.

Donaldson, T. 1982. *Corporation and Morality*. Englewood Cliffs, N.J.: Prentice-Hall.

———. 1989. *The Ethics of International Business*. New York: Oxford University Press.

Dorsey, D. 1994. *The Force*. New York: Random House.

Driscoll, J. W. 1979. "Working Creatively with a Union: Lessons from the Scanlon Plan." *Organizational Dynamics* 8 (Summer):61–80.

Dulworth, M. R., and B. L. Usilaner. 1987. "Federal Government Gainsharing Systems in an Environment of Retrenchment." *National Productivity Review* 6 (Spring): 144–152.

Duncan Baretta, S. R., and J. Markoff, 1987. "Brazil's Abertura: From What to What?" In *Authoritarians and Democrats: Regime Transition in Latin America*, edited by J. M. Malloy and M. A. Seligson, 43–66. Pittsburgh: University of Pittsburgh Press.

Durant, W., and A. Durant. 1961. *The History of Civilization*, vol. 8. New York: Simon and Schuster.

Durkheim, E. 1933. *The Division of Labor in Society*. Glencoe, Ill.: Free Press.

Dworkin, R. 1977. *Taking Rights Seriously*. Cambridge: Harvard University Press.

Entine, J. 1994. "Shattered Image." *Business Ethics* 8 (May):23–28.

Etzioni, A. 1993. *The Spirit of Community*. New York: Crown.

Ewing, D. W. 1977. *Freedom Inside the Organization*. New York: Dutton.

———. 1989. *Justice on the Job: Resolving Grievances in the Nonunion Workplace*. Boston: Harvard Business School Press.

———. 1990. *Inside the Harvard Business School*. New York: Times Books.

Ewing, J. C. 1989. "Gainsharing Plans: Two Key Factors." *Compensation and Benefits Review* 21:49–53.

Farnham, D. T. 1921. *America Versus Europe in Industry: A Comparison of Industrial Policies and Methods of Management*. New York: Ronald Press.

Fayol, H. [1949] 1967. *General and Industrial Management*. London: Pitman.

Foxenberger, B. 1994. "Team Bonuses Give Tangible Rewards." *Apparel Industry Magazine* 55 (February):12.

Freeman, R. E., and D. R. Gilbert. 1988. *Corporate Strategy and the Search for Ethics*. Englewood Cliffs, N.J.: Prentice-Hall.

Freund, W. C., and E. Epstein. 1984. *People and Productivity*. Homewood, Ill.: Dow-Jones Irwin.

Friedman, M. 1962. *Capitalism and Freedom*. Chicago: University of Chicago Press.

Fromm, E. 1941. *Escape From Freedom*. New York: Farrar and Rinehart.

Frost, C. F., J. H. Wakeley, and R. A. Ruh. 1974. *The Scanlon Plan for Organization Development: Identity, Participation, and Equity*. Lansing, Mich.: Michigan State University Press.

Fryxell, G. E., and M. E. Gordon. 1989. "Workplace Justice and Job Satisfaction with Union and Management." *Academy of Management Journal* 32:851–66.

Galbraith, J. K. 1958. *The Affluent Society*. Boston: Houghton Mifflin.

———. 1967. *The New Industrial State*. Boston: Houghton Mifflin.

———. 1973. *Economics and the Public Purpose*. Boston: Houghton Mifflin.

Geber, B. 1987. "Herman Miller: Where Profits and Participation Meet." *Training* 24 (November):62–66.

Gilder, G. 1981. *Wealth and Poverty*. New York: Basic Books.

Glaser, E. M. 1976. *Productivity Gains Through Worklife Improvement*. New York: The Psychological Corporation.

Gowen, C. R. 1990. "Gainsharing Programs: An Overview of History and Research," *Journal of Organizational Behavior Management* 11:77–99.

Graham-Moore, B. 1990a. "Review of the Literature." In *Gainsharing: Plans for Improving Performance*, edited by B. Graham-Moore and T. L. Ross, 19–47. Washington, D.C.: Bureau of National Affairs.

———. 1990b. "Seventeen Years of Experience with the Scanlon Plan: DeSoto Revisited." In *Gainsharing: Plans for Improving Performance*, edited by B. Graham-Moore and T. L. Ross, 139–173. Washington, D.C.: Bureau of National Affairs.

Graham-Moore, B., and T. L. Ross, eds. 1990. *Gainsharing: Plans for Improving Performance*. Washington, D.C.: Bureau of National Affairs.

Green, M., and J. F. Berry. 1985. "Trimming Corporate Waste Lines: The Participation Solution." *Management Review* 74 (November):35–39.

Hammer, T. H. 1988. "New Developments in Profit Sharing, Gainsharing, and Employee Ownership." In *Enhancing Productivity: New Perspectives From Industrial and Organizational Psychology*, edited by J. P. Campbell and R. E. Campbell, 328–66. San Francisco: Jossey Bass.

Hanlon, S. C., D. G. Meyer, and R. R. Taylor. 1994. "Consequences of Gainsharing: A Field Experiment Revisited." *Group and Organization Management* 19: 87–111.

Hart, O. 1995. "Corporate Governance: Some Theory and Implications." *Economic Journal* 105:678–689.

Hatcher, L. L., and T. L. Ross. 1985. "Organization Development Through Productivity Gainsharing." *Personnel* 62 (October):43–50.

Hatcher, L., T. L. Ross, and D. Collins. 1989. "Prosocial Behavior, Job Complexity, and Suggestion Contribution under Gainsharing Plans." *Journal of Applied Behavioral Science* 25:231–248.

——. 1991. "Attributions for Participation and Nonparticipation in Gainsharing-Plan Involvement Systems." *Group and Organization Studies* 16:25–43.

——. 1992. "Why Employees Support (and Oppose) Gainsharing Plans." *Compensation and Benefits Management* 8 (Spring): 17–27.

Hausman, D. M., and M. S. McPherson. 1993. "Taking Ethics Seriously: Economics and Contemporary Moral Philosophy." *Journal of Economic Literature* 31:671–731.

Hayek, F. A. 1944. *The Road to Serfdom.* Chicago: University of Chicago Press.

"Health Care Costs, Quality Top List of Human Resources Concerns." *Employee Benefit Review* 47 (September 1992):38–39.

Hofstede, G. 1994. *Uncommon Sense about Organizations.* Thousand Oaks, Calif.: Sage Publications.

Huse, E. F., and T. G. Cummings. 1975/1985. *Organization Development and Change.* New York: West Publishing.

Imberman, W. 1992. "Boosting Plant Performance with Gainsharing." *Business Horizons* 35 (November–December): 77–79.

Jay, A. 1967. *Management and Machiavelli.* New York: Bantam Books.

Jensen, M. C. 1993. "Presidential Address: The Modern Industrial Revolution, Exit, and the Failure of Internal Control Systems." *Journal of Finance* 48: 831–880.

Kakar, S. 1970. *Frederick Taylor: A Study in Personality and Innovation.* Cambridge: Massachusetts Institute of Technology.

Karl, T. L. 1990. "Dilemmas of Democratization in Latin America." *Comparative Politics* 23:1–20.

Katz, D., and R. L. Kahn. 1966. *The Social Psychology of Organizations.* New York: Wiley.

Keeley, M. 1988. *A Social-Contract Theory of Organizations.* Notre Dame, Ind.: University of Notre Dame Press.

——. 1995. "Continuing the Social Contract Tradition." *Business Ethics Quarterly* 5:241–256.

Kelso, L., and P. Hetter. 1967. *How to Turn Eight Million Workers into Capitalists on Borrowed Money*. New York: Random House.

Kidder, L. H., and C. M. Judd. 1986. *Research Methods in Social Relations*. New York: Holt, Rinehart and Winston.

Kieser, A. 1994. "Why Organization Theory Needs Historical Analysis—And How This Should Be Performed." *Organization Science* 5:608–620.

Kilburn, D. 1988. "The Power of Suggestion." *Business Tokyo* (April): 23–26.

Kilmann, R. H. 1984. *Beyond the Quick Fix*. San Francisco: Jossey Bass.

Kim, D. 1994a. "Factors Influencing Organizational Performance in Gainsharing Programs." *Industrial Relations* 35:227–244.

——. 1994b. "Causes and Correlates of Organizational Performance in Gainsharing: A Longitudinal Study." Unpublished paper, University of Wisconsin-Madison, Industrial Relations Research Institute.

Kirk, R. 1960. *The Conservative Mind*. Chicago: Henry Regnery.

——. 1988. *A Dispassionate Assessment of Libertarians*. Heritage Lectures, No. 158. Washington, D.C.: Heritage Foundation.

Kohlberg, L. 1981. *The Philosophy of Moral Development*. San Francisco: Harper & Row.

Kuhn, T. S. 1970. *The Structure of Scientific Revolutions*. Chicago: University of Chicago Press.

Lager, F. C. 1994. *Ben and Jerry's: The Inside Scoop*. New York: Crown.

Lawler, E. E. 1981. *Pay and Organization Development*. Reading, Mass.: Addison-Wesley.

——. 1986. *High-Involvement Management*. San Francisco: Jossey-Bass.

——. 1988. "Gainsharing Theory and Research: Findings and Future Directions." In *Research in Organizational Change and Development*, edited by W. A. Passmore and R. Woodman, 323–344. Greenwich, Conn.: JAI Press.

——. 1992. *The Ultimate Advantage*. San Francisco: Jossey-Bass.

Lawler, E. E., S. A. Mohrman, and G. E. Ledford. 1992. *Employee Involvement and Total Quality Management: Practices and Results in Fortune 1000 Companies*. San Francisco: Jossey-Bass.

Leana, C. R., and G. W. Florkowski. 1992. "Employee Involvement Programs: Integrating Psychological Theory and Management Practice." In *Research in Personnel and Human Resources Management*, edited by G. Ferris and K. Rowland, 10:233–270. Greenwich, Conn.: JAI Press.

Leana, C. R., E. A. Locke, and D. M. Schweiger. 1990. "Fact and Fiction in Analyzing Research on Participative Decision Making: A Critique of Cotton, Vollrath, Froggatt, Lengnick-Hall, and Jennings." *Academy of Management Review* 15:137–46.

Lenin, V. I. 1902/1963. "Letter to a Comrade on the Organizational Task." In V. I. Lenin, *What Is to Be Done?* Oxford: Clarendon Press.

——. 1904/1975. "One Step Forward, Two Steps Back." In *The Lenin Anthology*, edited by R. C. Tucker, 115–120. New York: W. W. Norton.

——. 1917/1975. "The Immediate Tasks of the Soviet Government." In *The Lenin Anthology*, edited by R. C. Tucker, 438–460. New York: W. W. Norton.

Lesieur, F. G. 1958. *The Scanlon Plan*. New York: John Wiley & Sons.

Levering, R., M. Moskowitz, and M. Katz. 1985. *The One Hundred Best Companies to Work for in America*. New York: New American Library.

Lewin, A. Y., and C. U. Stephens. 1994. "CEO Attitudes as Determinants of Organization Design: An Integrated Model." *Organization Studies* 15:183–212.

Lewin, K. 1947. "Frontiers in Group Dynamics: Concept, Method, and Reality in Social Science; Social Equilibria and Social Change." *Human Relations* 1: 5–41.

Lewis, M. 1989. *Liar's Poker*. New York: W. W. Norton.

Likert, R. 1961. *New Patterns of Management*. New York: McGraw Hill.

——. 1967. *The Human Organization*. New York: McGraw Hill.

Lindenfeld, F., and J. Rothschild-Whitt. 1982. *Workplace Democracy and Social Change*. Boston: Porter Sargent.

Locke, E. A., and D. M. Schweiger. 1979. "Participation in Decision Making: One More Look." In *Research in Organizational Behavior*, edited by B. Staw, 265–359. Greenwich, Conn.: JAI Press.

Locke, E. A., D. M. Schweiger, and G. P. Latham. 1986. "Participation in Decision Making: When Should It Be Used." *Organizational Dynamics* 14 (Winter): 65–79.

Locke, J. 1690/1960. *Two Treatises of Government*. New York: New American Library.

Lodge, G. C. 1976. *The New American Ideology*. New York: Alfred A. Knopf.

——. 1984. *The American Disease*. New York: Alfred A. Knopf.

Logue, J. 1991. "Democratic Theory and Atheoretical Democracy: Reflections on Building Democratic Enterprises in the American Economy." In *Managing Modern Capitalism: Industrial Renewal and Workplace Democracy in the United States and Europe*, edited by M. D. Hancock, J. Logue, and B. Schiller, 313–339. Westport, Conn.: Greenwood Press.

Maccoby, M. 1976. *The Gamesman*. New York: Simon and Schuster.

Machan, T. R. 1988. *A Passionate Defense of Libertarianism*. Heritage Lectures, No. 165. Washington, D.C.: Heritage Foundation.

——. 1990. *Capitalism and Individualism*. New York: Harvester Wheatsheaf.

——, ed. 1974. *The Libertarian Alternative*. Chicago: Nelson-Hall.

Malloy, J. M. 1987. "The Politics of Transition in Latin America." In *Authoritarians and Democrats: Regime Transition in Latin America*, edited by J. M. Malloy and M. A. Seligson, 235–258. Pittsburgh: University of Pittsburgh Press.

Malloy, J. M., and M. A. Seligson, eds. 1987. *Authoritarians and Democrats: Regime Transition in Latin America*. Pittsburgh: University of Pittsburgh Press.

March, J. G. 1962. "The Business Firm as a Political Coalition." *Journal of Politics* 24:662–678.

March, J. G., and H. Simon. 1958. *Organizations*. New York: John Wiley and Sons.

Markham, S. E., B. L. Little, K. D. Scott, and S. Berman. 1992. "Gainsharing Experiments in Health Care." *Compensation and Benefits Review* 24 (March–April): 57–64.

Markham, S. E., K. D. Scott, and W. G. Cox. 1992. "The Evolutionary Development of a Scanlon Plan." *Compensation and Benefits Review* 24 (March–April): 50–56.

Markham, S. E., K. D. Scott, and B. L. Little. 1992. "National Gainsharing Study: The Importance of Industry Differences." *Compensation and Benefits Review* 24 (January–February): 34–45.

Masternak, R. L. 1991/92. "Gainsharing Programs at Two Fortune 500 Facilities: Why One Worked Better." *National Productivity Review* 11:71–86.

——. 1993. "Gainsharing Boosts Quality and Productivity at a BF Goodrich Plant." *National Productivity Review* 12:225–238.

Masternak, R. L., and T. L. Ross. 1992. "Gainsharing: A Bonus Plan or Employee Involvement." *Compensation and Benefits Review* 24 (January–February): 46–55.

Mayo, E. 1925. "The Great Stupidity." *Harper's* July 151:225–233.

——. 1933. *The Human Problems of an Industrial Civilization*. New York: MacMillan Press.

McDonald, R. A. 1993. "Generating Bottom Line Performance." *Best's Review* 95 (September): 46–49ff.

McGrath, T. C. 1994. "Taping the Groove in Human Productivity." *Industrial Engineering* 26 (May):16–18ff.

McGregor, D. 1960. *The Human Side of Enterprise*. New York: McGraw Hill.

McNerney, D. J. 1994. "Team Compensation: Simple, Variable, and Profitable." *HR Focus* 71 (September):9–10.

Mendel, A. P., ed. 1979. *Essential Works of Marxism*. New York: Bantam Books.

Miceli, M. P., and J. P. Near. 1992. *Blowing the Whistle*. New York: Lexington Books.

Miller, C. S., and M. H. Schuster. 1987. "Gainsharing Plans: A Comparative Analysis." *Organizational Dynamics* 16:44–67.

Miller, K. I., and P. R. Monge. 1986. "Participation, Satisfaction, and Productivity: A Meta-Analytic Review." *Academy of Management Journal* 29:727–53.

Mises, L. von. 1949. *Human Action*. Glencoe, Ill.: The Free Press.

Mitchell, D. J. B., D. Lewin, and E. E. Lawler. 1990. "Alternative Pay Systems, Firm Performance, and Productivity." In *Paying for Productivity: A Look at the Evidence*, edited by A. S. Blinder, 15–94. Washington, D.C.: Brookings Institution.

Morgan, G. 1986. *Images of Organization*. Beverly Hills: Sage Publications.

Morlino, L. 1987. "Democratic Establishments: A Dimensional Analysis." In *Comparing New Democracies: Transition and Consolidation in the Mediterranean and the Southern Cone*, edited by E. A. Baloyra, 537–578. Boulder, Colo.: Westview Press.

Moskal, B. S. 1994. "General Tire." *Industry Week* 243 (October 17): 29–30.

Munsterberg, H. 1913. *Psychology and Industrial Efficiency*. Boston: Houghton Mifflin.

Murray, C. 1984. *Losing Ground*. New York: Basic Books.

Nader, R., M. Green, and J. Seligman. 1976. *Taming the Giant Corporation*. New York: W. W. Norton.

Nelson, D. 1980. *Frederick W. Taylor and the Rise of Scientific Management*. Madison: The University of Wisconsin Press.

Newman, S. L. 1984. *Liberalism at Wits' End*. Ithaca: Cornell University Press.

Novak, M. 1982. *The Spirit of Democratic Capitalism.* New York: Touchstone Books.

Nozick, R. 1974. *Anarchy, State, and Utopia.* New York: Basic Books.

O'Dell, C. A., and J. McAdams. 1987. *People, Performance, and Pay.* Houston: American Productivity Center.

O'Donnell, G., and P. Schmitter. 1986. "Concluding (But Not Capitulating) with a Metaphor." In *Transitions from Authoritarian Rule: Prospects for Democracy,* vol. 4, edited by G. O'Donnell, P. Schmitter, and L. Whitehead, 65–72. Baltimore: Johns Hopkins University Press.

O'Donnell, G., P. Schmitter, and L. Whitehead, eds. 1986. *Transitions from Authoritarian Rule: Prospects for Democracy.* Baltimore: Johns Hopkins University Press.

Olsen, F. A. 1979. "Corporations Who Succeed Through Communication: Three Case Studies." *Personnel Journal* 58 (December): 858–864+.

O'Toole, J. 1985. *Vanguard Management.* Garden City, N.Y.: Doubleday.

Park, J. C. 1995. "Reengineering Boards of Directors." *Business Horizons* 38(2): 63–69.

"Participative Management at Work: An Interview with John F. Donnelly." 1977. *Harvard Business Review* 55 (January-February):117–127.

Pateman, C. 1970. *Participation and Democratic Theory.* London: Cambridge University Press.

Payne, L. A. 1991. "Working Class Strategies in the Transition to Democracy in Brazil." *Comparative Politics* 23:221–238.

Perry, R. B. 1944. *Puritanism and Democracy.* New York: Vanguard Press.

Peters, T. 1988. *Thriving on Chaos.* New York: Alfred A. Knopf.

Peters, T. J., and R. H. Waterman. 1982. *In Search of Excellence.* New York: Warner Books.

Pfeffer, J. 1981. *Power in Organizations.* Marshfield, Mass.: Pitman Publishing.

———. 1992. *Managing with Power: Politics and Influence in Organizations.* Boston: Harvard Business School Press.

Pound, J. 1995. "The Promise of the Governed Corporation." *Harvard Business Review* 73 (2):89–98.

Preston, L. E., and J. E. Post. 1974. "The Third Managerial Revolution." *Academy of Management Journal* 17:476–86.

Przeworski, A. 1986. "Some Problems in the Study of the Transition to Democracy." In *Transitions from Authoritarian Rule,* vol. 4, edited by G. O'Donnell, P. Schmitter, and L. Whitehead, 47–63. Baltimore: Johns Hopkins University Press.

Puckett, E. S. 1958. "Measuring Performance under the Scanlon Plan." In *The Scanlon Plan,* edited by F. G. Lesieur, 65–79. New York: John Wiley & Sons.

Ramquist, J. 1982. "SMR Forum: Labor-Management Cooperation—The Scanlon Plan at Work." *Sloan Management Review* 23:49–55.

Rand, A. 1967. *Capitalism: The Unknown Ideal.* New York: New American Library.

Rawls, J. 1971. *A Theory of Justice.* Cambridge: Harvard University Press.

Reich, R. B. 1983. *The Next American Frontier.* New York: Times Books.

Reich, R. B., and J. D. Donahue. 1985. *New Deals*. New York: Times Books.

Remmer, K. L. 1991. "New Wine or Old Bottlenecks? The Study of Latin American Democracy." *Comparative Politics* 23:479–495.

Robinson, P. 1994. *Snapshots from Hell: The Making of an MBA*. New York: Warner Books.

Ross, T. L. 1990. "Why Gainsharing Sometimes Fails." In *Gainsharing: Plans for Improving Performance*, edited by B. Graham-Moore and T. L. Ross, 100–115. Washington, D.C.: Bureau of National Affairs.

———. 1994. "Self-Management and Gainsharing: A Winning Duo." *Journal of Quality and Participation* 17 (June): 10–15.

Ross, T. L., and D. Collins. 1987. "Employee Involvement and the Perils of Democracy: Are Management's Fears Warranted?" *National Productivity Review* 6:348–359.

Ross, T. L., and L. Hatcher. 1992. "Gainsharing Drives Quality Improvement." *Personnel Journal* 71 (November): 81–89.

Ross, T. L., L. L. Hatcher, and D. B. Adams. 1985. "How Unions View Gainsharing." *Business Horizons* 28 (July–August): 15–22.

Ross, T. L., L. Hatcher, and D. Collins. 1992. "Why Employees Support (and Oppose) Gainsharing Plans." *Compensation and Benefits Management* 8 (Spring): 17–27.

Ross, T. L., L. Hatcher, and R. A. Ross. 1989. "The Incentive Switch: From Piecework to Companywide Gainsharing." *Management Review* 78 (May):22–26.

Ross, T. L., R. A. Ross, and L. Hatcher. 1986. "The Multiple Benefits of Gainsharing." *Personnel Journal* 65 (October): 14–25.

Rothbard, M. N. 1978. *For a New Liberty: The Libertarian Manifesto*. New York: Libertarian Review Foundation.

Ruh, R. A., R. L. Wallace, and C. F. Frost. 1973. "Management Attitudes and the Scanlon Plan." *Industrial Relations* 12:282–288.

Sandel, M. 1982. *Liberalism and the Limits of Justice*. New York: Cambridge University Press.

Scanlon, J. N. 1958. "Profit Sharing under Collective Bargaining: Three Case Studies." In *The Scanlon Plan*, edited by F. G. Lesieur, 135–152. New York: John Wiley & Sons.

Schmid, R. O. 1994. "Structuring Gainsharing for Success." *Industrial Engineering* 26 (July): 62–65.

Schulhof, R. J. 1979. "Five Years with a Scanlon Plan." *Personnel Administrator* 24 (June): 55–62+.

Schultz, G. P. 1958. "Worker Participation on Production Problems." In *The Scanlon Plan*, edited by F. G. Lesieur, 50–64. New York: John Wiley & Sons.

Schuster, M. 1983a. "The Impact of Union-Management Cooperation on Productivity and Employment." *Industrial and Labor Relations Review* 36:415–30.

———. 1983b. "Forty Years of Scanlon Plan Research: A Review of the Descriptive and Empirical Literature." In *Organizational Democracy and Political Processes*, edited by C. Crouch and F. A. Heller, 53–71. New York: John Wiley & Sons.

———. 1984. "The Scanlon Plan; A Longitudinal Analysis." *Journal of Applied Behavioral Science* 20:23–38.

———. 1987. "Gain Sharing: Do It Right the First Time." *Sloan Management Review* 28 (Winter): 17–25.

Scott, W. G., and D. K. Hart 1971. "The Moral Nature of Man in Organizations: A Comparative Analysis." *Academy of Management Journal* 14:241–255.

Senge, P. M. 1990. *The Fifth Discipline.* New York: Doubleday.

Shepard, J. M., J. Shepard, J. C. Wimbush, and C. U. Stephens. 1995. "The Place of Ethics in Business." *Business Ethics Quarterly* 5:577–602.

Sheppard, B. H., R. J. Lewicki, and J. W. Minton. 1992. *Organizational Justice.* New York: Lexington Books.

Slater, P., and W. G. Bennis. 1990. "Democracy Is Inevitable." *Harvard Business Review* 68 (5):167–176.

Smith, A. [1759] 1976. *The Theory of Moral Sentiments.* Indianapolis: Liberty Classics.

———. [1776] 1976. *The Wealth of Nations.* 2 vols. Chicago: University of Chicago Press.

Solomon, R. C. 1993. *Ethics and Excellence.* New York: Oxford University Press.

Stone, C. D. 1976. *Where the Law Ends.* New York: Harper & Row.

Tannenbaum, A. 1986. "Controversies about Control and Democracy in Organizations." In *The Organizational Practice of Democracy,* edited by R. N. Stern and S. McCarthy, 279–303.

Tannenbaum, A., and R. A. Cooke. 1979. "Organizational Control: A Review of Studies Employing the Control Graph Method." In *Organizations Alike and Unlike,* edited by C. J. Lammers and D. J. Hickson, 183–210. Boston: Routledge & Kegan Paul.

Taylor, F. W. [1903] 1947. *Shop Management.* In F. W. Taylor, *Scientific Management.* New York: Harper & Row.

———. [1911] 1947. *The Principles of Scientific Management.* In F. W. Taylor, *Scientific Management.* New York: Harper & Row.

———. [1912] 1947. *Testimony Before the Special House Committee.* In F. W. Taylor, *Scientific Management.* New York: Harper & Row.

Towne, H. R. 1889. "Gain-Sharing." *Transactions of the American Society of Mechanical Engineers* 10:600–626.

U.S. Government Accounting Office. 1981. *Productivity Sharing Programs: Can They Contribute to Productivity Improvement?* Washington, D.C.: U.S. Government Accounting Office.

Vacs, A. C. 1987. "Authoritarian Breakdown and Redemocratization in Argentina." In *Authoritarians and Democrats: Regime Transition in Latin America,* edited by J. M. Malloy and M. A. Seligson, 15–42. Pittsburgh: University of Pittsburgh Press.

Valenzuela, J. S. 1989. "Labor Movements in Transitions to Democracy." *Comparative Politics* 21:445–472.

Veltrop, B., and K. Harrington. 1988. "Proven Technologies for Transformation." In *Corporate Transformation,* edited by R. H. Kilmann, T. J. Covin, and Associates, 330–349. San Francisco: Jossey Bass.

Victor, B., and C. U. Stephens. 1994. "Business Ethics: A Synthesis of Normative Philosophy and Empirical Social Science." *Business Ethics Quarterly* 4: 145–156.

Wagner, J. A. 1994. "Participation's Effect on Performance and Satisfaction: A Reconsideration of Research Evidence." *Academy of Management Review* 19: 312–330.

Wagner, J. A., and R. Z. Gooding 1987. "Shared Influence and Organizational Behavior." *Academy of Management Journal* 30:524–541.

Walton, M. 1991. *Deming Management at Work*. New York: Putnam.

Walzer, M. 1983. *Spheres of Justice*. New York: Basic Books.

Weber, M. 1947/1959. *Theory of Social and Economic Organization*. Glencoe, Ill.: Free Press.

Weiner, M., and E. Ozbudun, eds. 1987. *Competitive Elections in Developing Societies*. Durham: Duke University Press.

Welbourne, T. M., and L. R. Gomez-Mejia. 1988. "Gainsharing Revisited." *Compensation and Benefits Review* 20 (July-August): 19–28.

Werhane, P. 1991. *Adam Smith and His Legacy for Modern Capitalism*. New York: Oxford University Press.

White, J. 1979. "The Scanlon Plan: Causes and Correlates of Success." *Academy of Management Journal* 22:292–312.

White, J. K., and R. A. Ruh. 1973. "Effects of Personal Values on the Relationship between Participation and Job Attitudes." *Administrative Science Quarterly* 18:506–14.

Wrege, C. D., and A. G. Perroni. 1974. "Taylor's Pig-Tale: A Historical Analysis of Frederick W. Taylor's Pig-Iron Experiments." *Academy of Management Journal* 17:6–27.

Wren, D. A. 1979. *The Evolution of Management Thought*. New York: John Wiley & Sons.

Yin, R. K. 1987. *Case Study Research: Design and Methods*. Beverley Hills: Sage Publications.

Zahra, S. A. 1985. "Background and Work Experience Correlates of the Ethics and Effect of Organizational Politics." *Journal of Business Ethics* 4:419–23.

SUBJECT INDEX

Author Index